Practical Mediation:
A Guide for Mediators, Advocates, Advisers, Lawyers and Students in Civil, Commercial, Business, Property, Workplace, and Employment Cases

by Jonathan Dingle FSOM MCIArb FRSA with
John Sephton MSoM Chartered FCIPD & FCMI

Published in association with, and with all authors'
royalties going to, the Society of Mediators,
UK Registered Charity No. 1151526
Mediation, Education, Training

Zoey was always late to her
mediations but her entrances
were worth the wait ...

Law Brief Publishing

The authors gratefully acknowledge the permission given by Charles Pugsley Fincher, an Honorary Member of the Society of Mediators, to use a selection of his drawings in this work. Charles is an inspiring lawyer (slash) artist with an eagle eye for the absurdities of the profession: http://www.lawcomix.com/cartoonist.html

The authors are very grateful to John Sturrock QC for use of the section in Part One entitled "The Mediator's Log – A Mediation Story" which is © Core Solutions Group Limited and is from their website at: http://www.core-solutions.com/news-events/the-mediator-s-log/

Published 2017 by Law Brief Publishing,
an imprint of Law Brief Publishing Limited,
30 The Parks, Minehead, Somerset, TA24 8BT

www.lawbriefpublishing.com

Paperback: 978-1-911035-35-0

An expert mediator with a better than 95% settlement rate, Jonathan Dingle FRSA shares his internationally-known expertise gained over some three decades as mediator to the Elite Panel. A leading mediator trainer working from South Africa to New Zealand and India to Ireland, JD has been instrumental in the development of mediation in this country and especially the West Indies, where he is an Honorary Member of a number of Associations. He is a Member of the Chartered Institute of Arbitrators and a Fellow of the Association of Arbitrators (South Africa).

As a former Naval Officer John Sephton held senior positions in Human Resource Management within Career Management, Learning & Development and Strategic Workforce Planning. As a mediator his practice is focused upon workplace and employment and he is familiar with the wide variety of disputes that can occur in that environment, ranging from breakdowns in communication to bullying & harassment. He is a Chartered Fellow of both the Chartered Institute of Personnel and Development and the Chartered Management Institute.

Practical Mediation:

A Guide for Mediators, Advocates,
Advisers, Lawyers and Students
in Civil, Commercial, Business,
Property, Workplace, and
Employment Cases

Dedicated to the inspiration of Lord Gordon Slynn of Hadley, Sir Brian Neill, and Sir Henry Brooke without whom the Civil Mediation Council, and all it has achieved, would have withered on the vine.

For Jonathan, Alistair, and Isaac – future mediators

Contents

INTRODUCTION

Giraffe mediator breaks ice with lame joke.

Practical Mediation is an art not a science. A place for conversations not forced conversions. A platform for possibilities. A resolution process for conflict, litigation, disputes, or divorce.

As a process, it can be taught, learned, and applied. It is a tool, one of many, for people to use or abuse at their pleasure, or in their ignorance, as they interact with others. It is international and universal, the product of at least three millennia of human refinement.

Like those who choose, or are required, to engage in it – mediation is diverse; it can be provided in a rainbow of formats and with every degree of (in)formality. Perversely, mediation is capable of being gallingly badly run – yet finding glittering success; or of being brilliantly chaired – but producing nothing but a feeling of failure and wasted time. For as a process, it is the sum of its parts. A mediator can use the power imbued in mediation to enormous effect, if there is some willing-ness, however deeply hidden, to engage.

To understand mediation is easy: well taught it will be seen to be analogous to painting, or shoes, or dinner parties. To learn basic medi-ation skills should also be easy: everyone, bar sociopaths, already has the ideas of mediation hard-wired. A good tutor will enable most people to grasp the fundamentals in a week of intensive, immersive instruction.

To manage a mediation well is less easy: but with thought and practice it is something that most genuinely neutral and sufficiently interested people can be trained to do. To use mediation effectively, though, can be challenging: the authors' experience is that while many advocates and advisers are now skilled in mediation, some have much to learn.

This book is intended as a to guide civil[1], workplace, commercial, business, community and like mediators (new and old, neutral and bold); advocates, advisers; and students on the path to learning mediation skills, and to apply the tool to internationally accepted standards. It provides a full knowledge of facilitation and evaluation, and is designed as a course reference work for those studying mediation with reputable organisations in many jurisdictions.

The authors have crafted it as the source book for the training courses run by a leading faculty in the subject, that of the Society of Mediators. The Society is a well-established registered charity that through its School of Mediation based at 218 Strand in London provides training in the United Kingdom and around the world. Details of the Society, its charitable work and the training courses can be found at www.218Strand.com or by calling the National Mediation Centre which it operates on +44(0) 207 353 3936.

This living work offers much more than a practical manual for teaching: certainly it is the collective wisdom of more than fifty years of mediation experience from the faculty, and as such is a timeless piece for all those interested in using, choosing, or carousing mediation. But, in Part Six, it dares to offer more – a hope that through all the uncertainties of a world filled with strife, the principles of neutrality, self-determination, and reason can create in the future, an art and science of Practical Mediation that is truly diverse and adaptive.

---

1   But not family mediation – meaning mediations dealing with children, contact, residence, and family finance.

That is the idea that motivates the authors, the Charity's Trustees, and it is to be hoped, the readers and students who have engaged with this work. The authors pay tribute to the work of the Trustees and all those who have helped to create and inspire this book, the authors' royalties from which will go entirely to the Society to promote training, education, and free mediation. The authors welcome feedback to SOM@218Strand.com.

Jonathan Dingle & John Sephton
The Temple, London
September 2017

PART ONE –
ON MEDIATION

Mediation is now is a key form of what many commentators call Alternative Dispute Resolution (ADR). The 'alternative' here is to having a decision imposed by a judge in court. Thus mediation is advanced as a consensual process, based on self-determination, that involves the participants (or 'parties') in the dispute meeting (generally in person but sometimes through various online technologies) with a neutral third person. These participants may or may not be joined by their lawyers, advisers, or various supporters.

The supposed mutual aim of mediation, or indeed any ADR, is to find a resolution to the dispute or problem that the parties face. Whether that is the real aim, or whatever the motive, around 80% of the time those coming to mediation leave with an agreement of some description. More than 90% of people leave mediations expressing satisfaction with the process – a consumer rating that would be envied in most sectors of commerce.

Mediation is a confidential and 'without prejudice' neutrally moderated conversation that allows participants, should they wish, to explore potential solutions in what should be a safe environment. The neutral person, or mediator, may be active or passive, creative or a blank canvas: seemingly a guide, philosopher and friend on some occasions or perhaps little more than a post box on others. Usually the aim will be to find a mutually acceptable solution.

That solution need not be, and often is not, an outcome that a judge might or could properly impose through a decision in a court, which may be limited by legal constraints, rights, and precedents. Whilst it must not be immoral or illegal, unconscionable or oppressive, a solution can be quite distinct from an arbitral award. It is simply the unique resolution found by the parties in the mediation that is 'good enough' for them in all the circumstances.

Mediation may provide a *Fisher & Ury*[1] "win-win" outcome for the participants. As part of the search for a solution a skilled mediator will often look for the kind of added value which is often missed in mainstream negotiations, but can be a way of removing deadlock.

---

1 Getting to Yes (1981) https://www.amazon.co.uk/Getting-Yes-Negotiating-agreement-without/dp/1847940935

1.1 An Idea of Mediation

Practical Mediation is thus intended generally to be a forward-focussed conversation. It is preferable to avoid backward-looking recriminations and analyses. Some mediations require such introspection and implosions. Others do not. The past cannot be changed, but it can be cathartic to explore important experiences, even if the mediator is the only audience, and then, from the ruins, set out to rebuild relationships – if this is needed for resolution.

But the authors are clear: mediation is not an arbitration. Nor a trial. Nor yet a quiz. It does not require the mediator to know or to tell the participants the solution – or generally even to venture suggestions, although in evaluative mediation there may be options for this to happen as discussed later. Normally, the solution is for the participants to find. One that suffices to meet their needs, concerns, and interests. Control therefore remains with the participants. Mediation does not involve the mediator telling the participants what a judge may or will do, or who is right or who is wrong. Nor does it usually involve the mediator assessing the merits of the case: after all, the mediator may not be aware of all of the relevant information, or law.

Mediators are commonly not lawyers and, because participants generally bring their own advisors, mediators do not need to be experts in the law behind the dispute. Where mediators are invited and permitted to evaluate, under a clear contractual framework, they will still decline to do so if they do not believe that they have adequate information or knowledge.

There are many misconceptions of the role of the mediator, which may hinder participants agreeing to mediate. Those commonly encountered are:

- Mediation requires compromise from one or both participants – it does not: very often the outcome is unexpected and one that allows growth.

- The mediator is an evaluator – there should be no material evaluation by a mediator: any assessment of risk or merit is for the participants to decide.

- The mediator is an arbitrator – arbitration is a wholly different statute-based process involving legal assessment by, in effect, a private judge.

- The mediator will impose a solution – a mediator has no such power, or desire.

- The mediator will knock heads together – a mediator has no such role.

- The mediator will apply pressure on the participants – the only pressure that participants experience is that from their own assessment of risk.

- The mediator will advise the participants what to do – no, the participants must rely on their own judgment, or that of their advisers.

1.1.1 *Mediation and adding value*

The concept of adding value is demonstrated by the apocryphal anecdote known as *The Mediator's Orange*. It has been fondly told to generations of training courses and begins with a parent going into the kitchen to find two children arguing over the last orange in the fruit bowl. The parent intervenes, taking the fruit from the children and cutting it in half. Each child is given half of the orange. One child goes into the lounge and sits down to peel that half of the orange. The child does so, throws the peel in the bin, and eats the fruit. The other child stays in the kitchen, carefully removes the peel from the fruit, throws the fruit away, and uses the peel to flavour icing and bake a cake.

The knife represents the law: the equal division was a legal solution. But the outcome could have been very different had the parent asked: "Why do you want the orange?". Had that happened, and had each child answered honestly, then both could have had 100% more. The parent could have added value at no cost – with perhaps the chance to gain even better involvement with the hungry offspring.

Apocryphal, maybe, but a key tool for the mediator to use, in open or private sessions, is the question "why"? That question can, even if unanswered, cause participants to begin or further a process of reflection that allows at the very least some direction for the mediation to be established.

The authors suggest, and adopt as a theme throughout this work, that by floating questions mediators can add value to the process and so engage with the participants. Difficult or challenging questions, or reality testing, when conducted neutrally with no compulsion to answer, is part of that catalytic chapter in mediation that can be so enervating.

1.1.2   *The origins of the species*

Practical Mediation is not new. The authors acknowledge Sir Brian Neill's paper[2] which a decade ago noted that many outside the law, and in particular historians, were surprised that ADR processes have taken so long to come to the fore in contemporary Western society. Other civilisations embraced mediation long ago. There are references to mediation in Justinian, and before that historians speak of the Phoenicians using mediation in commercial disputes. In Greece a mediator was termed a προξενητης, or matchmaker.

In China there has been a long tradition of compromise where Confucian philosophy favours persuasion rather than coercion. In Kerala there is a similar history of negotiated settlement and appropriately the Indian Institute of Arbitration and Mediation is based in Cochin. There are many traditions where a neutral third party has

---

2   www.civilmediation.org/downloads-get?id=129

helped disputants reach an accord: the Quakers, as merely one example, have played a distinguished role.

But in the West, and despite Abraham Lincoln's enjoinder:

> 'Discourage litigation. Persuade your neighbors to compromise whenever you can. As a peacemaker the lawyer has superior opportunity of being a good man. There will still be business enough'

the practice until the 20th century was to use a third party as a judge in formal court proceedings – or more recently an arbitrator or adjudicator – to determine a dispute, rather than to enlist a neutral to assist the disputants to reach a conclusion themselves. The legal route, and the philosophy behind litigation, was adversarial, costly and time consuming

Gradually, however, with the rising complexity of law, increasing delays and the international nature of business, people began to question whether there might not be a more effective alternative to litigation. Conciliation procedures began to spring up in industrial relations, notably in the cotton and mining industries and in the US in 1896 the Conciliation Act was passed. Not long after that the US Department of Labor set up a panel of Commissioners of Conciliation to handle disputes. It is generally recognised, however, that it was not until the last third or so of the 20th century that serious attention was given to the settlement of disputes by mediation. The early drivers towards ADR in the New World were not, however, directly a response to the needs of clients for control or choice.

Rather the precipitators were the clogged court systems and prohibitive costs associated with traditional litigation. It became fashionable to criticise the use of courts and their Victorian values when a more Aquarian option was developing.

Morganthal obliquely refers to
his high-end legal fees.

ADR organisations in Canada, for example, emerged 30 or so years ago to become major clearing houses[3] for litigation through combining the skills of forward thinking QCs, recently retired judges and ADR practitioners keen on promoting access to justice – with the demands of the insurance industry. This cost-aware industry began effectively promoting the use of mediation in personal injury and clinical negligence claims to avoid leakage and reserve overruns. Lawyers and clients were initially suspicious of the spread of ADR. Volpe and Bahn reported in 1992[4] that lawyers in particular felt threatened or discomforted by a process they did not understand[5] [6]. Some felt they may not be able to charge the usual fees, or that reasonable expectations of profiting from costs may be thwarted[7].

---

3   For example: ADR Chambers http://adrchambers.com/ca/ has undertaken 50,000 plus mediations since 2013

4   See:
https://pdfs.semanticscholar.org/6dec/c7bf87b202658b82a852005ed2c14423a8c5.pdf

5   Even in 2016, Fromuso reported similar resistance: see http://www.civilmediation.org/downloads-get?id=754

6   The same was highlighted in construction law: see http://www.civilmediation.org/downloads-get?id=503

7   cf: Richbell's http://www.brownwelsh.com/Archive/The_Subversive_Lawyer's_Guide_to_Mediation.pdf

There is still some resistance to mediation in a number of outlying countries which, on examination, appears to say more about the litigators involved, or their financial interests, than the merits or otherwise of mediation. The UK Government, in contrast, came into mediation with the *Government Pledge* announced on 23rd March 2001 to embrace ADR and mediation, followed by the *Dispute Resolution Commitment*[8] a decade later. The savings and effectiveness are reported and reviewed therein, and wide-ranging resources including the *Small Claims Mediation Service*[9] and (the now unfunded) *National Mediation Helpline* that have been used to promote mediation.

A continent or more away, in South Africa, the Court-Annexed Mediation Rules which apply in the District and Regional Courts form part of Government's effort to transform the civil justice and enhance access to justice. The Rules of Voluntary Court-Annexed Mediation (Chapter 2 of the Magistrates' Courts Rules) were approved by the Minister and came into operation on 1 December 2014. The pilot project sites in (as of 2017) Gauteng and the North-West Province have met with some success in conjunction with the rationalisation process.

The objective of these Rules is to assist Case-Flow Management in the reduction of disputes appearing before Court and to promote access to justice. The Rules make provision for the referral of disputes for mediation at any stage during civil proceedings, provided that judgment has not been delivered by the Presiding Officer. Mediation adopts a flexible approach compared to the rigid and tedious legal processes which most often require services of a lawyer to present before court. Disputes are usually resolved in a reconciliatory manner and mediation, therefore, promotes restorative justice.

To assist with the implementation of the Mediation Rules the Minister appointed an Advisory Committee which will advise the Minister regarding the norms and standards for mediators and for the accredita-

---

8 http://www.justice.gov.uk/courts/mediation/dispute-resolution-commitment

9 http://www.justice.gov.uk/courts/mediation

tion of mediators for enlistment to the panel as required by the Mediation Rules[10].

Back in the United Kingdom, the Ministry of Justice offers (for England and Wales) direct access to mediators on a voluntary basis – through http://civilmediation.justice.gov.uk/ on a fixed fee basis. The site tells users (as of 1st September 2017) that:

Table 1: The cost of mediation via the online directory service

Amount you are claiming	Fees per party	Length of session
£5000 or less*	£50 + VAT £100 + VAT	1 hour 2 hours
£5000 to £15,000	£300 + VAT	3 hours
£15,000 to £50,000**	£425 + VAT	4 hours

* The mediator/mediation provider should agree in advance whether this should be dealt with in one or two hours. For the one-hour rate the option is available to facilitate settlement over the telephone if appropriate, and if the parties agree.

** If the claim is for more than £50,000, the fees will need to be agreed with the organisation providing the mediation.

Why has this happened? Cost and speed are certainly factors attracting governments and individuals, organisations and litigants to mediation worldwide in this age of austerity. Privacy and confidentiality are others.

It is important to understand the scope of mediation and how it can and should work. It is equally important to grasp that the process must be structured yet flexible, with a clear contractual framework that allows parties and mediator to know what can be done.

---

10 See: http://www.justice.gov.za/mediation/mediation.html#sthash.ZUMwjPCk-.dpuf

1.1.3   *The scope of mediation*

Mediation is a voluntary process for resolving disputes by mutual agreement. It differs fundamentally from both arbitration and judicial determination at a trial in that no decision is, or can be, imposed by the mediator. Any settlement arising at mediation will be one which the participants own, and have created for themselves. The mediator is a midwife rather than a parent.

Mediation can be applied to all, or to just a discreet part, of a dispute. Brown and Marriott[11] observe that a dispute is a class or kind of conflict which manifests itself in a distinct, justiciable issue; a disagreement over issues capable of resolution by negotiation, mediation, or third party adjudication. Mediation offers an impartial, mutually acceptable and neutral guide to help disputing parties through the *tangled thicket of their conflict*[12] to a resolution of their own crafting.

In contrast to a trial, mediation is a private process, normally paid for by the participants, conducted at a time, at a place, and by a mediator of their choice. It follows the principles of self-determination and works under an ethical code. See Section 10 (below) for the AoA(SA) Code of Conduct.

1.1.4   *Mediation: A legal or contractual process?*

For now, at least, in the United Kingdom mediation is a contractual process.

Spain (as from July 2012[13]), Austria (as from June 2003[14]), Ireland[15] and many other states have a mediation law, or court rules for medi-

---

11 <u>ADR: Principles and Practice</u> 3ʳᵈ Edition 2011 (paperback 2012)

12 Richard Weiler's expressive phrase

13 http://www.boe.es/boe/dias/2012/03/06/pdfs/BOE-A-2012-3152.pdf

14 http://portal.wko.at/wk/format_detail.wk?angid=1&stid=362257&dstid=0&titel=Austrian.Mediation.Act

15 Order 56A of the Rules of the Superior Courts (Mediation and Conciliation) 2010

ation, but in the United Kingdom there are presently none. Ireland has recently gone further than its Court Rules. In 2017 it published the Mediation Bill which is expected, at the time of writing to become law.

The Bill's objectives[16] are to:

- introduce an obligation on solicitors and barristers to advise parties to disputes to consider utilising mediation as a means of resolving them and, where court proceedings are launched, requires parties to proceedings to confirm to the court that they have been so advised and have considered using mediation as a means of resolving the dispute;

- in family law cases, parties will be required to attend an information session on mediation;

- provide that a court may, on its own initiative or on the initiative of the parties, and following the commencement of proceedings, invite the parties to consider mediation as a means of resolving the dispute;

- provide for the suspension of court proceedings in such cases to facilitate the mediation process;

- contain general principles for the conduct of mediation by qualified mediators;

- provide that communications between parties during mediation shall be confidential;

- provide that the parties to the mediation determine among themselves the enforceability of any agreement reached during the mediation process;

- provide that the costs of mediation must be reasonable and proportionate and not linked to the outcome of the process;

---

16 http://www.justice.ie/en/JELR/Pages/MediationBill2017

- make specific provision for the involvement of children in mediation in family law disputes;

- provide for the introduction of codes of practice for the conduct of mediation by qualified mediators.

In South Africa[17], as discussed above, there are pilot scheme rules[18] for Court Annexed mediation but more widely used are organisation's bespoke rules such as those of the Association of Arbitrators (Southern Africa[19]).

Thus, the participants will normally sign a Mediation Agreement with the mediator which defines the procedure and sets out what the participants and the mediator can and cannot do, before, at, and after the mediation. It is therefore not a creature of statute, and can exist entirely outside the current Civil Procedure Rules 1998 (CPR[20]) which defines the legal process.

There are several advantages to mediation being a non-judicial process. It follows that because the process is voluntary, contractual, and independent of statutory restriction, the solutions which the parties decide to adopt do not need – in most cases – to have anything in common with the orders to which a court or arbitrator are restricted.

Apologies, explanations, meetings with consultants, amendments to policies, staff retraining, changes in procedures, therapy, counselling, admission for further or new treatments and second opinions are just some examples of highly creative solutions which mediations devise and which judges cannot aspire.

---

17 http://www.justice.gov.za/mediation/mediation.html

18 http://www.justice.gov.za/legislation/notices/2014/2014-03-18-gg37448_rg10151_gon183-rules-mc.pdf

19 http://arbitrators.co.za/wp-content/uploads/2014/10/aoa_mediation_rules.pdf

20 https://www.justice.gov.uk/courts/procedure-rules/civil

1.1.5 *Mediation and English Rules of Court*

Although there is neither proscription nor regulation, the English CPR does seek to encourage ADR, and so by implication mediation:

Rule 1.4(1) obliges the court to further the overriding objective of enabling the court to deal with cases justly by actively managing cases. Rule 1.4(2)(e) defines active case management as including *encouraging the parties to use an alternative dispute resolution procedure if the court considers that appropriate and facilitating the use of such procedure.*

Rule 26.4(1)[21] provides that *a party may, when filing the completed allocation questionnaire, make a written request for the proceedings to be stayed while the parties try to settle the case by alternative dispute resolution or other means.* The court/judiciary can also stay the case if considered appropriate.

Rule 26.4A[22] says in the case of Small Claims (up to £10,000 in non-personal injury matters):

(1) Referral to the Mediation Service

26.4A

(1) This rule applies to claims started in the County Court which would normally be allocated to the small claims track pursuant to rule 26.6.

(2) This rule does not apply to—

(a) road traffic accident, personal injury or housing disrepair claims; or

(b) any claim in which any party to the proceedings does not agree to referral to the Mediation Service.

---

21 https://www.justice.gov.uk/courts/procedure-rules/civil/rules/part26#26.4

22 Also: https://www.justice.gov.uk/courts/procedure-rules/civil/rules/part26#26.4

(3) In this rule, 'the Mediation Service' means the Small Claims Mediation Service operated by Her Majesty's Courts and Tribunals Service.

(4) Where all parties indicate on their directions questionnaire that they agree to mediation, the claim will be referred to the Mediation Service.

(5) If a claim to which this rule applies is settled, the proceedings will automatically be stayed with permission to apply for—

(a) judgment for the unpaid balance of the outstanding sum of the settlement agreement; or

(b) the claim to be restored for hearing of the full amount claimed, unless the parties have agreed that the claim is to be discontinued or dismissed.

Rule 44.4(3)(a)(ii)[23] requires the court, in deciding the amount of costs to be awarded, to have regard to the conduct of the parties, including in particular *the efforts made, if any, before and during the proceedings in order to try to resolve the dispute.*

The pre-action protocols[24] contain standard wording on ADR, to the effect that:

"*The parties should consider whether some form of alternative dispute resolution procedure would be more suitable than litigation, and if so, endeavour to agree which form to adopt. Both the Claimant and Defendant may be required by the Court to provide evidence that alternative means of resolving their dispute were considered. The Courts take the view that litigation should be a last resort, and that claims should not be issued prematurely when a settlement is still actively being explored. Parties are warned that if this paragraph is*

---

23 https://www.justice.gov.uk/courts/procedure-rules/civil/rules/part-44-general-rules-about-costs#rule44.4

24 http://www.justice.gov.uk/courts/procedure-rules/civil/protocol

not followed then the court must have regard to such conduct when determining costs."

There is therefore much for the practitioner to consider and this is supported by, as has been mentioned earlier, the encouragement of the referral website[25] and the work of the Civil Mediation Council[26] as well as the Society of Mediators.

1.1.6   *Characteristics of Mediation*

Mediation is usually characterised by without prejudice discussions. These take place both in open (plenary) meetings with all the participants present and which the mediator will moderate, as well as in private and confidential meetings (caucuses) between individual parties, their advisers, and the mediator. The amount of time spent in private as opposed to open sessions will vary from mediation to mediation. There are no fixed times, or patterns. During both types of encounter, the mediator will seek to create an atmosphere where the participants focus on effective solutions rather than on past demands. The mediator in the most commonly-used form of the process does not resemble a judge or arbitrator: the mediator neither decides who is right or wrong, nor expresses an opinion. A mediator will not give legal advice or suggest what a judge might do but instead, by using core skills, acts as a facilitator to help the participants reach a settlement which they will own.

1.1.7   *Facilitative Mediation*

Facilitative Mediation is that in which most mediators are usually trained. Training usually takes place in one intensive week and is conducted by a CMC approved training school. It does not intrinsically require the mediator to have any deep specialist knowledge of the legal context of the dispute, although many mediators will be chosen because they have professional experience. It does require the mediator to be

---

25 http://civilmediation.justice.gov.uk/

26 http://www.civilmediation.org/

thoroughly trained in listening and questioning skills that are often wholly alien to judges and lawyers.

It is vital to understand that the mediator is not seeking to decide the case but instead to help the participants understand their own individual and common interests. Facilitative mediation is one form of a process called *Principled Negotiation*. This term was advanced by the late Professor Roger Fisher and William Ury[27] at the Harvard Negotiation Project (now the Global Negotiation Insight Initiative).

They noticed that traditional bargaining focused on defending positions rather than addressing underlying concerns. This led to a contest of wills, often resulting in a win:lose, lose:win or indeed lose:lose result. Fisher and Ury went on to develop the technique of Principled Negotiation which centres on negotiating on merit rather than on defending or attacking positions. Principled negotiation requires the negotiator to be soft or co-operative with the people and hard on the issues. The process aims to separate the people from the problem; to focus on interests not positions; to generate a variety of options before making decisions; and to base solutions on objective criteria.

Facilitative Mediators using the Principled Negotiation model will accordingly look to distinguish between positions and interests. This is a widely adopted model. A good mediator will not ask a participant to give an opening position but instead to indicate what, in general terms, the participant would like to achieve from the mediation. That may lead to an agreement that both participants want a solution that is, above all, fair.

Of course, getting from there to a solution is the mediator's skill but having established a common interest the process can begin. The mediator is likely to follow this by inviting the participants to tell their stories and to listen. In doing so, the participants will be gently encouraged to put themselves in the other person's shoes and to try to see the situation as they do. The mediator will emphasise that understanding the other position is not the same as agreeing with it. Where differences

---

27 See: *ibid* and <u>Getting to Yes</u> (second edition with Bruce Patton), 1997 ISBN-10: 0099248425

exist, the mediator will encourage the participants to discuss them rationally and involve each participant in the problem-solving process – rather than trying to convince them that only one solution is right, an often ineffectual hallmark common to many client-driven litigators.

From there, the mediator will look to focus on interests instead of positions. Positions are what participants actually want. Interests are why participants have decided upon the positions. Interests underline positions. To identify interests, the mediator may need to have addressed the human problems that may be behind the positions: and the storytelling is indeed an important part of that process.

People like or even want to be heard, especially in cases where an individual has been physically or emotionally injured or personally wronged. And one should not rule out the power of an apology in any form of business, commercial, family or other case. Humans appreciate sorry. Once a level of trust is established, the mediator can ask, usually in private and carefully avoiding any hint of opinion, probing questions that seek to reveal the active interests.

Questions such as *what is so important about this figure?* or *why do you need that result?* or *what does this mean for you personally?* can unlock deep levels of understanding.

The mediator may also invite a participant (and their advisors) to try to imagine being in the other person's shoes – and ask why then you would or would not accept the offer.

The answer can be tested against objective criteria and lead to a rapid opening of both participants' interests and the creation of possible solutions. It is not, however, the only technique that is deployed.

1.1.8   *Evaluative Mediation*

Less commonly used in disputes in the United Kingdom at least in 2017, Evaluative Mediation requires the mediator to form and express an opinion on the merits and/or potential settlement terms for the dispute. This is quite different to Facilitative Mediation.

Evaluative mediation needs to be considered with great care by the mediator and the participants. It can be very effective but requires a clear contract, explanation – and training in the process. It often happens that mediators, particularly lawyers or former judges who practice in specialist areas, are invited by participants (especially litigants in person) to give an evaluation or advice on some or all of the issues. Some participants want to be told the answer to their dispute. Some, including formerly intransigent insurers or over optimistic clients or their advisers, need the security blanket of a fresh opinion before changing their position.

Unless, however, the mediator has been contracted to perform an evaluative mediation, and the Mediation Agreement permits or requires such a foray, almost all mediators will (sensibly and properly) decline to offer an evaluative opinion. Facilitative mediators hold that it is the parties who have responsibility for the problem, and who will own the solution. If the mediator opines then the solution will not be theirs, but that of the mediator. It follows that the process is undermined by invasive opinions.

But sometimes the participants and the mediator agree in advance that the mediation should be evaluative, either from the outset or if Facilitative Mediation does not provide a solution. In that case, the Mediation Agreement must reflect this and provide for suitable measures to ensure a smooth transition to the evaluation process. So too must the means of offering the evaluation be stated: some mediators give written evaluations, others prefer to offer an oral assessment.

The means of delivery of the evaluation needs to be agreed and written into the Mediation Agreement. Sometimes, an evaluation is given to all the participants in a plenary session, somewhat akin to an arbitral award or a judge giving judgment. If this is the preferred solution, then the participants need to be aware of the implications, and particularly of the risks, of an open evaluation being given. Most mediators prefer an assessment of the strengths and weaknesses of a case, and sometimes the likely views of a judge, to be given to each participant in private. This may avoid some of the risks of the plenary session but means that neither participant can be sure what the mediator has said to the other.

In delivering the evaluation the mediator will be at pains to emphasise the neutrality of the role and to state that any settlement proposal appears to be the best commercial solution, given the facts and opinions disclosed. The mediator will emphasise that the evaluation is non-binding and should state that the opinion given in private will be substantively identical to both participants, albeit that there may be a different emphasis in each case. The mediator will make clear that an evaluation is made without blame or judgement. Furthermore, that where it differs from the advice previously given by the legal advisers the cause may be because the mediator has less knowledge of the case or because matters that have come to light at mediation have led to a different assessment.

This can be a real problem in Evaluative Mediation because clients may find the opinion of a subject-experienced mediator to be very influential. Where the opinion differs from the advice of the instructed lawyers there may be considerable embarrassment, loss of face, or conflict. Sometimes, mindful of this dilemma, mediators will offer a range of settlements to promote further negotiation – and thereby the ownership of the solution – by the participants. This is perhaps the strongest form of Evaluative Mediation.

Experienced evaluative mediators will generally not seek to justify their opinion with detailed references to facts or law. This is to avoid over-legalistic responses or challenges from participants who delve into the detail to find fault rather than to look to building a consensual solution. Having offered an evaluation, the mediator will give participants time to consider the opinion expressed and if necessary to reassess their negotiation position. The mediator may need to devise strategies for dealing with disappointed participants to keep them engaged in solution building.

There are structures and clear flowcharts in place to enable the process under the contractual agreement. Typical is that used by leading costs mediators in the United Kingdom under the CADR (Cost Alternative Dispute Resolution[28]) model.

This requires a proper description of the model by the mediator, and – if it is to be used – a certificate to be signed over and above the agreement to mediate contract. Mediators follow a flow chart that defines what they and the participants can expect of the process:

Table 2: CADR'S MEDIATION FLOW CHART

```
                    ┌──────────────────┐
                    │ CADR Standard    │
                    │ Agreement To     │
                    │ Mediate signed   │
                    └──────────────────┘
                             │
                             ▼
                    ┌──────────────────┐
                    │ Mediation day    │
                    │ begins with FM   │
                    └──────────────────┘
                             │
   ┌────────────┐            ▼
   │ Settlement │◄──  ┌──────────────────┐
   └────────────┘     │ Impasse reached  │      (Certificate
                      │ OPTIONS          │         signed)
                      └──────────────────┘
                             │
   ┌───────────┐  ┌─────────────┐  ┌──────────────────┐  ┌───────────┐
   │ Adjourn / │  │ Continue FM │  │ Private comment  │  │ Move to EM│
   │ End       │  │             │  │ and continue FM  │  │           │
   └───────────┘  └─────────────┘  └──────────────────┘  └───────────┘
                                                                │
   ┌──────────────────┐
   │ Opening session  │
   │ Select EM format │
   └──────────────────┘
         │
   ┌──────────────┐                           ┌──────────────┐
   │ Oral         │                           │ Written      │
   │ Non-Binding  │                           │ Non- Binding │
   └──────────────┘                           └──────────────┘
```

Submissions / responses (time limited)	Submissions / responses (time limited)
Mediator comment in open session	Mediator comment in writing
Reflection by participants (time limited)	Reflection by participants (time limited)
Extempore oral evaluation	Written evaluation delivered

---

28 http://www.costs-adr.com/

The risks of evaluative mediation must be understood. They require an informed decision by the participants and careful consideration by the mediator who should ensure that professional indemnity insurance covers such work. Competent evaluative mediators know that offering an opinion in mediation can be highly destructive to the process: once the mediator ceases to facilitate but instead assesses, the trust of and relationship with the participants may be lost. The mediator may be seen as biased, not worth dealing with, and even a hindrance to progress.

Indeed, the mediation may never come to life: some mediators report that where the participants know that there may or will be an evaluation there is a reticence to open up to the mediator, to stick firmly to positions, and not to risk exposing interests. The mediator is then restricted to a very limited range of information and may have to make an evaluation based on far less information than is likely available to the court or to the participants themselves.

It follows that whilst there are some circumstances where an evaluative mediation can be effective and undertaken either from the outset or when an impasse is reached, many mediators and advisers consider that the risks outweigh the advantages. Advisers and advocates sometimes fear that opponents will learn of as yet unexplored options, twists, or lines of attack from a mediator conducting an evaluation that they had not previously considered. They are wary of such a moment of illumination.

Mediators who step into the fray, without contractual permission, to offer advice, opinions, or solutions, do so at their peril. They will be considered by many to have assumed a mantle which is hard to reconcile with the confidential neutrality of the role. They will need to be insured and prudent.

1.1.9 *Mediation: a binding process?*

Mediation, whether facilitative or evaluative, only produces a binding outcome if the participants agree and sign a Mediation Agreement. This document is usually provided by the mediator, as seen in Appendix 1, or could be drafted by participating legal advisers. In either case it will be contractually binding.

It may be embodied in a court order where proceedings have already been commenced or where the approval of the court is required under CPR Rule 21.10[29].

Attendance at mediation is voluntary in the United Kingdom and many other jurisdictions, including South Africa. Mandatory schemes as pioneered in parts of Canada form no part of the domestic process. It follows that a participant is free to leave the mediation at any time if they wish, although most mediators will normally invite the participants to agree to a rule that they spend five minutes with the mediator in private before leaving, so as to find out what is wrong or to perform a final reality check.

It also follows that mediations may not always lead to a settlement on the day, or in the next few days (although, as will be seen below, most do). This may be no bad thing – having time to reflect and to consult can be vital – and mediators need to be aware of the damage that pressure and the hubris of wanting a deal can cause.

1.1.10 *Mediation and confidentiality*

Because of the without prejudice nature of mediation, if settlement is not achieved through mediation, any offers, comments, suggestions, concessions, proposals, or statements made by the participants during the course of the mediation are not binding on them and cannot be used or referred to in subsequent court proceedings.

There may be rare exceptions, however, if fraud or oppression is alleged. These questions were highlighted by the discussion of the dilemma

---

29 https://www.justice.gov.uk/courts/procedure-rules/civil/rules/part21#21.10

faced by mediator Jane Andewartha in the interesting 2009 case known as *Farm Assist*[30].

Mr Justice Ramsey, though an experienced High Court judge wholly familiar with the value of mediation, set out the factors which had led him to decide that in that case the interests of justice overrode the interests of the mediator in retaining the confidentiality of what had occurred in the mediation. The judge appears to have been particularly influenced by the fact that in support of its case DEFRA had applied illegitimate pressure or had acted in bad faith.

Farm Assist Limited was alleging that DEFRA had refused or failed to take a structured, reasoned, bilateral, reasonable or bona fide approach to the valuation of the Farm Assist account, and that in its witness statements it was relying on what the mediator had said in private sessions, or on conversations between the mediator and others, or on what had happened in the mediation.

The judge found that whilst the mediator had said clearly that she had no recollection of the mediation, that this did not prevent her from giving evidence. He pointed out that frequently memories are jogged and recollections come to mind when documents are shown to witnesses and they have the opportunity to focus, in context, on events some years earlier.

He ended his judgment by saying that whilst the mediator had a right to rely on the confidentiality provision in the Mediation Agreement, he considered that this was a case where, as an exception, the interests of justice lay strongly in favour of evidence being given of what was said and done.

---

30 Farm Assist Limited (in liquidation) v The Secretary of State etc (No.2) [2009] EWHC 1102 (TCC)

1.1.11 *Summary of Section 1.1*

Facilitative Mediation in particular is a much used and highly valued tool for Alternative Dispute Resolution, supported in the United Kingdom, South Africa, and common law jurisdictions by the courts largely through contractual mechanisms. Evaluative mediation is increasingly important but not without attendant risks and must be carefully delivered. Mediation is confidential and only exceptionally will that veil be lifted. Mediation is highly effective, resolving seemingly intractable matters where all else has failed in a quick, quiet and cost effective way. While neither the default option, or a panacea, nor a substitute for judicial precedent, for many it will be very much the future, especially in a time-poor world.

*Everyone sensed that the mediator wasn't simply
giving another phony deadline.*

1.2 An Idealised Mediation

1.2.1 *What is an Ideal Mediation?*

"An ideal mediation", like a unicorn, is rarely seen but easily imagined. Some commentators focus on how successful mediation is statistically as a process of Alternative Dispute Resolution – which of course it is! Research indicates that 85% of mediations are successful – meaning that a settlement is achieved on the day or shortly thereafter as a direct consequence. But what is success? Success for one person might mean something totally different to another. What we want and what we need are two totally different things.

The authors consider that for a mediator a successful mediation should be considered to be one conducted under the terms of the Agreement to Mediate and the Rules, where the mediator has behaved ethically and deployed appropriate tools to provide the opportunity for the participants to engage in safe conversations. By removing outcomes from the equation, and replacing it with process driven performance indicators, mediators are freed to focus on listening and effective communication rather than pushing reluctant participants towards a place they do not wish to go – at least as yet.

Primarily, then, an Ideal Mediation is about providing a process that is fair to all and gives the participants the opportunity to discuss their differences. If they wish, they can move forward towards a resolution that perhaps a judge could not impose and the mediator might not have considered. The participants will have kept ownership of the process, acted under the principles of self-determination, and designed their own outcome with which they are content.

1.2.2 *Beginning the process*

In a typical case, two individuals will have fallen into a dispute. In the instant example, the authors have in mind an employer and a former employee who has been injured at work and dismissed on medical grounds. Both parties (soon to become participants) are represented –

the Claimant by solicitors acting under a no-win no-fee agreement and the Defendant by solicitors instructed by their insurers.

Standard forms have been exchanged setting out the claim and the reply. Medical evidence is obtained but the parties cannot agree the level of damages. In traditional litigation there might be a CPR Part 36 Offer[31] and the claim might then be issued in the County Court Money Claims Centre in Northampton, or in the High Court.

In this case, however, as is now common, the solicitors have agreed to meet with a mediator before the claim is issued – there is sufficient time under the Limitation Act 1980 for this to happen (three years from the accident or date of knowledge) even though agreeing to mediate does not generally[32] stop the clock from ticking.

The solicitors source a mediator through the personal injury panel of Trust Mediation[33] and all those taking part in the mediation agree with the choice, having viewed the mediator's online CV. Thereafter, arrangements start to firm up using the panel's Registrar – Phil Hesketh. The Registrar ensures the basics are covered: the venue, the date, the time, and that an Agreement to Mediate is drawn up.

The mediator sends a letter or email to all, introducing the process and offering some thoughts about the approach to the mediation. Papers might be exchanged and possibly telephone calls made between the mediator and the legal representatives of those involved. The date is confirmed and the venue clarified.

A week or so before the day of the mediation, agreed papers ("the mediation bundle") arrive with the mediator by email. These have been prepared by the solicitors and the mediator notices that there is an agreed case summary and details of the offers made to date. All of this is confidential.

---

31 A formal offer to settle which can be made by Claimants or Defendants and which, if not beaten, can have severe costs consequences – see:
https://www.justice.gov.uk/courts/procedure-rules/civil/rules/part36#36.2

32 Without a written agreement to suspend Limitation.

33 See: https://www.trustmediation.org.uk/about-us/personal-injury-mediators/

The mediator reads the PDFs and then files them in an encrypted folder under a password on the iPad that will be taken to the mediation. The mediator also calls the venue to check all is well, and prints off a hard copy of the Agreement to Mediate for signature the next day.

1.2.3   On the day

On the mediation day itself, the mediator arrives in good time. The rooms are checked and the mediator is available to meet the participants and their representatives. They are settled into their respective private (or caucus) rooms. The mediator checks too that there is a plenary room available with sufficient seats in which the open session will take place.

The efficient reception has confirmed that there will be lunch and refreshments available. People do get tired and hungry even in ideal mediations, although mediators rarely find time for lunch.

1.2.4   The first open session

Once people are settled and refreshed the mediator invites everyone to assemble in the plenary room. Earlier private sessions have had the Agreement to Mediate signed and any fears that it might be difficult for some people to actually meet in person with the other participants dispersed. The mediator welcomes everyone and then goes through the checklist prepared for the introduction to the day. There is authority to settle on both sides of the table and plenty of time. Everyone is content to engage with standard ground rules relating to one person speaking at once and using ordinary business language.

After the introduction, the mediator invites the participants to say in turn what they would like to achieve from the day. At this stage, the mediator notices that the Claimant is hesitant but his counsel steps up. A succinct opening, which also pays tribute to the Defendant in coming to the mediation, is seen as helpful by the opposing barrister.

The Defendant's counsel therefore says, speaking directly to the Claimant,

> *"Can we agree on two things – first, our insured was in the wrong in exposing you to the accident that you suffered, and second, you deserve fair compensation?"*

The Claimant has no difficulty with either proposition. The Defendant barrister continues by saying that "…while there is no one present from the company, the legal team who are here are sorry for what happened and sorry too that you remain injured."

> *"Our job, though, is to come up with a settlement for you which we can justify to the auditors in Cardiff. So we are here to listen, to debate, and to make offers – and also seek what is fair"*

Further remarks are made but they do not lead to much. The mediator asks everyone in turn if they have completed their opening remarks, and then encourages an open conversation by asking questions, but being careful not to embarrass or accuse. The mediator's questions are searching and curious with the positive intention to encourage dialogue. The mediator uses neutral language to "separate the people from the problem" to help to identify what is really important to participants and their situation.

1.2.5   *Breaking into private sessions*

After a while, it is clear that no one wants to progress further around the table, but to take stock in their private rooms. At this point in our ideal mediation the mediator suggests that the participants enter into private sessions or caucuses. Thus, they adjourn to their private rooms and the mediator, on everyone's agreement, spends some time with each set of participants and their representatives in turn. The mediator agrees the timescale amicably such that for 20 minutes they would spend time with one set of participants and then offer a similar session with the other participants thus keeping everything equitable and fair to both.

In the private sessions our ideal mediator starts by saying, *"What was it that didn't come out for you in our plenary session?"* From this, conversations develop. The mediator seeks more and is curious whilst actively listening. This includes summarising and reflecting.

In this ideal mediation earlier entrenched views in the Claimant's camp start to thaw and the situation starts to be expressed from another perspective. The Claimant wants to return to work but needs a lump sum now to retrain and cover the risk of being slow to find work. There are also accumulated debts and a new automatic car to be purchased. Plus, the Claimant would like to take the family, who have spent two years acting as nurses and carers, to Florida for a well deserved holiday. Putting a price on all these items, the Claimant asserts that past special damages are worth £50,000, future loss a further £50,000 and general damages for his leg fractures, knee injuries, and bad back, at least £40,000.

This is rather less than the claim of £250,000 that was previously advanced and the mediator asks why? Counsel for the Claimant suggests that it is a result of a stock take and a more positive view of the future. The Claimant does not want, however, to make an offer yet – it is the Defendant's call as they asked for the mediation.

After 20 minutes, the mediator asks whether the Claimant has anything else to say and then suggests that it is now the right time to talk to the other participants. Before the mediator leaves this first private session the Claimant and his team are assured that all that has been said is confidential. Nothing will be disclosed or even hinted at.

1.2.6 *The opening offer*

The second private session then takes place with the Defendant and the mediator approaches it in the same or similar way. Very soon, however, the Defendant's counsel says that they were impressed by the Claimant in the open session and fear that a judge will see him as he is – an honest individual who has not exaggerated the claim. They want to make a prompt offer and it will be three times the previous tempter, which was £40,000.

From the £120,000 now on the table, there are benefits claimed since the Claimant lost his job of £12,000 and an interim payment on account of damages of £10,000 to be deducted. Thus if the offer were accepted, the Claimant would receive £98,000 in about three weeks, together with costs.

The mediator asks the Defendant how they want this transmitted – do they want to do so directly to the Claimant, through the lawyers or by using the mediator. To the mediator's surprise, the Defendant indicates that it detests the Claimant's solicitors and does not want to have anything to do with them in direct negotiation. Nor does the Defendant's solicitor want any counsel to counsel carving up of the case. The mediator is asked to take the offer through as a written document, marked "without prejudice" and in the pen of the Defendant's barrister. Only 15 minutes have elapsed since the mediator left the Claimant's room but soon the knock comes on the door.

The ideal mediator enters the private room and at once says:

> *"I have an offer – would you like to see it?"*

The Claimant does, and is impressed. The offer is a little light. It transpires that his ambition is £110,000 in hand in new money – in other words valuing the claim at £132,000 overall or 'gross'. The mediator enquires why and it is because the holiday will cost £5,000, the car the same and the Claimant plans to put £50,000 into a reserve, pay off £20,000 of debt and reserve the rest for retraining and the new business as a website designer.

1.2.7 Settlement

Eventually consensus is reached – at £132,000. Even in an ideal mediation nothing is binding until it is written down and signed. This document. the Settlement Agreement, the Claimant's counsel prepares adding a term whereby the Claimant's solicitors will receive £20,000 on account of their costs and disbursements with the rest of the claimed costs falling to be assessed by a judge if not agreed in due course.

The Defendant's solicitors are content with this plan, provided that there are 28 days to discharge the £130,000 to be sent to the Claimant's solicitors. In fact the Claimant will also lose a proportion of the £110,000 under the retainer with his solicitors – there is a success fee payable. This will actually mean that on the terms of the agreement the Claimant will get £100,000 net new money and the balance goes as costs to the solicitors. Everyone professes themselves happy with this outcome.

1.2.8 *Conclusion*

The mediator thanks the participants for their assistance and fades away. On this occasion, there has been some effective reality testing and some worthwhile probing, but overall, the importance of the mediator on this occasion was to overcome the ill feeling held by the Defendant's solicitors. There was nothing on the face of the papers to suggest this and the Claimant's lawyers will never know – but had it not been for mediation the matter would have been litigated, with all the delays, expense and uncertainty that would have involved. It had been a worthwhile day.

1.3   An Idol's Mediation

The idealised mediation set out in Section 1.2 above is just that – an edited version of a real, but far grittier, day. Mediations vary but the skills of experts remain constant. The authors are thus indebted to an idol, John Sturrock[34] for his permission to re-use the following mediator's story from Core Solutions Group[35] [36].

The Mediator's Log – A Mediation Story

1.3.1   The Day Commences: Engaging the Participants

0845: The mediator arrives at the venue, the office of one of the lawyers. These days, few parties seem to mind where the mediation is held, even if the location is that of the other's lawyer. More important is that the environment is comfortable and that the catering is good.

0846: The mediator's assistant is already here. She is able to brief the mediator on the room allocations and inform him that one of the parties has arrived. More importantly, they reflect on the late arrival of an expert report from one party the night before, wondering how that will affect attitudes in the other room. They speculate a little on how long the mediation may take but quickly remind themselves that mediation is like the proverbial piece of string…. and that it is impossible to predict the outcome or the timescale. The mediator reminds his assistant that the more they focus on the process and the less they worry about the outcome, the more likely it is that a satisfactory resolution will ensue. Easy said…

---

34 John Sturrock is the founder and Chief Executive of the Core Solutions Group, recognised as Scotland's leading provider of commercial mediation services. John Sturrock has been described in Chambers Guide to the UK Legal Profession as the "foremost mediator in Scotland", and is highly ranked in the UK and abroad. He is also a mediator at Brick Court Chambers in London. The authors have been glad of his input in ADR projects.

35 John does not advance this as an 'ideal' mediation but the authors offer it as a good starting point to analyse a long and complex commercial matter. Many mediations settle in four hours but all-day mediations are common.

36 http://www.core-solutions.com/news-events/the-mediator-s-log/

0901: In the corridor en route to the first private meeting with the claiming party. The mediator pauses and glances at the agreement to mediate to remind himself of the names of those attending. Remembering names is crucial and he often draws a mind-map of the players as an aid. But, occasionally, even that fails and he mixes up the names just at the wrong moment. An occupational hazard in a fast-moving day, where little things can make a big difference…

0902: Knocks on the door and enters. The atmosphere is slightly tense. That late report has had an impact on the lawyers in particular. The mediator looks around the room, finds the client and extends a hand. She is anxious and the mediator knows that his first task is to reassure. Building what the experts call "rapport" is the foundation for any mediator. If the client trusts the mediator and his or her ability to handle the day's discussions effectively, the whole process has a greater prospect of a successful outcome. The mediator introduces himself and his assistant to others in the room. He discusses briefly the late arrival of the report with the lawyer in charge of the case, a fairly senior litigation partner. His objective is both to recognise the inconvenience caused and to encourage a positive view of the fact that the position is now clearer. But there is no doubt that, as the latest in what is perceived as a series of impediments, this has not helped. The lawyer is concerned about whether he can properly advise his client. The mediator suggests an early meeting with the lawyer for the other party.

0909: The main conversation in this initial meeting is with the client. She is keen to explain her circumstances and the impact on her life, job and future of the events on the day in question. The mediator listens intently. He says little at this stage and uses the conversation to reaffirm the confidentiality of any discussions in that room, knowing that this will have been covered already by the lawyer who has considerable experience in mediation. When pressed for a comment on the behaviour of the other party's chief executive, the mediator reminds the group that his role is not to judge, pass judgment or offer a view. The client is clearly upset, not just by the events of the past but by the uncertainties of the day and the strangeness of the situation. The mediator explains how the day may unfold and makes clear that the client does not need to do or agree to anything with which she is not happy.

0924: There are some formalities to cover. This includes the question of decision-making when it comes to the crunch later in the day, as almost inevitably it will. Is there anyone else with whom the client needs to speak? If so, who and how will they be contacted? They discuss timing and whether anyone has any time pressure later in the day. The financial expert has a flight to catch at 6.30. Hopefully, his presence will not be required by then anyway though, as they have often invested a lot of time in the client's case, many experts like to be there until the end. That is not always a good thing if their influence is disproportionate…

Everyone else is able to stay for as long as it takes. The mediator encourages the lawyers in the room to begin thinking about what might be included in any resolution agreement. He reminds them that there is nothing worse than starting drafting from scratch after agreement is reached.

0927: That other document, the agreement to mediate, needs to be signed. It has been circulated, revised and checked in advance by all concerned and the senior lawyer confirms that all those in the room can sign. The mediator thanks everyone, checks whether the client has any other questions and leaves, heading for the next room…

10.03: Time for the gathering of all participants. The mediator's practice is to bring everyone together in one room for an informal meeting, some food, mingling and scene-setting. The mediator chats to his assistant and reflects on the purpose: humanising the process is important for people who may not have met before, or who may have formed views about their counterparts on "the other side". For clients, it can be a difficult moment (and can never be forced) which can lead to a sense of relief, acknowledgement or at least recognition. The last time the clients met before today's mediation was highly stressful for both.

10.11: The mediator taps a glass and begins what he customarily describes as his "carefully prepared, spontaneous, improvised comments". "Firstly, thank you all for coming …. This is not an easy matter….if it was, we wouldn't be here……the important thing today is that, for this to work, you need to help each other….the paradox is that it only works for you if it also works for you" he directs his remarks to the clients particularly. "This is a great opportunity.... Later in the day, you will have choices to make, ultimately, it will be entirely up to you ... I encourage you to make only one assumption today: that everyone is trying their best." He knows that this is a bit of a set-piece. He also knows that it is a useful way to mark the transition from the opening stage to the next series of more in-depth meetings.

10.17: Time for a break: first though, the mediator has asked the clients to stay behind and meet privately with him. This is one of those occasions when the lawyers are content for this to happen, judging that the clients can handle this without support. The clients sit, rather awkwardly at first, side by side. The mediator gestures with a hand and the "defender" client begins...

"I am glad we are here. I really want this to get sorted today. This should never have happened. I wish we had had this conversation a year ago..... but, when you did that to us......" The atmosphere changes...

1.3.2 *Exploring what it's about*

10.18: ...In that moment, the mediator has to decide whether to intervene or not. On such judgments could the success of the day depend. He has already undertaken not to allow the short meeting of clients to become tetchy, assuming that his presence would provide a check on any tendency to reopen old wounds. He chooses to remain silent, watching intently as the claimant reacts. "It wasn't my issue...if your team hadn't botched the job initially....." A pause: "Look, let's not get into that now. That's not why we are meeting here." "OK, you're right ..... As I say, I want to get this sorted."

"So do I, we need to move on." The mediator breathes an internal sigh of relief. The clients have corrected themselves, at least for the moment. It is far better this way. The whole point of the mediation process, after all, is to enable the clients to take responsibility wherever they can. This is not always easy, as some clients like to have their lawyers lead and do not wish to be exposed. Some lawyers are protective of their clients. There's always a balance to be struck.

10.22: The mediator senses that the purpose of the short meeting has been achieved: a re-engagement of the two key players and, apparently, a common understanding of the primary purpose of the day. Some-times, such a meeting can go on for a considerable period. On this occasion, it seems better to take stock now. He summarises the position:

"It's not unusual for this sort of thing to happen. It is unsatisfactory for you both but I see this frequently. The key now is to explore the options for a resolution. Your lawyers are here to help and you have expert advice too. For the first part of the day, we'll have each team set out how it sees things and what needs to happen. We've agreed that the claimant's team should go first and then the others can take a break and consider what has been said before setting out their picture. I'll come and see each of you in your rooms first, in about five minutes."

10.25: After a quick comfort break, the mediator returns to the main room to chat to his assistant. "What do you think?" he asks. "That was interesting," she replies. "I think there's quite a bit under the surface that might spring up again." The mediator agrees. He knows how volatile the situation might still be if the clients think that the other is not really making an effort or is seeking an advantage. This is where the expertise and common sense of the lawyers is really important. Lawyers face a number of choices: one is whether to be wise counsel to the client, acting as a modifying force if the client gets upset or angry, or to back up the client forcefully and reinforce any feelings of hostility. The mediator remembers a speech a few years back by Sir David Edward, then judge in the European Court of Justice, when he observed that the biggest risk to lawyers is over-identification with the client. "We'll go and have a quick chat in each room", he suggests…

10.45: The morning is moving on. It has been agreed that, at 10.55am, everyone will gather in the main room for the claimant's team to make a presentation. The room is laid out as a board-room with one long table and chairs on either side. "Hopeless", murmurs the mediator. He and his assistant set about unhinging the tables and moving them into a rather ramshackle triangle. A bit of adjusting and re-allocation of chairs and the job is done. They discuss who will sit where. The physical dynamics of what is known in the business as a "joint meeting" are important. The plan is to enable the claimant's team to sit in such a way that they can easily address the other team, without doing so directly across the table in a confrontational manner. Parties often poke fun at the mediator for this furniture rearranging but usually come quickly to appreciate the benefit which a more open arrangement brings.

11.01: "Let's get started." All the participants are now in place. The mediator turns to the lawyer for the claimant. "Peter, you are choreographing this I think. Do you wish to start? Just a quick word to the others. I'd ask you to listen to what is being said. Listen for something new. Don't just think about rebutting. You'll get your opportunity in a while and this is an opportunity to understand where Peter and his client are coming from today." The mediator has already talked privately to the defending team about the importance of appearing to be interested, making eye contact and acknowledging the presence of everyone in the other team. The benefit of the short private meeting of the clients is now clear: the awkwardness between them is at least reduced and it is easier for them to focus on what is being said.

11.05: The lawyer commences. His first point is about the late report. The mediator immediately realises that he has forgotten to convene the meeting of the two lawyers which he had proposed in that first meeting nearly two hours ago. There is a bit of friction which might have been avoided had he brought them together privately. The mediator is annoyed with himself but the moment has passed and, fortunately, the defending lawyer acknowledges the inconvenience and explains that his expert had been away on holiday until three days ago.

11.08: It has been agreed that the claimant will speak. She begins and it is clear that she is struggling with having to recall the events of several months ago. As her voice falters, there is a different kind of tension in the room...

1.3.3   *Exploration Continues: Getting to the heart*

11.09: "This has ruined my career and family. I had a solid professional role and a really good future. I have had to put everything on hold. I have been demeaned and humiliated. The cost to me is ......huge. I did everything I could. The Department wanted a fall guy and they chose me. I had warned about the time pressure. But no-one would listen. I stood up and was side-lined as a result. I went out on a limb and got the contract signed. You can't run a business like this." The mediator wondered if all the careful planning so far was about to go out of the window. And yet, this was exactly what she felt. Mediation is not about pushing under the carpet what needs to be said. Indeed, mediation is often represented as akin to having your day in court, except in a way which would be unlikely in a court under the conventional conditions of examining witnesses.

There was more scope here to say – and hear –what needed to be said – and heard. What this situation really tested was the skill of the lawyers in managing the expectations of clients and the mediator's careful steering beforehand. The defending party had been advised to expect this from the claimant. Their reaction was crucial however...

11.21: The claimant's lawyer had finished delivering a measured and yet direct analysis of his client's entitlement and the dangers to the defending team of not reaching agreement today. His experience in advocacy had come through, but not in an adversarial way. He had carried out his preparation meticulously, assessing the strengths and weaknesses on each side. He had not sought to hide the risks to his client.

Indeed he had played up the risks to all concerned. By doing so, he turned what might be thought to be his client's vulnerability into a positive. Be in no doubt, he had said, that the consequence of not resolving this will be bad for all concerned.

11.22: In the earlier days of mediation, convention had led to both parties making a "position statement" in the opening "joint meeting". Often, this just involved a forceful repetition of what was recorded in writing already. This mediator, in common with many others, reckoned that this tended simply to reinforce the antagonism and polarisation which had brought parties to this point in the first place. So, on this occasion, he had already flagged up that a break would occur when the claimant's team had set out their stall.

"Ok, thanks for the courteous way in which you have listened" he looked at the defending team. "And, Mrs A, thank you for the way in which you spoke, along with your lawyer. As I mentioned before, we are going to take a break now. We'll return to this room to hear what Mr B and his advisers have to say, not as a rebuttal but to build on what has been said already. Any concerns at this stage? Ok, please go back to your rooms. I'll check with both rooms shortly."

11.25: The mediator asked his assistant for an assessment. "That was just like the role plays in the training course," she said. "Everyone says that", came the reply. "In reality, I guess there are only a limited number of ways in which humans react to each other in conflict – all that changes are the facts and context." He had heard somewhere that there are four or five major themes in all literature, the human condition being universal. "We'd better go and see how the defending folk are getting on".

11.28: The atmosphere in the room was more relaxed than the mediator might have expected. The participants had a general reflection on what had happened and then moved to how the response would be handled. The mediator knew that it would be very easy for this room simply to try and refute the allegations made. Even done courteously, that might not work. Time for AA, RR, EE. This was one of his most used coaching tips, simple yet effective to engage people who genuinely needed to be valued and have their concerns acknowledged. Time for the flip chart...

11.48: Later than anticipated, but necessarily so as the next meeting was an important part of the first stage of mediation – and its conclusion – the parties reconvened in the plenary room. But there was one key person missing...

"Our client has decided that she does not want to be in this session". The claimant's lawyer was slightly sheepish as there had been no hint of this ten minutes ago when the mediator checked with her room. "She feels that it will be too much". The mediator knew that challenging this in front of the whole room would be insensitive. In any event, he always said to those concerned that they did not have to do or say anything that they did not wish to. It was the claimant's prerogative not to take part. And, yet, everything had been planned so that she could hear what the other party had to say. And had been planned to help everyone, including the claimant, to move forward. That was the point of AA, RR, EE.

11.54: The mediator knocked on the door and moved to the seat nearest to the claimant.

"How are you doing?" he asked.

1.3.4   *Moving on and summarising*

12.42: ....The last 45 minutes had been tough. The claimant had decided to listen to what the defending party had to say. Their lawyer had been careful not to inflame matters and had offered an expression of genuine regret to the claimant; not an apology as such, which was not appropriate, but a recognition that things had not worked out as anyone would have wished. While such an acknowledgement would often come from the client, on this occasion it was easier and better for it to be offered by someone who could be more dispassionate. The lawyer had also explained why his advice to his client was that a court would not find in the claimant's favour. While mediation is not simply about assertion of legal rights, it provides an opportunity to address the other client in a way which may be unique. For that client to hear, directly and in private, what her opposite number is being told by their lawyer gives a different perspective and often provides a better under-standing of risk. It reinforces the reality that, in litigation, respectable and well-regarded lawyers are offering different advice to their clients. At times like this, the mediator was often prompted to mention recent research which reveals that lawyers, like the rest of the population, tend to be over-optimistic about risk and the prospects of success.

12.45: It was now time to move on. The parties had lunch in their rooms. The mediator paused to take a couple of sandwiches but liked to keep moving. He was well aware that there was a lot of ground to cover before the day was over. If anything, the pace needed to pick up as the day progressed.

12.50: The mediator entered the defending party's room. There was a sense of relief that the most difficult part of the day, in personal terms, may have passed. The mediator joked about the excessive supply of sandwiches that they seemed to have been provided with. Lightness of touch is essential to maintain working relationships and to give some relief from the intensity of the day. It is often forgotten that people are condensing into one day that which may have taken months or years to build up and may take a similar time to resolve if these negotiations are not productive. "What do you think still needs to be said before we can move on to the next stage?" he asked.

13.10: It was time to summarise the discussions. "You are concerned that the claimant and her team are still unrealistic about what a court might do? And that you may need to run over the legal risks again..... Apart from that, the key now is to make progress on how to sort this out. Apart from the money side, what else is there to deal with? You have mentioned consultancy work and another project in the wings. How realistic is that? What about the reputational aspects? This was featured in the financial press some time ago, you said. How important is that? Can I suggest that you start to think in detail about these aspects and what you might say to the claimant?

On the legal analysis, my sense is that you won't need to rub this in. As a colleague of mine often says, you don't need to hear the penny drop. I think you should assume that they have heard you and got the message. You can't expect them to agree with you ...and remember their lawyer was fairly clear that they accepted they had risk...I would focus now on what you can do to help her to move on. Think about it in her shoes. Assume she has family members back home. If she accepts a deal today, what does she need to be able to say to them to explain what has happened? William Ury calls it the "victory speech"...you have to help her work out what she will say to her outside constituency... that may be as important as persuading her, especially if they have all invested a lot in this. OK, I'll leave you with that to work on...".

13.20: Back in the mediator's room, the mediator picked up a piece of fruit. His assistant asked about financial claims. "These are often a substitute, at least in part, for other things", the mediator responded. "Money seems to be the only way to address the wrongs but, if you leave money until later, you can often find other things of real value to add to the range of solutions. You need to find out what the parties really need, not what they say they want, or what the court pleadings say.

Often, they don't know themselves until you ask them although good lawyers will often have worked with them to explore their real interests in advance. What do you think the claimant really needs?" "A way to start back in business with a good project" came the reply. "She said that at one point early on in the second meeting." "Well spotted," said the mediator. "And, if so, we need to explore that soon...... Let's go and see how she is."

13.25: There was laughter in the claimant's room. "What's going on here?" asked the mediator. "I see you've not left any of the profiteroles. How was your lunch?" It was clear that the careful handling by the defending lawyer had helped to reduce the tension and removed the fear that the claimant had that she would be the subject of some sort of personal attack. "What more do you think you need to say, or that they don't understand, before we can move on to trying to resolve this?"

13.40: "In summary, then, while you are still not exactly happy with what was said, you accept their recognition of what you have been through? Let's close that chapter for now and look at what you really need out of this so that you can wake up tomorrow with this behind you and a new chapter to open. How would that feel?"

1.3.5 *The Experts Appear*

14.00: It was time for a meeting of the legal advisers. The mediator favoured working with the lawyers as much as possible. Just as bringing the clients together to talk could help to build bridges, encouraging collaboration by the lawyers was usually constructive. It gave them the opportunity to talk openly about the situation as they saw it, reminding their opposite numbers of the legal aspects but also focusing realistically on what could and could not be achieved.

Without breaching client confidentiality, they could often suggest courses of action or agree what might be said to clients to help them to make progress. The mediator would often ask apparently naïve questions in order to draw out the underlying issues. "What about the experts? Are they relevant anymore?" "Yes, we need to have their views on valuation and what should have been done with that other contract". "We certainly don't agree with your guy". It was clear that there was a source of conflict which might need to be addressed.

"How about bringing them together and asking them to present to each client directly?" asked the mediator. "It can often be really useful for the client to hear what is being said on the other side. Again, it's about understanding risk, not persuading either side that they are right or wrong." "But would we be present?" asked one lawyer. "I'm not particularly happy about them being alone with the clients".

"That's not a problem", replied the mediator, "but maybe your role can be as an observer in this session?"

14.20: It had been agreed that the mediator would meet with the experts first and discuss with them what the main differences were between them. Although they had prepared reports, as usual these played up the strengths of the party they had been asked to advise. The mediator knew from experience that, when experts actually sat down and talked through the issues together and gained a better understanding of the other perspective, the differences would often diminish.

Or, at least, the reasons for the differences would become clearer. It was remarkable how highly experienced professionals could reach different views based apparently on the same facts. The reason was usually an incomplete or (unconsciously) partial approach, reliant as they were on the information provided to them. It was far better that they reached greater consensus – or indeed made concessions – now, in this confidential process, than after several days of cross-examination in a court.

While this prospect troubled some lawyers, most appreciated the value of bringing clarity at this stage.

14.25: "What are the biggest differences between you?" asked the mediator. "Can you rank them in order, so that we can focus on what really matters? And can you identify why it is that you have these differences? When you've done that, I am going to ask you to come through to the main room together and take each topic in turn and I'll ask you to tell the clients where you differ and why." The experts knew each other well – and had a mutual respect – so, on this occasion, such a prospect was not too uncomfortable for them. (The mediator recalled some instances when this was not so. Such situations needed careful management).

Nevertheless, the mediator was aware that professional prestige was to some extent at stake, especially as the lawyers would be watching. After all, like others, the experts relied on the lawyers for work. Would that influence them? In theory, not at all. But even the mediator was aware that future revenue streams could have a sub-conscious effect on how a professional performed. Did that ever have any impact on mediators too, he pondered...?

14.45: The mediator had left the experts to talk and to prepare a rudimentary schedule of key issues. He gathered the others together, having made sure that he updated the clients on what was happening. It was that stage in the afternoon when people would begin to wonder if progress could be made. The mediator would use the term "wading through treacle" to describe the time it sometimes took to work through the issues. Experience taught him that trying to cut through things too quickly could backfire if niggling doubts or uncommunicated issues surfaced late in the day at a time when a resolution was in sight.

Patience was therefore the supreme virtue. On the other hand, dwelling overmuch on events in the past could cause the mediation to get bogged down. It was a fine balance, a judgment call each time…

14.55: "Ok, let's get started. This meeting is to invite the two experts to set out where they are coming from. They have a lot in common but there are a number of matters where you are each receiving different advice from them. You need to understand why and the implications for decisions you need to make today".

1515: There was a degree of frustration. One expert had rather dug himself in, or so it appeared. He looked less comfortable with the subject matter. All of this was useful, from the mediator's perspective.

The experts' performance at this stage was simply another fact in the overall matrix of risk. It gave the lawyer on that expert's side the opportunity to make an assessment of what might happen if the matter came to court. Again, better to know now…… On the other hand, the natural instinct was not to allow this to become undignified. The lawyer for the other party had already asked a rather dismissive question of this expert, notwithstanding that it had been agreed that the lawyers would simply observe. The mediator was quick to remind everyone of this ground rule. One of the mediator's roles at this stage was to ask apparently anodyne questions of both experts but, having read the papers in depth, he was able to identify some key issues. One question revealed that neither had considered a particularly significant consequence of a calculation they had each carried out.

15.30: A break had been taken for reflection in the private rooms. The mediator and his assistant pondered the cupcakes that someone had placed in their room. "I think we need to move on soon," observed the mediator. "We needed to show that the experts are unlikely to agree, nor to be persuaded by each other, but we can't let that become an impediment. It is what it is. Time for a reality check."…

1.3.6   Testing reality: "what if...?"

15.40: The mediator invited the lawyers into his room. Given the passage of time, conversation was now brisk and matter of fact. "I doubt that we'll get much more from the experts" suggested the mediator, "but at least the clients can now see that there is a different perspective from the other room. I would like to check up on that calculation though. What effect does that have?" The lawyers agreed that hearing the experts had been useful, perhaps more useful than might have been anticipated. "I think that my client was quite shocked to hear that there might be a different approach on that second point," said one, "but it's still difficult to get across the idea that a court may find against our expert." "And the calculation is frustrating," commented his counterpart. "Why on earth.....?" The mediator was aware that meetings like this were delicate and that neither lawyer wished to say anything that might appear to weaken their client's position. At the same time, and paradoxically, this kind of conversation was what loosened up the negotiations. It was important that the lawyers now did what they could to help their clients make the choice about whether to resolve matters today or not. The mediator reminded them of what he had said in that first gathering: that they needed to help each other.

15.51: As the lawyers departed, the mediator gestured to the claimant's lawyer to wait behind. "How do you see it?" he asked. "It's a bit of a struggle" was the reply. "This has left a deep scar". "How can I help?" asked the mediator. "I think she needs to hear from you. There is a limit to what I can say without losing credibility.....It's been a tough one." Such momentary asides often turned the day around.

16.03: "It's been a long day," acknowledged the mediator. The claimant nodded. "But it's important to remember that we are condensing into one day something that has taken months to get here and will take months – or longer – to resolve if it's left to some other process. Remember what we discussed about new chapters. Let's consider what would happen if this doesn't settle today". The mediator spent less time these days on BATNAS, WATNAS and risk analysis as many skilled lawyers now carried this out effectively with their clients. But, quite often, it remained useful for the mediator to act as an independent prompter of reflection on what would happen if agreement could not be reached. "What if you don't reach a deal today?" he asked. "I can't really contemplate that," replied the claimant. "This is eating my life up." "I can see that", said the mediator. "But you probably need to have a benchmark for deciding what will work for you." He turned to the lawyer" "What will happen next if there is no agreement today?"

16.27: It had been a tough session, with figures on the flip chart, the mediator's rudimentary decision-tree analysis, the usual conversation about the asymmetry of litigation and about the onus on the claimant to establish a number of things. The mediator frequently deferred to the lawyer, asking for his agreement or disagreement with propositions the mediator was putting. "Feel free to disagree," he would say to the claimant. "Or to reject any of this when I'm out of the room. My job is to raise all this with you, to make sure you have all the information so that you can make an informed choice".

He looked at his watch. "It's nearly 4.29" he said. "That's nearly always the low point in the day! This is the point when you wonder if this can ever move on. Well, it's remarkable how the pace can pick up. Let me ask you, what do you really need out of this now? Assume that the other team can't give you all you have asked for, and bear in mind the cost in money terms and in other respects of not reaching agreement, what realistically will work?"

16.43: Moving to the other room, the mediator's assistant asked what he thought would be the outcome. "I really don't know," he replied. "And the more I do this work, the less I am interested in the actual solution. I know that, if I let the process do its job, the more likely it is that an outcome will be reached. If I start to think about a particular result, I might influence things in that direction". The mediator knew, of course, that there would come a point where he would be testing and probing very hard around the consequences of not moving in particular directions and indeed might need to give an "impression" of what was and was not likely to work. It was a fine balance as always. And there was always the "Lord Not Very Bright" routine which he occasionally followed in each room as he speculated what might happen to the parties if a judge got out of bed on the wrong side....for them.

17.10: After a discussion about reputational risk and what the media might say if the matter became public, the mediator asked the defending client what he thought the claimant might need.

"If you were in her shoes…"

1.3.7 *Creative Problem-Solving: Moving Forward*

17.30: The exercise of getting in the claimant's shoes had been more cathartic than the mediator could have imagined. All the theory about viewing a situation through someone else's eyes, and the recent books about cognitive traps and confirmation bias and the like, were all very well but if, in practice, the theory fell flat, what use was it? The mediator referred to this material more now than ever before. After all, recent years had seen a proliferation of writing on such topics. And here, once again, at the right time and in the right way, assisting a party to alter his or her viewpoint, even if only for a few moments, enables a new perspective to be taken. The defending client has crossed a rubicon. He now understands at a deep level what had happened. That does not mean he agrees with it. But he understands.

"She'll need some help to go forward," he suggests. "A recommendation, some money, maybe a new contract. The money is hard. I can't see the board being happy about that. But she was good most of the time. I can say that. And I can put it in writing. I'd need to think about a contract. What it would look like. What we can realistically cover."

"Why don't you chat about that?" suggests the mediator.

"I'll need to talk to my contracts manager back at the plant".

"Remember the agreement you signed about confidentiality," warns the mediator. This was a grey area – he is keen to maintain the formality of confidentiality but not to let it get in the way. A discussion with a company colleague is perhaps covered by the agreement anyway.

"Tell you what, why don't I say to [the claimant] that you are looking at possibilities and that you'd like to talk to your contracts man. That way I can introduce the topic in a low key way and get her agreement to you doing so. Keeps us all covered. And can I mention the recommendation? I'll have a short meeting and let you know asap."

17.45: Back in the defending party's room, there is an atmosphere of business-like attention to detail. The whole mood has changed. "We can talk about a contract, needs to be short term but it may be enough to get back on the road again. And I can do a small cash payment as part of that contract. Not separate but within the payment provisions of the contract. Makes it more sellable." "What are the figures?" asks the mediator. What he hears worries him. He knows what is in the mind of the claimant from an earlier remark by her lawyer. "How will that go down?" he asks. "The danger is that you undermine your whole strategy by offering something so low that she considers it derisory and insulting. That could lead her in the opposite direction."

This is a flip-chart moment. He gets up and draws rudimentary lines on the sheet, showing with an "x" and a "y" the dangers of making what might be perceived as unreasonable proposals. He talks about the theory of first-mover advantage, never an easy one as it applies to both sides. Then he sits down and pauses.

"We need to think some more" opines the solicitor. "We can't afford to throw this away. There's the other matter to think about....." There is an anxious glance between client and advisor. A quick moving on. But, once again, in that moment, the mediator realises that there is more going on here than he will ever know. When observers talked about "justice" and the need for the mediator to make sure that "justice" is done, what they often did not appreciate is that there is nearly always more going on than the mediator will ever be aware of.

In his view, it could not be a mediator's job to assess the rightness or wrongness of a resolution, but just to make sure that the process works really well and that clients and advisers make as well-informed decisions as they can. They can always walk away, a point sometimes forgotten by those who would equate mediation with the judicial process. Nothing is binding until…

18.00: "Let's look at a realistic figure" suggests the mediator. "My impression is that you can go considerably further without in any way doing harm to yourselves. My sense is that even at £x, the claimant will be below anything that she would contemplate." This is tricky territory. "Impressions" and "senses" could convey ideas based on understandings the mediator had gained from his discussions in the other room.

"Is that what she said?" asks the client.

"You know I can't refer to anything said in the other room without permission. I won't be telling her your figures unless you authorise me to do so."

A mediator's stock response and such a fine line…

1.3.8 *Negotiating Towards a Resolution*

18.10: The mediator has checked with both rooms about refreshments. The catering staff have gone home and the coffee, in those ubiquitous flasks, is lukewarm. By this stage, people tended to nibble on biscuits and the sandwiches left over from lunchtime, which were becoming less edible by the minute. The more wary avoided the prawn sandwiches… It is agreed to keep going without a formal break in the hope that progress can be made soon. Mindful that this is nearly always the wish, the mediator nevertheless asks his assistant to remind him about trying to get some pizzas delivered in about an hour's time. He recalls those other occasions when early evening food had been provided by the venue. This had created opportunities for him to position the key decision-makers next to each other as they ate. In these moments, conversation often led to creative solutions, such as an offer to make a donation to charity in lieu of a contractual claim.

Honour was addressed and faces saved by such a proposal. The fact that the principals came up with it over food seemed to give it additional mileage. Ah well, pizza will have to do this evening. ...

18.12: Rather than taking the defending party's proposals direct to the claimant's room, the mediator needed to take time to find out what the claimant was now thinking after their previous discussion about the risks of not resolving today. Amazingly, it was nearly 90 minutes since their last full discussion. Far too long, thought the mediator, though he had popped in to mention the suggestion that the defending principal needed to discuss matters with the contracts manager – and generally to reassure that the reason he was taking so much time was because progress was being made. He had encouraged the claimant to go for a walk and get some fresh air. She had done this and seemed more focussed now as a result.

"I need to move on," she said, "What are they saying?"

The mediator was firm about not being, as he put it, a "mere messenger," nor did he see himself as a deal broker. He disliked taking offers and counter-offers back and forward, especially if these were at the extreme end of the spectrum. He viewed this as rather unsophisticated negotiation. Indeed, on occasion he had invited a party to convey their apparently derisory proposal direct to the other party. That usually led to further conversation..... He much preferred to draw parties together by managing expectations and helping them to get as close as possible before presenting them with formal proposals.

18.17: "They, like you, wish to see this brought to an end," he said. "And my sense is that they can move further than you might have thought earlier, indeed further than you might have expected. All that good work that you, your lawyer and your expert did in earlier meetings has had its impact, which is the whole point. Just as you have learned from them, too....", he added for balance. "Apart from the money side, what value would you place on a short term contract to get you back up and running again? And with a reference that emphasises the positive work you did on the project last year? How would these help you get started again?" The claimant looked relieved. "That could make a difference," she said. "I really need to get my confidence back. Where would it be? Who for? How long?" "These would all need to be discussed," responded the mediator, "but if we can get these moving in principle, I can get you round the table with them."

"But the money is important too," the claimant was again anxious, "I have lost a lot and all these legal costs....." Nearly always, in these situations, the legal costs became a relevant factor.

The mediator had seen emerging deals falter because the legal costs outweighed the sums in dispute, or at least those being contemplated in settlement. Not an easy moment for the lawyers either. One of the conundrums in litigation is that cost and time often obscure the real underlying issues. The mediator was tempted to quote Abraham Lincoln: discourage your neighbour from litigating. Point out that the nominal winner is often the real loser. In other words, victory in court will, in many instances, be a pyrrhic one.

18.30: The mediator now had a feel for what would work for the claimant. He began to talk about how the defending party was thinking, as he had been authorised to do. It was useful to be able to weave in their thinking after hearing from the claimant. The mediator could choose what to say and when. He was not a mere messenger. This enabled him to work with the parties to try and build the best possible solution. Or, as he would often say, ensure that each felt that they had achieved as much as they could. The value of a mediator should be that the claimant should know, for example, that she had pushed the other side to the maximum they would offer on the day, and the paying party should know that they were paying the minimum that a claimant would accept. That was, after all, the key role that a mediator could play, adding something that was sometimes too difficult to achieve in direct negotiations by parties themselves, who could never be sure just how far they could go without feeling compromised.

18.35: "May I take this to the other room?" asked the mediator. The claimant looked at her lawyer. He nodded. "It's time to make progress and there is nothing there that we don't want said to them."

1.3.9 *Getting down to specifics*

18.37: The mediator paused in his private room with his assistant. This was the time when it was easy to rush things. People were getting tired. A mediator's adrenalin could pump too fast as the end seemed to be in sight.

Many a false dawn…. This was the time when rushing from room to room trying to pin down a settlement could backfire. This was the time when a mediator could be tempted to take over the burden of resolution and implicitly (or explicitly) take on the responsibility for reaching a conclusion. It remained the parties' problem. They needed to remain responsible for it. It was a fine balance. The mediator had to encourage, cajole, test reality, resist inappropriate game play, be prepared to let them blow it, and yet…. "What do you think..?" asked the assistant. "Let's see" came the reply.

18.40: "How are you getting on with the terms of a contract? I think we should try to get that worked up before dealing with the money. And the wording of the reference?" The mediator had decided to take the initiative on this occasion in the defending party's room. "In my experience, it is usually best to deal with the non-monetary aspects first if possible. It is often the case that the money claim is a substitute for other things. Or at least in part. I have seen large claims significantly reduced when other elements are on offer. Value is not just found in the cash. The trouble is that we tend to view these disputes through the lens of what a court can do, which is always going to be more limited….." He realised that his attempt to be encouraging was turning into a bit of a homily. Not the best use of time at this stage…

18.45: "So, that is what we can do" the client has summarised the position after his further conversations with his contracts manager. "That's helpful" responds the mediator. "I appreciate that this is not easy. How about the reference?" It is clear that not much work has been done. He turns to the lawyer. "I wonder if you and [the claimant's solicitor] could have a short meeting and try to come up with a wording? It's really more than a reference, this will be important for the claimant as she seeks to build a new approach to her business. …. Now, onto the numbers…. One of the problems is going to be costs. Have you any idea what these might be for her?" After a quick discussion, the mediator reveals the total, as he has been authorised to do. There is apparent shock all round.

"It is what it is," the mediator is aware that, in this room, the costs are probably even higher and that the expressions of surprise are a little overdone. "Last time you told me what you can do overall on the figures. My sense is that the claimant will need a good bit more, probably starting with a "2". But let's see how we get on with the contract and the reference."

18.50: "I'd like to take these specific terms to her and invite the lawyers to try and get the bare bones of a reference." The seed has been planted on the number. It is time to use the other aspects to help lever the parties to a place where they could make choices. "By the way, have you got the resolution agreement in draft? Let's not leave that until the end." This is the first time that the mediator has hinted that he thinks that resolution might be in prospect. And he is careful with his caveat. "I don't want to pre-empt anything and don't assume that we are home and dry but I don't want to spend another couple of hours drafting from scratch if you do resolve this in the next hour." Often, he invited parties to start to put together a resolution agreement quite early in the day. It helped to keep the lawyers (especially if there were a number of them) occupied and focussed on looking ahead to an agreed outcome rather than dwelling on the past.

1910: The short meeting with the claimant has gone well. The contractual proposals seem to be broadly acceptable. The mediator has now called the two lawyers into his room. Ostensibly this is to discuss the terms of the reference. But, in reality, it is to get them talking about the figure which will help their clients complete an agreement. "There is still a bit of a gap" says the mediator. "What can be done?" He is content to let the lawyers chat for a few minutes. This is where skilful and courageous lawyers are able to do their best. Some of the best lawyering in mediation occurred at moments like these. After all, most disputes were resolved by lawyers negotiating like this.

The mediator took the view that his role, wherever possible, is to help the lawyers and their clients to regain their ability to negotiate with each other. The mediator's role then begins to diminish. As ever, there is a balance to be struck. If it was easy, they wouldn't be here. In reality, however, the heavy lifting has been done to a large extent. There would still be the odd dangerous moment however…

1.3.10 *The End Game*

19.26: It is really down to the money now. Everything else is slotting, like a complex jigsaw puzzle, into place. That fact alone gives the process momentum and gives the parties the incentive to persevere and reach a conclusion.

It was often forgotten that research – and experience – showed that most people, even in the most difficult of disputes, wish to resolve matters and move on. For everyone, risk aversion, sunk costs, intuition, confirmation bias and so on could operate to impede that desire. But, in the end, the mediator muses, the human instinct is more cooperative than combative and his job is to harness that instinct and help the players to override the contrary motivations.

19.28: Back to the claimant's room. "How are you bearing up?" the mediator inquires. "Time for pizza?" He knows that blood sugar levels will be low and there is still a bit of ground to cover. It will help to have some food to sustain the teams at this stage. Fortunately, there is a take away pizzeria nearby. One of the legal team offers to check with both rooms and do what is required. Hawaiian is the mediator's prefer-ence…."We are getting there" the mediator says, "Perseverance is now the key – and reality. Where have you got to on the figures?" He can see that the lawyer has been working on the flip chart. No attempt is made to conceal the figures from the mediator. He invites them to talk him through what is written up.

The approach appears to be to focus on what the claimant really needs to be able to walk away and get started afresh, with costs paid. This re-alignment from entitlement and rights to needs and interests is refreshing and the mediator is quick to acknowledge that. It seems that what she needs is still higher than what the defending party is able to offer but the gap will be closer now. "I think they will struggle with that", the mediator offers a view. "Of course, we don't know, it's in their interests to sort this too. But I think we need to get a move on. Can I take this analysis to them? I don't think you compromise yourselves by showing this. It may just help them to understand better what they need to do." He wonders about inviting the lawyer or even the claimant herself to present the figures to the other side but quickly concludes that he can probably do so more effectively. At least at this stage. ...

19.47: "So, there we are" the mediator summarises to the defending team.

"From her point of view, and that of her advisers, this makes sense and moves them away from that figure beginning with a "2". It's time to bite bullets I think. Maybe even time to formulate an offer."

"Could you give us some time to think?" the lawyer is looking thoughtful. "Of course…"

1950: The mediator's assistant looks at her pages of notes. "Could we not just have got to this in the first hour….." "What do you think?" smiles the mediator. "Ask yourself how likely that would have been given what we saw and heard early on. You have to give it time. That is what is frustrating for people of course. At the end, it sometimes seems so obvious. But if it was that easy…we wouldn't be here. It's necessary to go through the stages. It's only a day after all and they have been at this for months. And if they don't resolve it……"

There was a knock on the door. "Can we have a chat?" It is the lawyer for the defending party. "Come in" replies the mediator. "Here is what we think we can do….." the lawyer begins to set out his and his clients' thinking.

20.02: "Go back and see if that is possible" suggests the mediator. He has heard enough to know that the gap is closing significantly. There still has not been a formal proposal put on either side. That was how the mediator liked to work. Avoiding putting either party in a situation where they were fixed to a position, boxed in or needing to save face. Trying to minimise the offence which could be caused by over- or under- pitching. If he could help to manage the movement on numbers so that each party felt it was being listened to, was not compromised and was getting the best deal it could, that was the objective.

A knock on the door again. "We can do that but there's not much more room," says the lawyer. "That's really helpful, thank you," responds the mediator. "May I take that and use that in my own way?" "Over to you," is the smiling reply.

20.15: The mediator deliberately changes his approach. It is more business-like, matter of fact. He looks at the claimant. "I think there is scope for some movement. I'd like to have a chat with your lawyer if I may?" The claimant indicates that she is comfortable with this. By this stage, the trust built up over the day is such that no one is in doubt that both lawyer and mediator are working for a solution in the best interests of all concerned. They leave the room and head for comfortable chairs in the foyer.

The building is deserted now.

"Here is where we are," says the mediator. "It's about the best they can do. I might get another 10k out of them. But only if your client can say she would accept that sum if offered. Can you help her with that?"

The bluntness of the question seems quite in order at this stage. "Leave it with me" the lawyer is already on his feet, heading back to the room to speak to his client.

20.23: "She can do that" the lawyer comes back to the foyer. "Ok, I'll be back soon. Wait here." The mediator leaves and returns shortly after with the other party's lawyer and addresses him in front of his counterpart.

"Here's where we are…… If you can offer that, perhaps on the basis that if the claimant says she will take it you can make the offer, I think we are going to get there." He looks at the claimant's lawyer for confirmation. "Agreed" comes the affirmation.

20.35: "Well, here we are," the mediator welcomes the two principals to his room. "Seems like a long time since we first met together this morning. Lots of water under the bridge…. I prefer, if possible, for the principals to complete the deal if they can. I think you are both able to do so. You have broad agreement now on the contractual matters and the reference. The lawyers still need to get the wording right but, with goodwill and good sense, that can be done briskly this evening in the resolution agreement. And I think you are nearly there on the figures."

He turns to the defender client who immediately reacts. "I would like to thank you for all your time today. I know it has not been easy," he says directly to the claimant. "But we want this to end well. So we are prepared to offer you…"

The claimant leans forward with a hand outstretched.

"Thank you," she says quietly. "That works for me. I can move on now. If only we'd had this conversation three months ago…"[37]

---

37 The authors acknowledge John Sturrock's work and invention in putting this work together: and his candour in reflecting points where others may have worked in a different manner. Every mediation is different and every mediator learns from each instance the neutral's role is taken.

1.4   An Idle Mediation

1.4.1   *The mediator and the 17 camels[38]*

As discussed through the medium of Sir Brian Neill's Vienna conference history lesson[39], although mediation is sometimes perceived as having "come from the USA", in fact, it seems likely that mediation originated in the Far East, where mediation has a long and honourable tradition of resolving conflict. The fable of the Mediator and the Seventeen Camels, however, comes to us from the Middle East, and like all the best fables, it is a bridge to the truth. The authors offer it, with due caution as to the method adopted and mindful of the paucity of camels in London, as a parable that shows how a neutral's reality testing, looking in at the matter without any interest in the outcome, may be a catalyst.

> *"Once upon a time, a Mediator was riding through the endless wastes of the desert on his camel. The Mediator had been riding for a long time and as he scanned the sea of sand that surrounded him, he was pleased to see the palm trees of an oasis on the horizon. He turned his trusty camel towards it and made for the oasis.*
>
> *But, as the Mediator neared the oasis he realised that all was not well. Raised voices drifted across the sand towards him, and he caught the unmistakable glint of sunlight on drawn swords. By the time the Mediator arrived in the oasis it was apparent that a full blown conflict was about to break out. Anxious to help (or, perhaps, seeing the opportunity for an unexpected bit of business) the Mediator enquired as to what the problem might be.*
>
> *The sad story was soon told. An old, and important member of the tribe had died. He had provided for the distribution of his worldly goods in his will, and, as was common in those days, in that part of the world, he had divided his goods between his three sons, giving the*

---

38 The authors acknowledge the retelling of this idle tale by expert mediator Martin Plowman in 2013 as set out on the Mediation 1ˢᵗ website http://www.mediation1st.co.uk/?p=the.story.of.the.mediator.and.the.17.camels

39 Supra – page 8

most to the oldest, and least to the youngest. The eldest son was to receive one half of the estate, the middle son was to receive one third of the estate and the youngest son was to receive one ninth of the estate. That in itself would not have triggered a conflict, for the principle was not unusual, but the difficulty lay in the fact that the man's estate consisted entirely of seventeen camels.

In a part of the world where wealth was measured in camels this was a significant fortune.

The difficulty, however, was that seventeen is a number that can be divided by neither two, to give the eldest son a half, nor by a third nor a ninth to give the next two sons their proper shares. Hence the impending conflict. The eldest son, not unnaturally, felt that he should have a bit more, but his younger brothers, again understandably, felt that as their older brother was already receiving the most it was he who should give something up.

The only compromise that had been suggested was to kill all seventeen camels, to weigh the meat, and then to divide the estate that way. Unfortunately, whilst it was superficially attractive this solution was, in the searing heat of the desert, and before the age of the deep freeze, simply not practicable.

So swords had been drawn, and the members of the family were about to fall upon each other, when the unexpected chance that a Mediator should suddenly appear out of the desert gave them a glimmer of hope, and they enquired of the Mediator whether he could help.

A fee was negotiated, and paid by each of the brothers out of their own assets[40], and the Mediator then said "I shall give you my camel".

---

40 To this day, mediators acting for fees are paid in advance to ensure that there is no question of any stake in the outcome – and they are generally paid equally by each of the participants unless other arrangements apply (for example under the NHS Resolution mediation scheme or in workplace mediations.

The Mediator's suggestion provoked amazement, with some asking how that was supposed to help, and others questioning the Mediator's sanity.

The Mediator went on to explain:

"Now you have eighteen camels. Eighteen is divisible by two, so the eldest son can have nine camels. Eighteen is divisible by three, so the middle son can have six camels and eighteen is divisible by nine, so the youngest son can have two camels". Satisfied, and overjoyed to have avoided a conflict, each of the sons took his camels and returned to his tent.

Moreover, since nine plus six plus two comes to seventeen, the Mediator's camel was left over and the Mediator was able to climb back onto his trusty camel and to resume his voyage across the desert".

The moral of the story is? As Martin Plowman[41] says – probably to check your maths when drafting a will, but also, and more importantly, that the input of an independent Mediator can transform even the most difficult of disputes.

1.4.2   Summary of Part One

Part One is intended to demonstrate that mediation is a polymorphic activity. But what of the authors' allusion[42] to painting, to shoes, and to dinner parties? How is this justified? Like painting and shoes, there are designs and styles, sizes and practical considerations of a near-infinite variety. The precise strokes of the Old Masters or the abstract images of Miro may have their place in the narrative of a mediation. Every day is a different day.

---

41 http://www.mediation1st.co.uk/?p=mediators

42 *Supra*, page 6

Similarly, the red-soled perfection of Christian Louboutin[43] is probably not going to wear well in a neighbourhood dispute in Catford nor should a mediator attempt to stamp size-12 CAT boot prints all over any mediation – the terrain is very much that of the participants, the mediator an invited visitor who should leave no trace at the end of the process.

Best of all, a mediation is comparable with a dinner party. The mediator might be regarded as the host – providing a welcome, refreshments, a guide to the venue, and generally a table. The host and mediator will introduce the guests, perhaps offer a grace, and then stimulate conversation. But the best hosts, like the best mediators, will let the talk flow, stepping in if it flags, attending to the guests' needs and seeing that all is well.

Some hosts will have private conversations, and may ask provoking questions once rapport has been built. So too with mediators. But neither will force guests to any point, and, at the end of the day, mediators like a good host, will prefer quiet satisfaction to noisy applause.

---

43 Other brands, or more properly designers, are available

PART TWO –
ON MEDIATORS

2.1   The Mediator's World

Kenneth Cloke[1], director of the Centre for Dispute Resolution in Santa Monica, California is a mediation giant. His view of the context in which mediators operate is interesting:

> *"The primary purpose of mediation is to create a controlled "chain reaction," in which the conflict is allowed to explode and implode without damaging the parties. The implosion fuels self-awareness, while the explosion allows them to identify the dysfunctional systems that cause the conflict. The chain reaction starts with deeply honest, empathetic questions that defuse or disarm the parties' defensive mechanisms, allowing truth and positive feelings to reach their target"*

Explosions and implosions may seem the business of ordnance disposal experts and big-bang theorists but there is, for all that, much to be learned from this analysis. In *Mediating Dangerously*[2] he expressed the thought that in mediation sometimes it is necessary to push beyond the usual limits of the process to achieve deeper and more lasting change. He suggested ways of getting to the outer edges and dark places of dispute resolution, where risk taking is essential and fundamental change is the desired result.

---

1   As Director of the Center for Dispute Resolution, Kenneth Cloke has served as a mediator, arbitrator, attorney, coach, consultant and trainer. Ken specializes in resolving complex multi-party conflicts which include: community, grievance and workplace disputes, collective bargaining negotiations, organizational and school conflicts, sexual harassment and discrimination lawsuits, and public policy disputes. Ken also provides services in designing conflict resolution systems for organizations. He is an internationally recognised speaker and author of many books and journal articles.

2   (2001) https://www.amazon.co.uk/Mediating-Dangerously-Frontiers-Conflict-Resolution/dp/0787953563

It meant opening wounds and looking beneath the surface, challenging comfortable assumptions, and exploring dangerous issues such as dishonesty, denial, apathy, domestic violence, grief, war, and slavery in order to reach a deeper level of transformational change. Mediating Dangerously[3] sought to show conflict resolution professionals how to advance beyond the traditional steps, procedures, and techniques of mediation to unveil its invisible heart and soul and to reveal the subtle and sensitive engine that drives the process of personal and organizational transformation. This echoed experiences in South Africa and Belfast.

In his recent work, The Dance of Opposites[4], Cloke considers what is success and failure in mediation, and how we should re-examine our approach to conflict resolution. He quotes Churchill – that success is going from failure to failure without losing your enthusiasm.

This to the authors summarises a particular aspect that is key to being a skilled mediator. Mediators who focus on "success", whatever that may be in their minds, tend to find resolutions for others take a deal of time to achieve. Those who focus on process find that the techniques of mediation create for the participants the success that they want, which is very often not at all what the mediator may have envisaged at the start of the day.

Thus, skilled mediators are those who can bring intelligent and deft touches to conversations, who are prepared to invest time and create rapport, who are not afraid of appropriate difficult conversations, and perhaps most crucially neutrals ready to lose the desire to state the solution or fix the problem. Skilled mediators can see that without owning the problem the knowledge to resolve it is unlikely to be theirs – but precisely because they do not own the problem they can bring and apply tools to create a safe workshop.

To do so is exhausting through the concentration it needs, but rewarding. In 1974, the late Robert Pirsig set out to resolve the conflict

---

3 Which is obviously not a style recommended in week one of a new mediator's practice.

4 See: http://www.kennethcloke.com/Pdf/The_Dance_of_Opposite_Flier.pdf

between classic values that create machinery, such as a motorcycle, and romantic values, such as experiencing the beauty of a country road. Thus, Zen and the Art of Motorcycle Maintenance[5] saw a search for understanding and the meaning of quality. It did so through the idea that encouraging the telling of a tale can pass on concerns and wisdoms so as to remove conflict.

Mediators encourage the telling of stories, of tales, the sharing of experiences and ambitions, as a way of resolving these tensions and conflicts. They can be across the common table in the plenary[6] (or open) session, or in candid confidential discussions in a caucus (or private) session. Mediators must therefore be enthusiastic listeners, willing to prefer the voices of the participants to their own. Mediators who talk more than 10% of the time should ask themselves 'why?' – how are they helping process and have they built a rapport. But the authors jump ahead – we should first ask: who can be these paragons of virtue?

5 https://www.amazon.co.uk/Zen-Art-Motorcycle-Maintenance-Inquiry/dp/0099786400

6 Plenary here meaning open to all participants – but not (almost always) the wider public: what is said or done in the plenary session is confidential and without prejudice and cannot usually be disclosed to anyone else.

2.2   Who Can Be a Mediator?

In short: almost anyone and everyone, without restrictions of background or age, culture or gender, provided they are possessed of sufficient capacity and a little patience. In fact some of the most intuitive mediators are young children who have been trained to resolve playground disputes in their schools. It might be that children are free from some of the baggage of later life and thus more easily disinclined to be judgemental and assumptive in their dealings with each other. Certainly, such attributes are desirable in mediators.

But as adults and professionals, it is a natural phenomenon to assess and consider those we meet and work with – perhaps making assumptions that later turn out to be wholly mistaken. As mediators we cannot (and should not seek to) escape our characters, but we can train the mind to apply the techniques and tools of neutrality, that ultimately may make us more functional and emotionally intelligent individuals, as well as mediators.

For the doubters, consider the experience almost everyone has of mediating with other people informally. It may be in calming or resolving difficult situations, whether that has been in business, amongst friends, or with our families. Indeed, whenever people walk a busy pavement they negotiate unconsciously to avoid collisions. That unconscious competence as a walker is a foretaste of what mediators seek to achieve in their practice.

Who then comes forward to seek that competence? Those attending mediation training courses come from a wide variety of backgrounds. Often, there will be lawyers and doctors. The lawyers, usually as a result of the increasing court promotion of ADR, and the doctors because they recognise a need to seek positive outcomes to complex patient and workplace issues including complaints. Perhaps the majority, though, are business people, teachers, human resource practitioners, scientists, and those seeking a change of career. Others are people returning to work or looking to add mediation to a broader skill set to apply in their professional lives and in all that they do as part of their vocation. The door welcomes all.

Some mediators want to evaluate and that desire may relate to a particular skill set. The training for the role is separate. But all would-be mediators, as part of their training, are encouraged to read widely and think deeply – not about the law or solutions, but about the human psychology and relationships that underpin conflict.

This has been described as the application of emotional intelligence although there are many other ways of looking at the skill. The term is often related to a 1995 work by Daniel Goleman, a psychologist and science correspondent for the New York Times. "Emotional Intelligence" reportedly sold five million copies in 40 languages worldwide[7]. Three years later, Goleman published "What Makes a Leader?"[8] Goleman discounted both the traditional Intelligence Quotient (IQ) and an individual's technical skill and competence as being the sole measures of a person's abilities.

In his original work Goleman had identified five characteristics that he claimed an individual with a relatively high level of emotional intelligence would display. The context of the research being that, visionary leaders and highly effective managers express these "softer skills" when dealing with others. These are:

- Self-Awareness;
- Self-Regulation;
- Motivation;
- Empathy; and
- Social Skill.

It seems to the authors that these offer a skeleton for a useful self-checklist to mediators, both before embarking on training and during their own work. They reflect the insights that mediators should themselves have, and those that they wish to foster within the conversations they

---

7   In fact, the term emotional intelligence (EI or EQ) was probably first coined by psychologists – John Mayer of the University of New Hampshire and Peter Salovey of Yale.

8   Goleman, D., *What Makes a Leader?* Harvard Business Review 1998

develop with participants. As ever with mediation, nothing should be considered definitive but it is helpful, the authors believe, to identify characteristics that assist process.

In "What Makes a Leader?" Goleman included a summary table that the authors have adapted below to relate to the mediator – rather than the leader in the workplace. A mediator is less a leader than a moderator or facilitator, but there are parallels. The columns with the characteristics and definitions remain Goleman's but the "Hallmarks of the Mediator" are the adaptations of the authors.

Table 3: THE CHARACTERISTICS OF EMOTIONAL INTELLIGENCE

Characteristics	Definition	Hallmarks in the Mediator
Self-Awareness	The ability to recognise and to understand your own moods, emotions, and drivers, as well as their effect on others	Self-confidence Realistic self-assessment and reflection of skill and competence A self-deprecating sense of humour
Self-Regulation	The ability to control or to redirect disruptive impulses and moods The propensity to suspend judgement – to think before acting	Trustworthiness and integrity Consistency in personal doing Comfort with ambiguity and the unknown An openness to change and acceptance that others may wish to do things differently
Motivation	A passion to do something for reasons that go beyond money and status A propensity to pursue goals with energy and persistence	Strong drive to assist others to achieve Optimism, even in the face of failure A strong commitment to and belief in the mediation process
Empathy	The ability to understand the emotional make up of other people Skill in treating people according to their emotional reactions	Expertise in building relationships Cross-cultural sensitivity An ability to provide a "service above self" to the participants
Social Skill	Proficiency in managing relationships and building networks An ability to find common ground and build rapport	Effectiveness in leading others, without directing in order to assist others in achieving Doing the right thing in the right way at the right time Fostering a sense of purpose

To Goleman's Table the authors would add one additional character-istic – curiosity. We return to that below observing that it is one of the privileges of the mediator to enquire.

It is the authors' view, then, that there are many factors, qualities, and attributes that crystallise in a skilled mediator. Often they will do so in different combinations and it is important that they do. We are all unique and that is to be celebrated – the authors do not seek to train clones of themselves. Everyone will bring their own style to mediation. Yet, Goleman's work and the five characteristics of Emotional Intelli-gence are a sound place to start that personal journey as a mediator and to understand what is required to succeed.

Emotional Intelligence can be learned. Neuroscience suggests that Emotional Intelligence sits largely within the human brain's limbic system, which governs feelings, impulses and drives. Research indicates[9] that in order to get the limbic system to learn it is best achieved through motivation, extended practice and feedback[10].

Interestingly, however, the majority of working and professional training uses learning and development focused on a part of the brain called the neocortex. Doctors and lawyers are particularly trained in this manner: to think analytically and logically using a structure of rules or hierarchies. The neocortex governs this human analytical and technical ability. It is that part of the brain that deals with concepts and logic. In short, being 'a professional'

In contrast, mediation training exercises and stretches the limbic brain. Nimbleness of thinking, listening, and consideration of drivers is para-mount. This is probably why, on the first few days of mediation training, the authors often hear student delegates saying, *"I am having to leave lots of baggage behind to grasp the process."* or *"This is so right – but so counter-intuitive to my day job."* By the end of the week, however, most have found that the two skill sets are complementary not contra-

---

9 See eg: Wagner and Tendler, Haifa (2015) https://elifesciences.org/articles/03614

10 See also: http://neurosciencenews.com/learning-memory-emotion-limbic-system-2393/

dictory and their professional skills multiply. This includes the renewed ability, first learned by age four, to step into another's shoes[11].

Many find that becoming or being a mediator is about learning to temper old learned 'professional' habits and adapting the neutral self to engage with the feelings, impulses, and drives of others. In other words, activating or reapplying the mediator's innate Emotional Intelligence.

It is sometimes claimed that Emotional Intelligence increases with age. Some use this to suggest that grey[12] or silver hair (hidden by dye or not) is a pre-requisite in a mediator. Perhaps that perception is predicated on becoming wise and more sagely with age drawing on life's experiences and encounters? Present research suggests not[13] – although the perception continues.

Interestingly, younger adults reported to Atkins and Stough (through significant batteries of tests and anecdotally) being better able to prevent strong emotions from interfering with their work than either middle-age or older adults. This result contradicts the view, on self-reporting measures, that older adults are more likely to claim that they successfully control their emotions because they feel that they should be able to do so (Carstensen et al., 2000).

It follows that the authors see no barrier through age or any other factor to becoming a mediator. Whilst older mediators may be the popular choice for legal professionals, perhaps to inspire earlier confidence in their clients or to bring wisdom from a demonstrably successful career, there is no reason in principle or practice why younger mediators should not thrive. The authors have seen successes at both ends of the spectrum.

---

11 See recent research summarised in *Nature* (2017)
   http://www.nature.com/articles/ncomms14692#abstract

12 See: Suzanne Rab (2017) http://kluwermediationblog.com/2017/03/21/do-you-need-grey-hairs-to-mediate/

13 See: Atkins, Paul & Stough, Con. (2005). Does Emotional Intelligence change with age?

Effective mediators are, therefore, certainly those who are willing, at least through the duration of their appointment, to look at differing perspectives whilst considering the feelings of others; of being non-judgmental whilst being confident about process; and of maintaining a curious, and energetic, neutrality. These techniques can, as the authors believe, be grasped and applied by most people. All of them feed into the central skill, reported most often, as the ability to build a rapport. That more than anything is how skilled mediators, who themselves lack any power to impose a solution, nevertheless often assist even bitter disputants to agreement.

Of course, serious mediation training and substantive expertise are critical, as is a keen analytic mind. But according to a survey by Northwestern University law professor Stephen Goldberg[14], veteran mediators believe that establishing rapport is more important to effective mediation than employing any specific mediation techniques and tactics.

To gain parties' trust and confidence, rapport must be genuine: "You can't fake it," one respondent said. Before people are willing to settle, they must feel that their interests are truly understood. Only then can a mediator assist in reframing problems and allow them to float creative solutions.

Goldberg's[15] various respondents could report only their own perceptions about why they succeed, of course. A detached observer or the parties themselves might have very different explanations. Indeed, one of the tenets of mediation practice is to work subtly so that parties leave feeling as if they have reached accord largely on their own, a strategy that is meant to deepen their commitment to honour the agreement.

---

14 See: 2010 paper, at https://www.pon.harvard.edu/daily/mediation/what-makes-a-good-mediator/

15 See: http://www.law.northwestern.edu/faculty/profiles/StephenGoldberg/

In an earlier study by mediator Peter Adler[16], his colleagues explained their success by discussing "the breakdowns, breakthroughs, and the windows of opportunities lost or found." By contrast, participants in the same cases remembered the mediators only as "opening the room, making coffee, and getting everyone introduced."

This research perhaps offers two lessons. One is the importance of relationship building, especially in contentious situations. Some measure of trust is required before people will open up and reveal their true interests. The other is that a hallmark of an artful process is that others do not feel manoeuvred or manipulated. Skilled mediators apply both lessons.

2.2.1   *An exercise – the thin red line*

The authors offer with due deference an exercise adapted from a student game used by Tammy Lenski[17], an eminent American trainer, to consider trust, rapport, communication, and win:win in mediation. It also helps people to think about negotiating styles.

Students see a line on the floor made with red masking tape. Students must find a partner and stand facing each other on opposite sides of the line. They are told that they are about to play a game and that the object is to get your partner to come over to their side of the line.
The leader then tells the students that if they can do that, they will win. And not only will they win, but the leader will pay the winner $1,000 in monopoly money. The leader then gives the students 60 seconds to play. What happens next is predictable. First of all, across all groups, people typically rely upon three approaches:

---

16 See http://www.mediatehawaii.org/peter-adler/

17 See: https://lenski.com/ – Tammy has written a useful guide call Making Mediation Your Day Job that helps mediators do precisely that: it is supported by a website with weekly newsletters. Both are recommended.

(1) Persuasion.
(2) Trickery.
(3) Force.

Persuasion: most people will attempt to persuade their partner to come over to their side of the line. They try to offer compelling arguments why they deserve the money. Sometimes, too, one partner will persuade the other to postpone gratification and come over to the other side on the promise that if the game is played again it will be their turn to collect the $1000.

Trickery: In some cases, people will promise to split the money while secretly intending to renege. An unscrupulous few will trick their partners, reaching out to shake their hand as a sign of good faith and then suddenly pull their unsuspecting partner across the line.

Mediator Trick #273: "The Mom Phone Call"
Used to break deadlocked mediations.

Force: Some players will try to use intimidation or brute force to drag their partner across the masking tape line.

This is not surprising. In real-world negotiations, people rely on these same approaches. Persuasion is very common: efforts to convince the other person that the speaker is right and the listener wrong, or to hand over something that is wanted. Trickery and force or intimidation remain perennial favourites because for some people, negotiation is a form of warfare. Unless there is blood on the sand, the negotiation is a failure.

These approaches often come up short. With persuasion, people often get nowhere – it becomes an endless round of "Yes, but...". With trickery, some might get the monetary results, but they also destroy trust. Not only will that person never do business again, they will tell others to stay away too.

And the problem with treating negotiations like a battle is, after all the time and energy you invest in the negotiation, the warrior has made an enemy instead of someone who might be willing to do business in future once again. So back to the exercise.

When the leader stops the game and asks who won, the results are interesting. Typically, there are three outcomes, in order of most frequently occurring to least frequent:

(1) Neither partner wins anything, since both failed to get the other to step across the line (approaches used: persuasion, trickery).

(2) The partners split the $1,000 if one agrees to cross the line to the other side (approaches used: persuasion, trickery).

(3) One partner wins, the other partner receives nothing (approaches used: trickery, persuasion or force).

There is, however, a rarely used fourth approach which yields an equally rare outcome. This approach enables both partners in a pair to each get $1,000. A win-win, in fact. The authors wonder if the reader has discerned the mediatory approach – stepping into each other's shoes.

All the partners have to do is switch sides. That is it.

The problem though is that people do not usually think of doing that. When you tell them that the winner gets $1,000, people figure in each pair only one can emerge a winner. It does not occur to them that both could win. There is nothing in the directions that forbids it. The directions are clear: If you get your partner to come to your side of the line, you win $1,000. That is it. But people hear the word "win" and they're already thinking about the other side of that coin: lose. It's what puts the "zero" in zero sum[18] game. People therefore compete.

That competitiveness forecloses any other results but lose/lose, win/lose or a 50/50 split. People waste time figuring out how to divide the pie instead of inventing ways to expand it.

Lenski suggests to her students that in their negotiations they consider how much value are you leaving on the table? Is the desire to keep that competitive edge blinding them to more profitable outcomes? This myopic view is illustrated by expressions such as 'a larger slice of the pie', which imply that 'the pie' has a fixed size and that net benefit cannot be improved by growing a bigger pie. That is, that people can only become richer by making others poorer; or that increasing labour productivity or immigration causes unemployment. In economics, this is known as the 'lump of labour fallacy' or more generally as the 'zero sum fallacy'. Many economic situations are not zero-sum, since valuable goods and services can be created, destroyed, or badly allocated in a number of ways, thus creating a net gain or loss of value to various stakeholders. Specifically, all trade is by definition positive sum, because when two parties agree to an exchange each party must consider the goods or money it is receiving to be more valuable than the goods it is delivering. In fact, all economic exchanges must benefit both parties to the point that each party can overcome its transaction costs – or the transaction would simply not take place.

These lessons are not just for mediators to consider and apply in discussions with participants. They work for negotiators and lawyers, and

18 These games involve only two players; they are called zero-sum games because one player wins whatever the other player loses. See for example, the analysis at https://neos-guide.org/content/game-theory-basics and the fallacy analyses for example at https://yandoo.wordpress.com/2013/06/18/the-zero-sum-fallacy/

indeed anyone who has to deal with people in routine everyday – as well as complex settings. It follows that much can be learned but almost everyone has the rapport skill: very few people are an isolated rock, and even those who consider themselves slow to engage should remember this: sometimes those least believing in their abilities turn out to be the best students.

2.3   How to Succeed as a Mediator

It is often said of mediation that a suitably qualified mediator should be able to mediate any subject matter in dispute. It is not necessary to have, the argument goes, a detailed knowledge of the subject or law of the dispute for a successful mediation. Rather it is a mastery of process that is essential, allied to the skills and competencies of the mediator as a mediator.

There are others who take a different view, suggesting subject expertise is needed. The authors' view is that both arguments are sustainable. But neither has primacy – for that decision lies with the participants or in most cases their representatives who will call for CVs – mediators should read Part Four below for the guide to choosing a mediator to get a consumer's view and apply the reverse telescope.

Along with a CV, a mediator will commonly be asked to perform a conflict check and state what they would charge for the mediation. It may be that the mediator is on panel and that the fee is part of the mediation provider's offer. CVs are usually viewed by both participants and their lawyers and advisers.

The behaviour of human beings is always fascinating: people generally eschew mediating dangerously preferring security and confidence. That may begin with whom they select to take a mediation forward. In the authors' experience the gatekeepers or buyers will tend to select those who have knowledge of the area in dispute.

But this is not a universal rule. In some ways, and in the main, people are looking for reasons not to select rather than positive criteria upon which to select. If a mediator can demonstrate competency, or suggest good reasons why they should be preferred, then participants may select neutral skills over traditional subject knowledge.

Thus in setting-out as a mediator perhaps it is important to self-reflect on a number of questions as follows:

- What constitutes personal success as a mediator?

- How much mediation work is it desired to undertake

- Will the mediation work be the mainstay of employment or form part of a wider portfolio?

- What areas does the CV naturally lend itself to mediate?

- How is the mediator's existing network going to help?

- How is the mediator going to get started?

There are more and this list of questions is not exhaustive. Tammy Lenski is a good guide[19].

Once the mediator has a mediation-specific CV and has defined the target areas for business then it is all about marketing and gaining experience. For the former, not only can Lenski assist but discussions with established and successful mediators such as Dom Collis of Collis Mediation[20] or other tutors on a training course should assist.

For the latter, observations are needed. After that a well-trodden path is gaining experience through co-mediating[21] with a community mediation group offering pro-bono mediation in neighborhood disputes – and in some instances restorative justice. There is real scope to learn from other practitioners, not just in observations but through co-mediating and new practitioners should welcome these chances.

Joining organisations such as the Society of Mediators and the Civil Mediation Council and taking part in events through such communities of like-minded people. Some modest financial outlay may be required and when work does come it may initially be pro-bono but it will be valuable experience. Advanced courses[22] can also assist in the journey.

---

19 See: https://www.amazon.com/Making-Mediation-Your-Day-Job/dp/0990332721
   2014 edition

20 https://www.collismediationltd.com/mediator-profiles/

21 See Part Four of this work, below with guidance on co-mediation

For legally qualified mediators perhaps the journey is "easier" as many legal practices now offer mediation and have qualified mediator solicitors and barristers within their firms and chambers. This may provide an opportunity for others to observe and to build a practice.

Fundamentally, however, as Lenski says, new mediators should use their mediation skills to create a market. In her book[23] Lenski invites practitioner into "Marketing like a Mediator" and to progress through "Uncovering Interests" to "Setting Your Practice-Marketing Agenda": by this means a blueprint for success is developed.

Basic ideas such as choosing a market that speaks to your passion sound simple, but how many mediators actually do this? The authors have noted that most mediators are passionate about what they do, but when it comes to marketing themselves, they hide their passion in a cloak of neutrality.

It makes good sense to meet the needs of the market and to talk to potential clients. But too often mediators preach to the converted, which is, other practitioners and groups that have adopted mediation. In doing so they fail to look beyond their kin – in short they fail to go to the balcony[24] to see the untapped mainstream.

Whilst mediators try to sell dispute management services and solutions, they all too often fail to ask potential clients what would help them sleep better at nights, increase their profit margins, or make their workforce more content. Instead the authors see too many mediators working to and then infuriated by the maxim in *Field of Dreams*. We have built it, whatever it is, mediators say, and they have not come!

Lenski suggests that mediators can succeed by developing "niche" markets in their practice areas. One of the many strengths of her work is that it shows how mediators can use the Internet to reach out to that

---

22 For example at http://www.218strand.com/products/

23 Supra

24 See *Getting Past No*

niche. Blogs provide opportunities for mediators to brand themselves as experts. Yet there remain, a decade on from Lenski's first edition, few mediation blogs or for that matter websites, as compared to the number of mediators.

None of revolution: Lenski says that "there's not a single new idea" in her book. But there is: her synthesis of existing marketing ideas into a "mediator friendly" process is more than that. It opens new ways of problem solving, which is what mediators are supposed to do.

2.4 Progressing on the mediation journey

The mediation journey will not necessarily be easy. Achieving success is as rewarding as it is challenging. There will be great moments and others that the authors would describe as "sub-optimal" – but tremendous learning opportunities. Some mediators think of their vocational journey in terms of transitioning through four phases:

- Unconscious incompetence;
- Conscious incompetence;
- Conscious competence; and
- Unconscious competence.

A good foundation in basic mediation training should leave the new mediator at the "conscious incompetence" level and able to progress effectively from there. For being a practising mediator requires thought and self-reflection to ease the learning journey. It is worthwhile keeping a journal, mindful of confidentiality issues, in which the new mediator can self-reflect and really delve into their practice. It is often worthwhile talking challenging situations through with a mediator colleague – again suitably redacted.

For those considering becoming a mediator who are unsure of any aspect of the requirements, training, or the background to the vocation, do not hesitate to contact the Society for an informal, confidential, impartial and obligation-free discussion: call +44 (0) 207 353 3936 or email the Charity's advisors using <u>SOM@218Strand.com</u>. There will be neither pom poms nor obstacles, but a realistic set of options provided after listening, as mediators can do.

Parker's pom-poms annoyed everyone at the negotiations.

2.5   What a Mediator Does

In the first third of this book, the authors have described in general terms what a mediator does and how a mediation may be managed. Rapport and curiosity, listening and appropriate neutrality have been discussed. This Section will develop these ideas through introducing technical matters which form the basis of a mediator's toolkit.

Mediation training at the Society of Mediators' School[25] in London[26] focuses on the agreed foundations that together constitute the "mediation process." These fall into four categories:

- Administration;
- Process;
- Soft Skills;
- Ethics (considered in Chapter Three).

Each of these categories have various subsections. They are taken in turn.

---

25 See eg: http://www.218strand.com/categories

26 In accordance with the criteria and requirements laid down by both the Civil Mediation Council and the Chartered Institute of Arbitrators in the United Kingdom, and (amongst others) the Association of Arbitrators of Southern Africa in Johannesburg. These meet or exceed international norms and are routinely developed.

2.6   Administration

2.6.1   *Before the day of the mediation*

Prior to the mediation there is almost always contact between the mediator and the participants[27] or their representatives, usually by email, and sometimes by telephone focussing on housekeeping. Most mediators will send, on appointment, an acknowledgement email letter describing the arrangements and the rules by which the mediation will take place. This will often have a PDF guide attached or a link to a webpage with more information and is routinely shared with the lay clients if the representatives so desire.

It follows that the email, and any PDF or website link must be well thought through, offering clear and accurate information in a manner that begins rapport building. Mediators should think, in preparing their materials, how a person who has not mediated before might respond to the data, and write accordingly. Technical language should be avoided.

The mediator will want to check who is attending, that the venue has enough seats and room space[28], what car parking arrangements there may be, and whether lunch, or other refreshments have been commissioned. The mediator will also wish to:

---

27 By participants the authors mean those taking part in the mediation: they are sometimes referred to as disputants (although that emphasises the dispute and is less used) or parties (although that stresses the legal nature of the matter and suggests mediation is a litigious process, so it is also discouraged as a term). Similarly mediators try to refrain from referring to "sides" and on the day will call participants by their chosen names.

28 Ideally there should be one plenary room with seats for all the participants and their respective representatives, and a break out room for each set of participants. The mediator themselves is unlikely to need a private room. The mediator should check on arrival that the rooms are sound-proof and sufficiently far apart so that should the participants indicate that they wish to avoid direct contact this can then be achieved.

- carry out a conflict check to ensure that there is no reason to decline to act: if there has been past professional contact this must be disclosed and thought given as to whether the contact should disqualify the mediator from acting – it is not always the case and providing such contact is relatively limited, purely professional, and disclosed the participants may well be comfortable with the mediator;

- ensure that there is a copy of the Agreement to Mediate[29] with all participants or their representatives together with any Mediation Rules that may apply;

- invite the participants to confirm the names of any representatives, counsel or attorneys who will be present, and check who is the point of contact[30];

- invite the participants to agree what if any documents, papers, materials, reports, witness statements, pleadings, or other items should be read by the mediator ahead of the day[31], and how they will be delivered[32];   and

- invite the participants to send them private summaries, not to be shared, sometimes referred to as "confidential position state-

---

29 This is the contract that is discussed below and at Annex B. It must be signed before any substantive matters are discussed and is the basis on which the mediator operates, ensures due process, and gets paid.

30 Usually this is obvious – sometimes though there are unusual circumstances. It is important for all emails relating only to process and housekeeping to be copied to all participants to avoid any suggestion of bias.

31 Very often a quasi-trial bundle or brief is prepared but it is not actually necessary. The mediator will want background but, as they are not deciding matters, the most helpful materials are details of any offers and costs, the arguments raised to date, the procedural steps if any, and key witness statements, reports, or documents.

32 Increasingly, mediators are sent password protected PDFs. It is vital that mediators register as data controllers in the United Kingdom jurisdiction and have encrypted and secure devices that may receive any such materials.

ments" setting out what they hope to achieve from the day: these documents, if used, will be "mediator's eyes-only" and not brought to the mediation but destroyed beforehand to avoid the risk of a breach of confidence.

The mediator will, if the mediation date is more than a few weeks ahead when the initial email is sent, continue email contact as a countdown to ensure that the matter is proceeding. A significant number of 'mediations' settle before the day and the mediator will wish to keep an active diary. It is important that mediators set out their overtime and cancellation charges[33] clearly in advance as part of the Rules or contractual documents.

2.6.2 *The day before*

The day before a mediation, in addition to having read any and all papers[34] that have been sent, the mediator will check the logistics and probably email each of the participants or their representatives to ensure they have all they need. A mediator will check that there is a printed copy of the Agreement to Mediate available for all to sign on the day, so that everyone knows that the document governs the day, and that any feedback forms or other panel requirement documentation is available.

It is important to understand that when the mediator reads the papers that have been sent the mediator is not seeking the answer, the solution, or the probable outcome.

For a start, were it so obvious that a neutral on picking up the papers could say "Eureka" then it is much more likely that the participants

---

33 Typically mediators operate a sliding scale whereby a mediation cancelled or postponed more than four weeks in advance incurs no fees, whilst those up to 14 days away incur a 33% fee, up to a week away a 66% fee, and those less than a week the full fees. In addition, the mediator's terms for any non-refundable travel and hotel fees will need to be set out clearly in writing with the participants upon appointment. Where a mediator is working as a member of a panel, it will usually be the panel's administrator that will deal with these aspects.

34 The "bundle" or mediator's brief.

would have had their Greek bathtub moment many weeks earlier. It is hubristic to assume that a mediator will know more with less contact.

Rather, the skilled mediator reads the papers to be familiar with their content, to be curious as to what lies beneath, to wonder what is really going on, and to be able to listen intelligently on the day. The mediation bundle is a menu to savour not a crossword to answer.

A mediator should not Google[35] to find out more about the facts, or seek to look up the law or cases, unless they are engaged to evaluate. A mediator is not engaged to decide anything so selective or random Googling is likely, if deliberately or inadvertently mentioned, to cause participants to wonder what the mediator has been told or is doing. There is a real risk of a perception of bias.

Where a mediator is concerned that some potentially vital document is not in the mediation papers care needs to be taken about whether to ask for it: there may be good reason why it is absent and the representatives may have agreed not to include it. Equally, one participant may not be aware of the potential document and to ask for it might be akin to giving advice if they are unrepresented. On the other hand, if the mediator would thereby be proceeding on a basis that would lead to an oppressive and manifestly unjust process there would need to be thought given as to how best to raise the matter, or whether to start the mediation at all.

Such ethical dilemmas, which are covered in more detail below, are actually rarely troublesome for long. Mediators should go back to first principles and consider what the Agreement to Mediate says, and what the Rules state. The answer is usually obvious but if not, or in any event, troubled mediators may wish to contact their mentor[36] or panel

---

35 Other search engines are available. On the subject of search engines, mediators should be aware that using an engine to consider a particular mediation's subject matter may well be a breach of confidentiality due to the information sharing policies that most engines have. Great care should be taken in respect of all data.

36 The Society of Mediators has a mentor policy for all who train with it and many other organisations have a similar availability – would be mediators should check before they sign-up for membership or training.

registrar to discuss the point if it is not clear. In raising ethical points, mediators should avoid emails and couch the situation in neutral terms such that the identities of the participants is hidden.

Finally, mediators should consider dress. For many a business suit is it, but increasingly mediators eschew ties to distinguish themselves from lawyers and judges. The authors say simply this – mediators should wear whatever they feel most comfortable for the work.

2.7 Process

2.7.1 *On the day – getting started*

The first rule is to arrive early. Very early. Clients are never late – merely delayed. Mediators are never late. Period. Experienced mediators will aim to arrive an hour before the agreed start time and book a train or seek a route that easily allows them a coffee and a stroll well before that hour. The simple reason is that there is little less comforting to stressed lay participants and their representatives than wondering where the mediator is and when they can start. The higher reason is that the mediator needs to get in the zone.

The authors generally tell participants that they will arrive 30 minutes before the start time, so that they have 30 minutes in hand by virtue of the planned hour's grace period. In practice, the authors are always at a neutral venue at a time to greet every participant as they arrive, show them where the private rooms are, where the coffees and toilets are and to discover and give any information about fire exits, drills, or other untoward happenings.

Past experiences that have caused bemusement to mediators who failed to make such enquiries are the Olympic Victory parade in 2012 outside a well known mediation centre in Fleet Street with record crowds and a brass band to boot, and the early closure of the building by reason of a civil service dispute which left the mediator and her participants to be rescued from the third floor by the Cardiff fire brigade. Always make basic enquiries of the venue about such matters on arrival and keep door and wifi codes to hand.

This is not simply a matter of efficiency. It will be recalled that the essence of a mediator's art as defined by Goldberg[37] is creating rapport. An understanding of the basic needs in life – coffee, toilets and wifi, communicated well and early, is a good start to that rapport building.

So too is listening carefully to who is who – immediately after meeting people for the first time skilled mediators without perfect recall like to

---

37 *Supra* – see Section 2.2

make a note about who is in each room. This can sometimes be gleaned from the sign in sheets at reception if something is missed but is a good way of beginning to check logistics – are there in fact enough chairs in the plenary room and have enough lunches been ordered. These are good things to check at this time.

Once the participants arrive and are settled, and have been given a few minutes to set up their rooms, most mediators like to go in and have a private administrative word with each in turn. It is important that, before this is done, the intention is mentioned to the other participants along with a time estimate for the stage. Communication and transparency by the mediator is a key matter.

In the private room before anything else, the mediator will make a gentle introduction and show some genuine humanity. Some mediators like to enquire about the journeys, about any pressures on parking or time, and to check that everyone has the same papers. The mediator will then ask for the master copy of the Agreement to Mediate to be signed and, absent any other observations on process, will go and repeat the same thing in the other private session.

One thing that a mediator will check on process is who is coming into the plenary session. It is not mandatory for all participants and their representatives to attend, but many mediators encourage this so that everyone hears the same briefing from the mediator at the same time, and sees who else is here.

Sometimes there is a reluctance on the part of some lay participants to be in the same room, and mediators do not force anyone to do anything. That said, a careful re-assurance about the mediator's role as a moderator, and agreed rules on who will speak and the language used can assist the process.

A word on language, in both its senses – most mediators encourage the use of business-like speech and politeness, but are not afraid of emotion and passion. They will have in mind a line that should not be crossed. It will certainly be where one participant is clearly upset and may be when a mediator is distracted from doing the required job. But mediators should avoid being unduly protective over industrial terms where all participants are clearly happy.

In terms of native language, the mediator must not act as an interpreter or translator. There must be a common native language for the mediation and if translation is needed then a neutral person should be engaged on whom the mediator can rely. If a mediator seeks to translate then not only is there a risk of error but the mediator may be accused of bias or of putting into their own mouth the thoughts of one of the participants. It must not happen.

For the avoidance of doubt, the provision of an interpreter or a signer is not a matter for the mediator unless set out as such in the Agreement to Mediate. Such skilled assistance can cost as much as a mediator and it is important that the fees are clearly marked as born by the participants in some proportion or other. If an interpreter is used then one of the first things that a mediator will need to check is that the person who is invited to sign the Agreement to Mediate has actually had it explained to them in the relevant language in full.

Once the preliminaries have been done, then unless the participants want to discuss settlement without the mediator before the day really begins (and especially when counsel are involved for the first time this is by no means uncommon) then the mediator will invite everyone into the plenary room for the first open session.

2.7.2   In the mediation plenary room

The mediator will have checked the chairs and the layout of the room. Sometimes there is little flexibility but generally there are ways of improving the topography of most rooms. The basics, such as ensuring that the sun is not streaming into a person's eyes and that the mediator can make eye contact with everyone in the room should be obvious.

But what of the layout of the room? Who should sit where? The authors are nowadays very relaxed. As long as the mediator can be in a neutral place, where all can be seen, then the locations of clients and lawyers, experts or observers can take care of itself. Indeed, skilled mediators try to avoid fixed seating and sometimes, especially with lawyer-only sessions should these occur, encourage lawyers to sit one side of the table collaboratively with the mediator opposite. These practical measures vary and experience plays a strong part in feeling what is the most advantageous use of the space available.

Once at the mediation as part of the "Welcome and Introduction," the once seated, will be invited by the mediator to confirm their names, their roles, and how they would like to be referred to during the mediation. The mediator will usually begin and encourage first name terms, but sometimes this will be resisted. It will not trouble the mediator and is part of the participant's self-determination to insist on a title, a surname, or some other appellation.

It is, however, highly recommended that at this point the mediator draws-up a table map recording the participant's names and roles. This is a very practical way to avoid confusion and embarrassment, especially when at times there is a lot to think about.

2.7.3   The Opening

The mediator's Opening is an opportunity for the mediator to set the scene for the day. There are some basic principles and these are included in an example opening checklist below at Annex A.

Mediators will develop their own individual styles – nevertheless, it cannot be recommended strongly enough that a structured opening is essential for what follows during a mediation. It is a good idea to prepare a printed opening checklist and have it at hand to refer to during the introduction. Doing this gives even the most experienced mediator confidence and it conveys a professional approach to the task, to the participants, and their representatives. Some mediators refer to it in much the same way as a pilot does their pre-flight check and invariably there will be several minutes of formal housekeeping as the pilot, or rather the mediator, prepares the room for the runway.

2.7.4 *The Mediator's Role*

As part of this the mediator will wish to confirm their role. It falls into three discrete areas

- As captain of the mediation process;
- As the facilitator during the process; and
- As the trusted neutral intermediary between the parties.

It is also sensible for the mediator to explain to the participants what the mediator's role is not. Most mediators confirm that their role is not to offer advice, either legal or otherwise and it is not to do anything to encourage any of the participants to decide upon a particular course of action or settlement. It is simply to be independent and neutral, using appropriate skills and methods to provide a fair and equitable process offering the participants an opportunity to settle their dispute should they so desire.

2.7.5 *Authority to Settle*

In signing the Agreement to Mediate it is also important that the mediator checks and confirms that the participants have "Authority to Settle"[38], in particular in the following situations:

- If a lawyer is representing a participant who may not be attending the mediation;

- If one of the participants is a firm, company, public body, or unincorporated body it is important that someone attends who can settle up to the maximum value of the claim (this may be an express condition in the mediation agreement); and

- If there is a situation where a participant only has authority to settle to a certain prescribed limit it may be that in the Heads of Agreement / Settlement that it specifies subject to authorisation.

---

38 See: Blake, S., Browne, J., & Sime, S. (2013) The Jackson ADR Handbook, Oxford University Press, paragraphs 4.07-4.08 & 14.52

That can be risky as there is no binding settlement until author-ised and a settlement agreement signed. It may be that it is best to adjourn the mediation until the relevant authority is obtained.

In normal course the important point to check here is that the parti-cipants have the authority to settle and are thus self-determinant in terms of the outcome. In practical terms, most participants will state that they do have authority, will have confirmed it beforehand, and will repeat that assurance in the private meeting before the start of the plenary session. It is, however, helpful for all participants to hear from each other that there is authority in the room – it builds some confid-ence in process.

2.7.6 *Confidentiality and the Concept of Without Prejudice*

It is trite to say that save in very rare circumstances every mediation is 'confidential' and also 'without prejudice'. This state of affairs lasts until a settlement is agreed, written down, and signed by all concerned. Even then the terms agreed may be stated to be confidential.

By signing the Agreement to Mediate, or the Observer's Confidentiality Agreement that is appended, the participants and those involved agree to this confidentiality. From the mediator's perspective the following terms (or ones like them) usually apply:

- During the mediation itself, the mediator will not disclose to anyone any statement said to him or her in private without the consent of the person who made that statement, and shall never disclose that statement to any person after the mediation.

- Following completion of the mediation, all information (whether given orally, in writing or otherwise) produced for, or arising out of, or in connection with, the mediation passing between any of the parties and/or between any of them and the mediator and made for the purposes of the mediation shall be and remain confidential other than as set out in the Settlement Agreement and any terms thereof.

- The mediator shall not retain any documents or electronic records made or obtained for the purposes of the mediation other than the signed copy of the Agreement to Mediate. The Mediator will promptly destroy or delete all materials sent or given to them at the conclusion of the mediation, including any notes taken other than the signed copy of the Mediation Agreement.

- The without prejudice principle is to protect from disclosure any communication made in mediation between the participants with a view to settling the dispute. It is to encourage participants to be is free and as open as possible with regards the use of information and communication to allow proposals for a settlement to emerge during the mediation.

- If such communications were not protected the mediation process would potentially be undermined, in that if anything were allowed to be said in subsequent litigation the participants would be unlikely to engage in any meaningful discussion at mediation. Within a mediation the without prejudice rule exists for the benefit of the participants and it can be waived by them: it is arguably not a privilege of the mediator.[39] That said, many mediators will quite properly decline to act where such rules are to be waived.

2.7.7   *Ad hoc rules*

Mediators report that it is useful to ask the participants if they would like to establish any particular rules for their mediation. Often at this stage the participants say nothing. Most have not mediated before[40] and

---

39 Blake, S. etc The Jackson ADR Handbook, Oxford University Press, 5.17 – 5.26, 13.59 – 13.63

40 The authors strongly recommend that mediators do not ask, whether in open or private session, or at all, their participants if they have mediated before. For a start, it makes no difference: every mediation is different. But much more risky is a situation, which occurred when one of the authors was acting as counsel, where none of the other lawyers or participants has been to a mediation before but the author

have little to base any such rules upon. So, after a short pause the mediator might choose to say something like:

"People often tell me that it's useful if we could all agree to be polite and not to talk over each other" (or that it is good that only one person speaks at once).

At this stage there may still be a reluctance to say anything, so the mediator might choose to say:

"For me that would be a great idea as sometimes I do find it hard to hear if there is a lot of talking."

"It is your mediation but is that something you might all wish to agree to in this mediation?"

Once that has been agreed the mediator might then say:

"Thank you – Are there any other rules you might like to consider to help us today?"

This process of establishing rules also serves to give, or perhaps better to emphasise that the participants have ownership of their mediation.

2.7.8   *Opening Statements*

One of the first tasks is then to invite 'Opening Statements'. Thus a mediator might say:

"In order to start the mediation it would be useful to me to hear what you would like to achieve today: there is no need to go back over the history, I have had the papers you have kindly provided and read them. I am interested in what you see as the best use of the day – who would like to go first?"

---

had attended more than a thousand – many more than the mediator concerned. An imbalance was immediately created in the room.

It can be that amongst the participants there is reticence at this point to say something. The mediator can overcome this by acknowledging the fact and respectfully saying:

"Someone does have to go first."

If there is still difficulty it might be worth the mediator saying:

"I appreciate your reticence. However, in my experience it is often that those present at mediations agree that it is the participant who is perhaps closest in similarity to a claimant in legal proceedings that conventionally goes first."

After the opening statements it really is a matter of sensing what has emerged. A sound technique is to simply summarise what each of the participants has said and invite them to add more if they so wish, with a view to developing the conversation.

2.7.9   Venting

There is always a risk at this stage that the participants may vent their anger and frustration. "Venting" is understandable, given that they may have been in conflict or dispute for some time and psychologically venting is a form of release. The mediator has a number of choices, yet if in establishing the ground rules earlier in the mediation the participants have agreed not talk over each other and be polite, there is opportunity for the mediator to refer back to this in a gentle and respectful way.

Clearly, if the venting continues and it begins to disrupt the mediation a firmer line may be needed. If the participants have representatives present, such as the lawyers, a good approach can be to seek help from the lawyer to calm the client. It is always good to acknowledge people's behaviour in a respectful way as it indicates empathy and an emotional awareness of where they might be.

Sometimes this can be done by breaking down the vented statement by openly taking notes and asking for assistance in ensuring the précised note is accurate. If this approach is adopted, then the mediator will naturally repeat it for the other participant(s).

2.7.10 *Management*

Throughout the mediation and particularly in these early stages, the mediator needs to have in the back of their mind the management of the process. This encompasses timings, acknowledging needs, and keeping people on track, such as by moving into private sessions (caucus) in a timely manner should that assist.

In general, the purpose of private sessions is to:

- Provide the participants with an opportunity to discuss their case on their own or with the mediator – and thus to allow for thought and planning the settlement in response to what has been established in the opening session;

- Enable the mediator to meet privately and explore opportunity and reality test possible solutions;

- Enable participants to consider and reflect on proposals from the other participants; and

- Enable offers to be developed and communicated in a positive way.

Private sessions also offer a break and a chance for refreshment. The mediator will be aware that they are not the only one engaged in a high concentration activity and that regular periods of quieter reflection encourage effective process. It may be that the mediator needs to assess when a private session is appropriate, and suggest it, or it may be that one set of participants asks to go into private session. A mediator should not decline such a request.

Time can be used to advantage by reminding participants that the clock is ticking and the agreement is that the mediation will complete by specified hour. It is remarkable how quickly time disappears during mediation. It is thus important to manage the private sessions, as it is very easy to agree to say 20 minutes with one set of participants and suddenly find that 35 minutes have elapsed. In contrast those participants waiting for their private session may well find the clock appears to run slowly. Mediators must be adept timekeepers.

2.7.11 *Flexibility*

Mediations almost always reveal the unexpected, which makes the mediator's role absolutely fascinating – but as a result real flexibility is key ability for a mediator. It is the participant's process and provided what they wish to happen is within ethical boundaries then mediators should adapt. Skilled mediators often refer to the process as structured yet flexible and this concept recognises individual needs.

2.7.12 *Offers*

Dealing with "offers" can at times present challenges to the mediator. As always it is best to keep things a simple as possible. Consider the following scenario –

The mediation is going well, having had a positive opening and a series of private sessions. The mediator is in private session with one set of participants and they are keen to make an offer, which with the assistance of their representatives is now well-defined in their minds and suitably framed. For the mediator, at this point the question might be to confirm how they would like to present this offer to the other participants. This can be done in a number of ways:

- The mediator can convey the offer having ensured that it is written down accurately on a piece of paper; or

- The mediator can invite the participants to consider making the offer themselves face to face or through any representatives.

If it is considered best that the mediator transmits the offer to the other participants, it is essential that is conveyed accurately and unambiguously. The authors therefore strongly recommend that it is written down by and checked by the participants. This ensures too that the participant's handwriting is on the paper, demonstrating commitment, and avoids the risk of the mediator appearing to be aligned with the offer or the offeror.

In transmitting the offer, the mediator should take the offer to the participants in their room and immediately upon entering the room say:

"I have an offer – would you like to see it?"

In their training courses and in mentoring mediators in live mediations, or as counsel, the authors have seen many variations of the above, which generally lead to confusion and misunderstanding. The mediator has neither right nor remit to delay handing over an offer – the authors believe that save in exceptional circumstances the only thing to do with the transmission of offers is to keep it simple as described above.

Who would not want to see an offer?

It is also a chance to inject energy and movement into the process and to learn from reactions much about the motivations of the offeree.

2.7.13 *The Settlement Agreement*

As the mediation continues and offers and counter offers are exchanged there may well be a point when the participants perhaps come into open session and agreement is reached. At this point the mediator will confirm in broad terms what has been agreed with each of the participants.

Nothing agreed in a mediation is binding unless it is recorded in writing and signed by the participants. This is known as a Settlement Agreement. The Settlement Agreement can take a number of forms such as, a formal written contract, an exchange of letters, with other legal documents depending on the nature of the dispute. Whatever form is chosen it is important that the mediator ensures that all participants do not leave the mediation until a settlement agreement has been produced and signed. It is usual if the participants are represented by lawyers that they look at the task of developing the settlement agreement and many come prepared to do so with laptops and appropriate administrative support. At this stage the mediator might find him or herself less engaged in the process, yet it is essential that the mediator is at hand to assist when required in helping all to iron out any disagreement at this stage.

In the event that no settlement is reached, although that may be disappointing it is important that the mediator at least clarifies the position before dispersal. In some cases is necessary to adjourn the mediation for further work or research to be done and then reconvene at a later date, going back into formal or telephone mediation finally to resolve the dispute and reach a Settlement Agreement.

2.8   Soft Skills

Soft skills and their deployment by the mediator make each process of mediation unique. Delivering the soft skills to the mediation process is infinitely variable. Each mediator will develop their own personal style as their practice develops. The section below considers what are the fundamental soft skills but as practice grows others may emerge. At the top of the list is rapport which is more than simply being comfortable.

Making your client comfortable with you.

2.8.1   *Rapport*

Building "rapport" is, as Goldberg discovered, essential in the delivery of effective mediations. If communication is really going to work between two people, such as between the mediator and a participant or between the participants it is widely acknowledged that they need to be in rapport. The Oxford English Dictionary definition of rapport is:

> *"A close and harmonious relationship in which the people or groups concerned understand each other's feelings or ideas and communicate well."*

Jenny Rogers[41] in her book "Coaching Skills" describes the building of rapport beautifully, linking it with congruence and empathy, such that if these are achieved simultaneously then rapport more broadly is about a way of being with another person. It is about matching body, voice-volume, breathing, gesture, space, language, pace and energy to enter the other person's world.

Mediators do need to be curious to the extent of being nosey, and to encourage participants to "walk in the other person's shoes." There must be no judgement of the other person but more a valuing of the other person alongside oneself.

Experience indicates that to master this area of mediation skill does take practice and considerable amounts of self-reflection. Participants can challenge a mediator to the core here and competence is achieved with experience and may well be hard earned in the process.

Established well, rapport can move to being something akin to an elegant dance[42] between the participant and mediator. Mediators should, however, be aware factors that can intervene to break rapport down. For example:

- Fear – the mediator's own, which stems from not valuing your own self or being self-conscious. Mediators should remember that this is a natural response to a challenging situation. To overcome it, if it happens, consider taking a few minutes just to relax and refresh.

- To counter fear, there are techniques such as visualisation: this suggests taking a few moments to visualise something that is enjoyed, perhaps by reference to a personal photograph on the iPhone if not in the wallet, which can quickly offer an effective counter. Hard-nosed litigators suggest with scorn that it is quite easy to discount such techniques, but as a mediator it is important to acknowledge personal feelings and the personal

---

41 Rogers, J., (2008). Coaching Skills: A Handbook, 2nd Edition, Open University Press.

42 Cloke, K., (2013). The Dance of Opposites, Good Media Press.

context: both will influence the approach the mediator takes to the mediation.

- Over eagerness – especially through the mediator's understandable human need to be liked, can create an impediment. It may prevent effective challenging, probing, and questioning. Mediators need to establish an interested distance from the participants, a professionally aware conversation that is at once open and guarded.

- Transference – it might be difficult to suspend judgement about things such as the other's values, clothes, nationality, religion, or personality. Unconscious bias or prejudice may leak out. Mediators must learn to consider what they are expressing and saying, and how their language (both verbal and non-verbal) may convey adverse or inappropriate meanings or timbres to the participants. Mediators must learn to be adroit and culturally sensitive, to avoid stereotypes and to understand diversity.

- Bias – by imposing or imagining actual or implied values onto a participant. There is no need to do so as the mediator makes no decision and should have no concern as to the values of a participant. The mediator is interested only in offering a process.

- External preoccupation – on the mediator's part by taking the stresses of the personal life into the mediation and losing focus. A mediator must be capable of operating in what sports people call 'The Zone' and to exclude the unnecessary and external influences. The day is the participants and the mediator should eschew emails and messages in time that they have bought. To do otherwise is to diminish the participants.

The search for rapport is common to all mediations but it gets easier. As mediators (like new parents) gain experience they relax and their confidence is transmitted to the participants (as parents do to babies). The more the mediator realises that slow is the new fast, and takes the time to establish rapport and learn about the people, the faster a mediation progresses. Mediators should learn to savour the opportunities before they enjoy the meal. Rushing food is never a good idea.

Mediator Ordering Dinner

2.8.2 *Body language – and its relationship to rapport*

Dr Albert Mehrabian undertook early work research on body language and non-verbal communication in the mid to late 1960s. Professor Mehrabian is now the Emeritus Professor of Psychology at UCLA. The results of Mehrabian's research[43] established that when an individual is speaking, the listener focuses on the following three types of communication:

- Actual Words – 7%

- The way words are delivered (tone, accents on certain words, etc.) – 38%

- Facial expressions – 55%

The percentage figure indicates the degree of importance the listener places on that type of communication. It is important to place this in context. Professor Mehrabian's work focused upon the specific communication of feelings and emotions when the importance of tone and

---

43 Mehrabian & Ferris., (1967). Inference of Attitudes from Nonverbal Communication in Two Channels, Journal of Counseling Psychology, Vol 31, 1967, pp. 248-52

facial expression are perhaps more important than in everyday communication, such as when in dispute. Nevertheless the research was conclusive in identifying the importance of body language and nonverbal clues in communication.

Quoting Professor Mehrabian:

> *"Please note that this and other equations regarding relative importance of verbal and nonverbal messages were derived from experiments dealing with communications of feelings and attitudes (i.e., like-dislike). Unless a communicator is talking about their feelings or attitudes, these equations are not applicable."*

The value of Mehrabian's research is not necessarily specific to everyday communication but more importantly what happens in emotional communication, such as that encountered during a mediation. There is a great deal of literature on body language. For the reader it is often that what is being described becomes over complicated and of course, there may be cultural differences overlain as well. Similarly, there is much in the literature about eye contact. Eye contact generally works to establish rapport and the conventional rules appear to be:

- The closer you are the less eye contact you should make.

- Therefore the further away the more you should make.

- Long infrequent glances are more beneficial than short frequent glances.

- Eye contact should always be available, if people make eye contact do hold it. If you look away a lot they won't trust you.

- Direct eye contact effects fluent and frequent speech

- No eye contact releases people to talk about their hidden secrets – i.e. Freud's seat was behind and at right angles to his patients' couch.

- Consider positioning and room layout to gain the most from available eye contact.

Returning to body language, mediators should be aware that there are many ways that a mediator can suggest that they are not engaged and break rapport. Common examples of these mismatches include:

- Fiddling impatiently / unknowingly with an object;

- Clock watching;

- Staring without blinking into the other person's eyes;

- Waggling a foot;

- Sitting with crossed arms;

- Turning the chair slightly away indicating disinterest

- Cross locking legs and other blocking body language suggests a lack of confidence;

- Sitting back in the chair when the other is leaning forward suggests detachment;

- Touching the face or having a hand in front of the mouth while talking suggests timidity;

- Rubbing the nose, or looking away, might suggest dissonance;

- Scowling or frowning disapproval; and

- Avoiding eye contact might suggest lack of confidence or disapproval.

There are many more. It is worth reading a good non-verbal communication guide[44] to gain insights into how mediators may be perceived, and what participants may be demonstrating. It is the unspoken dialogue, the messages that people exchange without sounds, that can be so telling in establishing and maintaining a relationship.

---

44 For example, a useful guide is Non Verbal Communication, Burgoon et al (2010/2016) reproduced at https://books.google.co.uk/books?id=KaZY-CwAAQBAJ&lpg=PP1&pg=PT2#v=onepage&q&f=false

This is all the more crucial where the time for rapport building is limited and the butterfly accordingly fragile.

2.8.3 *Trust*

Following the financial crash of 2008/09 and a series of corporate scandals across the world many commentators considered that levels of trust in professionals hit all time lows. The bigger picture across the globe is not the issue here but the essence of the process of mediation is trust. Clearly trust may not abound at the start of the mediation – but the mediator can do much to engender a sufficiency of trust amongst the participants. With this creation and building of trust the foundations can be established such that innovative and well thought through solutions can be developed based on cooperation and partnership.

So what is trust? Two classic definitions follow:

> *"A psychological state comprising the intention to accept vulnerability based upon positive expectations of the intentions or behaviour of another."* (Rousseau et al 1998)

> *"An individual's expectation that some organised system will act with predictability or goodwill."* (Maguire and Phillips 2008)

Research at the University of Bath with the CIPD identified that for individuals to be trusted they needed to show four key attributes, which were termed "The Four Pillars"[45]:

- Ability – a demonstrable competence in whatever they are doing;

- Benevolence – a concern for others beyond their own needs and having benign motives;

---

45 CIPD, Research Report (Reference 5746), Where has all the trust gone? March 2012; CIPD & University of Bath, Research Report (Reference 6525), Cultivating trustworthy leaders, April 2014; and CIPD & University of Bath, Research Report (Reference 6701), Experiencing Trustworthy Leadership, September 2014

- Integrity – adherence to a set of principles acceptable to others encompassing fairness and honesty (Mayer et al 1995); and

- Predictability – a regularity of behaviour over time (Dietz and Den Hartog 2006).

In the mediation context it is clear to the authors that these Four Pillars describe the key ingredients for a mediator in order to generate sufficient trust to create an effective process. If this is achieved then trust will manifest itself in terms of:

- Enhanced participant engagement and commitment;

- A feeling of empowerment to resolve the dispute;

- Positive sentiment; and

- Increased co-operation, the sharing of information and knowledge, as well as the desire to solve the problem.

University of Bath (2014) research revealed additional benefits of high-trust relationships including

- Feelings of safety;

- Feelings of pride; and

- Feelings of inclusion.

The soft skills the mediator typically deploys all contribute to an environment that is safe, inclusive and that delivers a positive outcome. Conversely, it is worthwhile being able to recognise the signs of when trust is waning.

- An increasing feeling or feelings of vulnerability amongst the participants;

- A lack of relationship-building, resulting in an introverted and silo-mentality towards the conflict;

- A reluctance to engage in the process as a result of feeling unsafe to do so;

- Defensive and / or disruptive behaviour;

- A visible increase in anxiety and stress levels amongst participants;

- A negative approach and attitude that is evident; and

- Threats to walk-out and leave the mediation.

If encountered these can be approached in a number of ways:

- Perhaps moving to private session and asking what might be causing the problem and how they are feeling;

- Engaging the help of lawyers and representatives present;

- Taking a break to refresh; and

- Confronting the problem through position shifting – inviting participants to look at matters from the others' perspective.

2.8.4   *Active Listening*

The "Golden Rule" the authors have long adopted derives from Hypocrates:

> *"Listen, listen, listen – and don't make matters worse!"*

Many mediators find, at least at some point in the mediation, that listening can be rather challenging. The ability to listen is influenced by individual feelings at the time, how much pressure the mediator is under and how well the mediator feels they are doing. There is much literature[46] on the psychology of listening and current research and presentation broadly identifies three levels of listening. These levels are

---

46 For example: Imhof; The Cognitive Psychology of Listening (2010) at http://acla-sites.com.ng/wp-content/uploads/2017/02/andrew_d-_wolvin_listening_and_human_communicatibookfi-org.pdf#page=112

described below with an indication to attempt to describe when an individual might be listening at a particular level.

<u>Listening at Level 1</u> – This is listening at the other person's level and is really all about self, not the other person and as such, in a mediation, it can be disastrous. Signs that the listener is at Level 1 include:

- Asking for more facts such as "How many" – "When?" – "Who?" – "What's the history?" When the participant hasn't mentioned them;

- Noticing an inner dialogue that results in you asking yourself such questions as,

    ○ "What can I ask next?"

    ○ "Was that a good enough question?";

- Wanting to give advice; and

- Talking about you with "I" and "Me."

<u>Listening at Level 2</u> – Here the listener and the other person are as one in an absorbing and deeply focused discussion that is characterised by:

- Rapport with body language, voice and energy levels matched;

- A flowing conversation, yet with the other person doing most of the talking;

- The listener is picking up on language, skillful and short questions are asked concentrated on the other's agenda;

- The listener is summarising, reflecting and clarifying in order to extend the other's thinking; and

- The listener hears what is not being said, as well as what is and is listening for underlying meanings.

Effective and valuable dialogue takes place at this level. Mediators can certainly regard Level 2 listening as their default level.

Listening at Level 3 – At level 3 the listener is becomes more aware of:

- Emotion;

- What risks might be taken in the conversation;

- What are the other person's underlying choices and what is really at stake; and

- The listener trusts his or her intuition that there may well be an emotional or intellectual connection with the other person.

Level 3 is a moment of real connection that most people seldom achieve in normal everyday conversations.

It may not be appropriate in some mediations, particularly where the participants are unrepresented, because the level of rapport may exceed neutral boundaries. For this reason, the authors encourage Level 2 as the default setting for mediators.

When it comes to listening, therefore, mediators should be ruthlessly honest with themselves. They should have no self-delusion about their listening skills. These can be tested through various exercises. At Annex C to this book there is a self-reflection sheet that may be a useful exercise to assess current listening skills as part of more general reflection on mediation skills and competencies.

By way of a touchstone, the authors suggest that a maxim when mediating is:

"Listen to understand, not to respond.[47]"

Such an approach, which runs counter to the images and personas of fast-talking lawyers or commentators, leads to real richness of process. It

---

47 See for example the video by Tom Yorton (2015) at http://rethinked.org/?p=7533

opens up opportunities to probe, to précis, to reflect and to reframe. Each of these techniques requires consideration of questioning.

2.8.5 *Open and Closed Questions*

Effective questioning in mediation stems from a mediator having listened to understand. Just as listening can be honed so can a mediator's skill at asking questions. The first stage is understanding the use of open and closed questions – and how they relate[48].

It is trite that the difference between an open and closed question is quite straightforward: a closed question is one that can, should the respondent choose, generate without perversity a simple "yes" or "no" answer.

In contrast, an open question seeks much more information and cannot properly be answered with a bare "yes" or "no." The closed question may be used to shut down a dialogue: the open to explore. Some open questions seek facts from the respondent, such as,

> *"What would you like to achieve today?"*
>
> *"What is the impact the conflict is having upon you?"*
>
> *"What has brought us here today?"*

These work well in finding out certain things from the participant and might lead, or should lead to deeper questions such as,

> *"If this conflict is resolved what would that allow you to do?"*
>
> *"How would you like to move forward with this?"*
>
> *"Why is what you have just told me important to you?"*

---

48 A useful consideration of the two genres is in Oxborough et al's paper (2010) https://www.researchgate.net/profile/Gavin_Oxburgh2/publication/40764681_Th e_question_of_question_types_in_police_interviews_A_review_of_the_literature_f rom_a_psychological_and_linguistic_perspective/links/53e4e8890cf2f-b748710fc6b/The-question-of-question-types-in-police-interviews-A-review-of-the-literature-from-a-psychological-and-linguistic-perspective.pdf

It follows that, to be effective, a mediator should aim to use appropriate questions which are concise but focused. Generically, powerful questions used in mediation

- raise self-awareness by encouraging thinking and offering challenge;

- are to the point in order to seek a truthful response;

- are relatively short using about 7 to 12 words:

- seek discovery: and

- will most probably start with the words "why," "what," or "how".

Clearly the types questions asked in an early open (plenary) session may well differ from those asked in private sessions, where deeper more probing questions can usually be asked without fear of embarrassment or compromise. At Annex D there is a list of questions that are useful when in private session.

To gauge how strongly a participant might feel about the issue questions can be asked to quantify a fact or feeling. "On a scale of one to ten, where ten is the most strongest you have felt about an issue and one the least, give me a number that indicates the importance of what you just told me."

If the answer comes back at three or four, the issue is probably of no real consequence to the participant and it might be that they are over-emphasising its importance vocally with words. If on the other hand they say seven or eight then the mediator should take note and seek a deeper understanding through further questions.

2.8.6 *Reflective listening*

Reflective listening is an advanced way of listening and responding to another person that improves mutual understanding and trust. It is an essential skill for mediators and participants alike, as it enables the listener to receive and accurately interpret the speaker's message, and then provide an appropriate response. The response is an integral part of the listening process and can be critical to the success of a negotiation or mediation. Among its benefits, reflective listening

- builds trust and respect,
- enables the disputants to release their emotions,
- reduces tensions,
- encourages the surfacing of information, and
- creates a safe environment that is conducive to collaborative problem solving.

Though useful for everyone involved in a conflict, the ability and willingness to listen reflectively is often what sets the mediator apart from others involved in the conflict.

Even when the conflict is not resolved during mediation, the listening process can have a profound impact on the parties. Jonathon Chace, associate director of the U.S. Community Relations Service, recalls a highly charged community race-related conflict he responded to more than 30 years ago when he was a mediator in the agency's Mid-Atlantic office. It involved the construction of a highway that would physically divide a community centered around a public housing project. After weeks of protest activity, the parties agreed to mediation. In the end, the public officials prevailed and the aggrieved community got little relief. When the final session ended, the leader of the community organization bolted across the floor, clasped the mediator's hand and thanked him for being "different from the others."

"How was I different?" Chace asked. "You listened," was the reply. "You were the only one who cared about what we were saying."

William Simkin, former director of the Federal Mediation and Conciliation Service and one of the first practitioners to write in depth about the mediation process, noted in 1971[49] that "understanding has limited

---

49 William Simkin, <u>Mediation and the Dynamics of Collective Bargaining</u> (BNA Books, 1971)

utility unless the mediator can somehow convey to the parties the fact that [the mediator] knows the essence of the problem. At that point," he said, "and only then, can (the mediator) expect to be accorded confidence and respect."

Simkin was writing about more than the need to understand and project an understanding of the facts. Understanding "is not confined to bare facts," he said. "Quite frequently the strong emotional background of an issue and the personalities involved may be more significant than the facts." He suggested that mediators apply "sympathetic understanding," which in reality is reflective or empathic listening.

Empathy is the ability to project oneself into the personality of another person in order to better understand that person's emotions or feelings. Through reflective or empathic listening the listener lets the speaker know:

> *"I understand your problem and how you feel about it, I am interested in what you are saying and I am not judging you."*

The listener unmistakably conveys this message through words and non-verbal behaviours, including body language. In so doing, the listener encourages the speaker fully to express themselves free of interruption, criticism or direction. The mediator will not agree with the speaker, even when asked to do so. It is usually sufficient to let the speaker know: "I hear you and I am interested in being a resource to help you resolve this problem."

Reflective listening is a core skill that will strengthen the interpersonal effectiveness of individuals in many aspects of their wider professional and personal lives. The power of empathic listening in volatile settings too is reflected in Madelyn Burley-Allen's description of the skilled listener. "When you listen well," Burley-Allen says[50], "you:

---

50 Madelyn Burley-Allen, <u>Listening the Forgotten Skill</u>, (John Wiley & sons, 1982). Burley-Allen is a former president of the American Listening Assn.

1. acknowledge the speaker,

2. increase the speaker's self-esteem and confidence,

3. tell the speaker, "You are important" and "I am not judging you",

4. gain the speaker's cooperation,

5. reduce stress and tension,

6. build teamwork,

7. gain trust,

8. elicit openness,

9. gain a sharing of ideas and thoughts, and

10. obtain more valid information about the speakers and the subject."

To obtain these results, Burly-Allen says, a skilled listener:

1. "takes information from others while remaining non-judgmental and empathic,

2. acknowledges the speaker in a way that invites the communication to continue, and

3. provides a limited but encouraging response, carrying the speaker's idea one step forward."

2.8.7 *Empathic Listening in Mediation*

Before a mediator can expect to obtain clear and accurate information about the conflict from a party who is emotionally distraught, it is necessary to enable that party to engage in a cathartic process, according to Lyman S. Steil[51], a former president of the American Listening Association. He defines catharsis as "the process of releasing emotion, the ventilation of feelings, the sharing of problems or frustrations with an empathic listener. Catharsis," he continues, "basically requires an

---

51 Lyman K. Steil, "On Listening...and Not Listening," Executive Health, (newsletter, 1981). See also, "Effective Listening," by Steil, Barker and Watson, McGraw Hill, 1983 and "Listening Leaders," Beaver Press, forthcoming, 2003

understanding listener who is observant to the cathartic need cues and clues.

People who need catharsis will often give verbal and non-verbal cues, and good listeners will be sensitive enough to recognize them. Cathartic fulfilment is necessary for maximized success" at all other levels of communication.

"Cathartic communication," Steil continues, "requires caring, concerned, risk-taking and non-judgmental listening. Truly empathic people suspend evaluation and criticism when they listen to others. Here the challenge is to enter into the private world of the speaker, to understand without judging actions or feelings."

Providing empathic responses to two or more parties to the same conflict should not present a problem for a mediator who follows the basic principles of active listening. The mediator demonstrates objectivity and fairness by remaining non-judgmental throughout the negotiation, giving the parties equal time and attention and as much time as each needs to express themselves.

Parties to volatile conflicts often feel that nobody on the other side is interested in what they have to say. The parties often have been talking at each other and past each other, but not with each other. Neither believes that their message has been listened to or understood. Nor do they feel respected. Locked into positions that they know the other will not accept, the parties tend to be close-minded, distrustful of each other, and often angry, frustrated, discouraged, or hurt.

When the mediator comes onto the scene, he or she continuously models good conflict-management behaviours, trying to create an environment where the parties in conflict will begin to listen to each other with clear heads. For many disputants, this may be the first time they have had an opportunity to fully present their story.

During this process, the parties may hear things that they have not heard before, things that broaden their understanding of how the other party perceives the problem. This can open minds and create a receptivity to new ideas that might lead to a settlement. In creating a trusting environment, it is the mediator's hope that some strands of trust will begin to connect the parties and replace the negative emotions that they brought to the table.

Madelyn Burley-Allen offers these guidelines for empathic listening:

1. Be attentive. Be interested. Be alert. Create a positive atmosphere.

2. Be a sounding board – allow the speaker to bounce ideas and feelings off you while assuming a nonjudgmental, non-critical manner.

3. Don't ask a lot of questions. They can suggest you are "grilling" the speaker.

4. Act like a mirror – reflect back what you think the speaker is saying and feeling.

5. Don't discount the speaker's feelings by using stock phrases like "It's not that bad," or "You'll feel better tomorrow."

6. Don't let the speaker "hook" you. This can happen if you get angry or upset, allow yourself to get involved in an argument, or pass judgment on the other person.

7. Indicate you are listening by

   • Providing brief, noncommittal acknowledging responses, e.g., "Uh-huh," "Go on", "Tell me more", and "What else".

   • Giving nonverbal acknowledgements, e.g., head nodding, facial expressions matching the speaker, open and relaxed body expression, eye contact.

   • Invitations to say more, e.g., "Tell me about it," "I'd like to hear about that."

8. Follow good listening "ground rules:"
   - Don't interrupt.

   - Don't change the subject or move in a new direction.

   - Don't rehearse in your own head.

   - Don't interrogate.

   - Don't teach.

   - Don't give advice.

   - Do reflect back what you understand and how you think the speaker feels.

The ability to listen with empathy may be the most important attribute of mediators who succeed in gaining the trust and cooperation of parties to intractable conflicts and other disputes with high emotional content. Among its other advantages, empathic listening has empowering qualities. Providing an opportunity for people to talk through their problem may clarify their thinking as well as provide a necessary emotional release.

2.8.8   *Summary of Section 2.8*

Soft skills well deployed create a mediation environment rich in rapport, thought, creativity, and opportunity. In many ways it can be considered to be a "Thinking Environment," an expression coined by Nancy Kline in her book "Time to Think."[52] It is commended to mediators and all those interested in extracting information.

Nancy Kline offers ten components which the authors have adapted to draw parallels with mediation:

- Listen – "Listen, listen, listen and don't make matters worse."

---

52 Kline, N., (1999). Time to Think – Listening to Ignite the Human Mind, Cassell Illustrated. The website offers useful insights at http://www.timetothink.com/meet-us/nancy-kline/

- Ask Incisive Questions – Seek facts and deepen.

- Establish Equality – Giving equal turns in private sessions and keeping to the mediation agreement and agreed rules, whilst being flexible.

- Appreciate – Acknowledge the participants' input and assistance of lawyers / representatives.

- Be at Ease – Manage the process carefully and be mindful of time but give the participants space.

- Encourage – Work to make it fair to all as it is not a competition.

- Feel – Find out how people feel and recognise the emotions they are experiencing.

- Information – Establish and define each participant's reality and seek to identify the crux of the matter.

- Make it human – The mediation is the participants' process.

- Create diversity – Recognise differences and the various perspectives, as they matter.

2.9   Further Techniques

2.9.1   *Clarifying*

What a word or phrase means to one person may have a totally different meaning to another person. This can even be the case in using everyday parlance, particularly words that could be described as strong. Consider the following:

Mediator: *"Steve, please could you tell me how you now feel about Tom?*

Steve: *"Gosh, thinking about Tom I get a feeling of hate in me."*

Mediator: *"Hate – that's quite something to say about Tom?"*

Steve: *"This whole thing has made me really angry and it is driving me to distraction ..."*

Mediator: *"I appreciate that but as you have told me Tom is your business partner and you have been very successful together in the past."*

Steve (after a silence) ...... *"perhaps hate is too strong a word to use but he has still made me mad for what he did."*

Not all dialogues might be so easy but the point is, whether it is words or facts, the mediator needs to clarify as it promotes thinking and creates common understanding.

2.9.2   *Probing*

Probing is a follow-up technique which seeks to explore in more detail a thread in the dialogue. Probing means asking questions to drill down to the deeper meaning, or perhaps to understand inconsistencies. It is part of the Socratic[53] toolkit and is widely used in interrogations. Probing

---

53 See:
  http://www.umich.edu/~elements/fogler&gurmen/html/probsolv/strategy/cthinking.htm

may involve funnelling down from broad questions and getting more focused to identify the crux of an issue.

It must be done permissively and sensitively, making the subject aware that they do not have to answer any of the mediator's questions. It can be described a playing the Devil's Advocate and as such allows for some wide latitude.

2.9.3 *Reality Testing*

As possible solutions to a dispute start to emerge, reality testing is a useful technique in private sessions. Reality testing involves "techniques used to adjust perceptions that do not conform to the realities of the situation[54]." In conflict resolution, it is a process that may be helpful when negotiations breakdown. Sometimes, a party to a negotiation will think they have an alternative or option that is better than what they will get through negotiation. (Fisher, Ury, and Patton called this a better BATNA[55]).

If a party thinks they have a good BATNA, then they may refuse to agree to a settlement, causing an obstacle in the negotiation process. If the BATNA truly is better for that party than the proposed agreement, then the agreement will have to be abandoned, or changed to accommodate that party[56]. However, a party's BATNA is often unrealistic. If a party is refusing to agree to a settlement based on an unrealistic BATNA, then the mediator or opposing party may seek to engage the reluctant party through reality testing.

---

54 Douglas H. Yarn, <u>The Dictionary of Conflict Resolution</u>, (San Francisco: Jossey-Bass Publishers, 1999), 372 and at
http://eu.wiley.com/WileyCDA/WileyTitle/productCd-0787946796.html

55 BATNA or "Best (Better) Alternative to a Negotiated Agreement" is a term first introduced in Roger Fisher, William Ury, and Bruce Patton, <u>Getting to Yes: Negotiating Agreements without Giving In</u>. Second Edition. New York: Penguin. 1991

56 Heidi Burgess and Guy M. Burgess, <u>Encyclopedia of Conflict Resolution</u>. (Denver: ABC-CLIO, 1997), 254 and at http://www.colorado.edu/conflict/encyann.htm

The actual process of reality testing "involves asking hard questions about each parties' power and options.[57]" Either the mediator or the opposing party must work with the resistant party to explore the reasons why it considers that its BATNA is as good as it seems – and what may happen if they stick with it.

There are many reality-testing questions one may ask.

For example, it might be that a participant seeks from another a sum of money to settle the dispute. Perhaps £100,000 is mentioned as an appropriate sum in private session. For the mediator a number of simple reality testing questions can spring to mind such as:

"How feasible is that possibility for you?"

"Why have you chosen the figure of £100,000?"

"How was that figure made up – please tell me more?"

But reality testing more generally involves bringing into play in the security of private sessions (caucus) some objective criteria or other litmus test. The mediator might thus, in the same example, ask on a more sophisticated level as to how a Court might deal with the claim should the matter not settle. Better yet, the mediator might ask:

If a judge were to ask you to explain the £100,000 demanded what would be your best point? And where would you feel most exposed?

If you were arguing the point from the perspective of the other room, what arguments would you advance – with what level of confidence?

By getting the participant to explore costing[58], a mediator can sometimes achieve a similar aim. In trying to reach an agreement in Northern Ireland, mediator George Mitchell reportedly told the parties that (in effect) if they did not reach an agreement, thousands more

---

57 *ibid*

58 Or cost benefit analysis – see Spangler:
  http://www.beyondintractability.org/essay/costing

people would likely die. "And history will hold you accountable," he told the negotiators. "Do you want to be responsible for that?".

If a party is reluctant to try mediation, preferring litigation instead, the mediator – or lawyer – might ask, "If you sue them, who do you think will win? Why? What are the strengths of your case? What are the strengths of theirs? Have you asked counsel to review your assumptions? How much will a lawsuit cost? How long will it take? What will happen in the meantime? Is it worth waiting when the outcome is so uncertain?"

Reality testing may also make reference to recent decisions, comparable cases, or the effect of delay on the business, on costs, and on the loss of management time, focus, and sleep on a problem that could otherwise be solved.

Mediators can often usefully ask lay participants what value they place on their time that will not be recovered if the dispute were to rumble on, and what they would do with the time that would otherwise be committed to the goal of litigation for a few dollars more. There may be other motivations, as in the 1965 spaghetti western[59] – revenge may have its price and mediators need to probe and reality test to find them.

2.9.4 *Reframing*

The authors are indebted to Brad Spangler's 2003 work[60] on reframing in mediation. Spangler suggested that participants enter into conflict resolution processes with their own interpretation of the problem: what issues are in dispute, why the problem has arisen, and how best to resolve the conflict[61]. The way in which a party describes or defines a conflict is known as framing. One of the first things a mediator does in

---

59 http://www.imdb.com/title/tt0059578/

60 Spangler, Brad. "Reframing." Beyond Intractability. Conflict Information Consortium, University of Colorado, Boulder. Posted: November 2003 http://www.beyondintractability.org/essay/joint_reframing

61 Christopher Moore, The Mediation Process (San Francisco: Jossey-Bass Publishers, 1996), 217.

the mediation process is to get the parties to explain their view of the problem. This allows the sides, as well as the mediator, to see how each is framing the conflict[62].

In most cases, these initial statements will reveal very different views of the dispute. For example, opening statements tend to use adversarial language. They often place blame on the other side, attribute negative qualities to the other side's personality or identity, and demand that the other side comply with their demands[63]. Such conflicting frames spur antagonism and prevent the parties from reaching an acceptable and effective agreement. Reframing is the opposite of framing:

> *"Framing refers to the way a conflict is described or a proposal is worded; reframing is the process of changing the way a thought is presented so that it maintains its fundamental meaning but is more likely to support resolution efforts[64]."*

Participants can engage in reframing on their own, but generally it becomes the mediator's role to restate what each party has said in a way that causes less resistance or hostility. In other words, the mediator helps participants communicate and redefine the way they think about the dispute, the better to enable cooperation between opposing sides.

The ultimate goal of reframing is to create a common definition of the problem acceptable to both parties and increase the potential for more collaborative and integrative solutions (see win-win[65]).

The process of reframing can occur quickly if parties are receptive to it, or it may take more time if they are not. In many cases, parties are not aware of the true nature of the conflict. They know they are angry, that they have been wronged, and that they want retribution. However, they

62 From http://www.colorado.edu/conflict/peace/treatment/jtrefram.htm.

63 Jay Rothman, Resolving Identity-Based Conflict (San Francisco: Jossey-Bass Publishers, 1997), 23-28.

64 Bernard Mayer, The Dynamics of Conflict Resolution (San Francisco: Jossey-Bass Publishers, 2000), 132.

65 Both in Fisher &Y Ury's work (*supra*) and Splangler http://www.beyondintractability.org/essay/win-lose

may not be able to identify the problem clearly. With the assistance of a mediator and the passing of time, the parties are given the chance to explore the nature of the conflict. Through this process they will hopefully begin to understand the underlying causes of the conflict. Once parties begin to truly understand each other's point of view, it makes it easier for them to think about solutions that will work for both sides.

While reframing is often all that is needed to find a win-win solution in many conflicts, in the seemingly intractable conflicts that are the subject of many mediations, reframing is helpful, but not sufficient. Often in these conflicts, disputants need not only to identify mutual interests, but also need to examine underlying needs.

When the parties understand the underlying causes of the conflict in terms of interest and needs, it becomes more possible to begin thinking in terms of innovative solutions, or at least possible conflict management strategies that allow the conflict to be pursued, but in less destructive ways.

Mediators and facilitators vary in the degree of direction they provide to parties in the reframing process. Some will simply ask probing questions and then sit back and let the parties work out the issues themselves. Asking "deeply honest" or challenging questions that force the parties to reveal their true feelings can be very effective at facilitating communication (see Empathic Listening[66]).

For example, the mediator may ask, "What did he do that you disliked?" "What would you like for him to have done?" "What would you like him to do now?" "How should he start?" "What should he say?" "How would you respond if he did?" [67]

On the other hand, the mediator may take a more directive role and specifically suggest new ways of defining the problem (reframing) that may be more constructive. Sometimes skilled mediators try to reframe issues that are unresolvable in a way that diverts attention away from

---

66 *Supra* and at http://www.beyondintractability.org/essay/empathic_listening

67 From: Kenneth Cloke, Mediating Dangerously (San Francisco: Jossey-Bass Publishers, 2001), 39 and *supra*.

that type of issue and toward aspects of the dispute that can be resolved[68].

How a skilled mediator approaches the reframing process necessarily depends heavily on the type of conflict at hand. Generally speaking, it is easier to help reframe interest disputes[69] than reframing value conflicts over issues such as guilt, rights, or facts[70]. As noted above, the goal of reframing is to develop a mutually acceptable, or at least workable, definition of the problem on which solution finding can then work.

Therefore, when redefining interest-related issues, it is crucial to include all essential interests of both sides in the new definition. A common way mediators accomplish this is to shift the level of generality or specificity of the issue[71].

For example, the mediator may expand the number of issues to be considered rather than just sticking with the parties' narrow conception of the problem. By listening carefully to the parties' position statements, mediators seek to identify the underlying interests of those positions. By shifting from specific interests, such as a pay increase, to more general interests such as overall employment benefits, mediators can help generate more feasible options for settlement[72].

Value conflicts, on the other hand, are normally more difficult to reframe. These conflicts have a tendency to polarize the disputants.

When parties possess strictly opposed value-based viewpoints there are a few techniques a mediator can use to reframe the issues so they will be

---

68 From http://www.colorado.edu/conflict/peace/treatment/jtrefram.htm.

69 See: Spangler http://www.beyondintractability.org/essay/interest-based-bargaining

70 See: the 2003 original article by Maise now updated to the April 2017 context of United States intolerance by Burgess at http://www.beyondintractability.org/essay/intolerable-moral-differences

71 cf: Bernard Mayer, The Dynamics of Conflict Resolution (San Francisco: Jossey-Bass Publishers, 2000), 135.

72 See: Chris Moore The Mediation Process (1996) http://www.colorado.edu/conflict/peace/moor7538.htm

more ripe for resolution. The first technique is to translate values into interests. For example, if there is a dispute between people about the value of wilderness as opposed to jobs, it would be very hard to resolve which is more important. The question always develops: for whom? Wilderness will be more important for some; jobs for others.

But if the particular dispute is reframed in terms of interests: some groups want a particular piece of land preserved as wilderness, and others want jobs, there might be a way to provide jobs serving people going into or coming out of the wilderness. Or development might be allowed to take place somewhere else in exchange for a wilderness designation on the contested land. By trading off interests, not values, agreement can sometimes be reached.

A second strategy for dealing with value conflicts is to identify over-arching, super-ordinate goals that all parties can accept and cooperatively work toward. In the abortion controversy in the United States, for example, the two sides are probably never going to agree about whether abortion is moral or not.

But they might agree on the idea that people should be helped to avoid having unwanted babies. They might then work together to try to prevent unwanted pregnancies and to provide options for women who still are faced with that dilemma.

People often explain their circumstances, emotions, and ideas through the use of metaphors, analogies, proverbs and other imagery. Thus, another approach to reframing is using new metaphors to describe the situation. Using metaphors that both parties relate to can help open up communication and increase understanding of the conflict and possibilities for resolution[73].

The final technique for value conflict reframing is avoidance. This means the mediator either avoids identifying or responding to the value difference(s) directly, or reframes them so the parties agree to disagree on certain points.

---

73 Bernard Mayer, The Dynamics of Conflict Resolution (San Francisco: Jossey-Bass Publishers, 2000), 136-137.

There are a few final points about reframing to keep in mind. Much of the reframing process is "about changing the verbal presentation of an idea, concern, proposal, or question so that the party's essential interest is still expressed but unproductive language, emotion, position taking, and accusations are removed." Therefore, it is important that mediators are careful with the language they use to reframe problems. Value-laden language and strong positions or demands should be reformulated. The challenge is to convert polarizing language into neutral terms, removing bias and judgment, without diluting the intensity of the message or favouring either side.

For example, Mr. Smith says, "This obnoxious jerk has not paid his rent in 3 months!" The mediator translates that into, "So you are upset that you have not received your monthly rent payment from Mr. Williams for the last three months?"

Lastly, parties must be explicit about the issues that divide them in order for the mediator to successfully help reframe the problem in terms that facilitate agreement. Often there is a cycle of exchanges between the parties and the mediator. As parties become more comfortable with the conflict resolution process they become more explicit about their issues.

Ultimately, the acceptance of the reframing of an issue "is a result of timing and the psychological readiness of the parties to accept the definition (or re-definition) of the situation."

2.9.5 *Curiosity*

The Concise Oxford Dictionary defines curiosity as, "an eager desire to know, inquisitiveness". In The Making of a Mediator: Developing Artistry in Practice[74] "Artistry" is defined as "a mind-set-a commitment to curiosity and exploration, to excellence and learning". The authors of the present work espouse the artistry of curiosity.

---

74 Lang & Taylor (2000) at http://www.beyondintractability.org/bksum/lang-making

At the opening ceremony of the 2012 Paralympic Games, Professor Hawking said this[75], which the authors suggest should be high in the thoughts of every mediator:

"Ever since the dawn of civilisation, people have craved for an understanding of the underlying order of the world. Why is it as it is, and why it exists at all. But, even if we do find a complete theory of everything, it is just a set of rules and equations. What is it that breathes fire into the equations, and makes a universe for them to describe? We live in a universe governed by rational laws that we can discover and understand. Look up at the stars, and not down at your feet. Try to make sense of what you see, and wonder about what makes the universe exist. Be curious."

2.9.6 *The Golden Thread or Threads*

In applying some or all of the above techniques the mediator is often seeking to identify what can be termed the "Golden Thread" of the tapestry of the conversation. These threads can appear as if, "out of nowhere," and it is for the mediator to pick up on the cues and clues, be curious and probe further. They are sometimes prefaced by "would it help if" or "do you know, I really to want to settle today" comments.

Tugging the golden thread may unravel the whole tapestry and allow the conversation to move in more productive directions.

These threads are the mediator's rewards for carefully played soft skills.

---

75 http://www.ctc.cam.ac.uk/news/120829_newsitem.php

2.10   How to Select a Mediator

Mediation is a relatively new field in the United Kingdom and, as yet, as discussed in Part Three, there is no statutory regulation. The Civil Mediation Council operates a pilot scheme for the accreditation of mediation providers, but the scheme is presently voluntary. The authors acknowledge that most mediators are committed to doing a good job and genuinely want to help people resolve their disputes.

YOUR OPPONENTS ARE OVER IN
THEIR CAUCUS ROOM LAUGHING AT
YOUR COUNTEROFFER. ARE YOU
JUST GOING TO SIT THERE AND
TAKE IT OR WHAT?

Bob's days as a mediator were numbered...
But, he was having a great time.

2.10.1   *The process of choosing a mediator*

Nevertheless it is still important for participants to choose a mediator carefully[76]. Because no easy formula can predict mediator competence, the consumer must do some groundwork before selecting a mediator[77].

---

76 The author, Jonathan Dingle, also wrote about this in detail in 2006 – in First Catch Your Rabbit for the Westminster Law Society: see http://www.clerk-sroom.com/downloads/63-How-to-choose-a-mediator.pdf

77 See also http://www.huffingtonpost.com/mark-baer/how-to-select-the-best-mediator-everyone-must-read_b_6172870.html from 2014

First, the user should understand something of the mediation process. After assimilating the basics, perhaps from reading Part One of this work, the following five step process[78] may assist in choosing a mediator:

1. Decide what you want from mediation
2. Get a list of mediators
3. Look over mediator's written qualifications
4. Interview mediators
5. Evaluate information and make decision

2.10.2 *Decide what is wanted from the Mediation*

A consumer should rigorously review the goals for the session. Is this a matter for discussion or robust denial? Does it need an evaluative mediator who suggests options in order to help move the parties towards agreement? Or, does this require a mediator who resists offering opinions so the parties feel responsible for their agreement?

Think about past attempts at negotiation and problems with those attempts. What are the choices if mediation does not work?

Think about the abilities that are affordable and available. What are the strengths and weaknesses of the competing negotiators? What are the other party's strengths and weaknesses? What are the emotional limitations?

Think about the dispute and the context in which it must be resolved. What is the time frame? Is this a commercial dispute between experienced insurance company representatives, or is it a personal matter requiring sensitive decisions? The approach or model that commercial parties might prefer may differ greatly from the one preferred by a mother and father.

---

78 The authors acknowledge that this section has been partly excerpted from the Consumer's Guide to Mediation published by the Alaska Judicial Council. See: www.ajc.state.ak.us/Reports/mediatorframe.htm

Consider the budget. How much can be spent might limit the choice of mediator or mediation panel. Many mediators and dispute resolution firms or services can help participants understand what services would be best for your dispute. Some will contact the other party to the dispute to introduce the concept of mediation.

2.10.3 *Compile a Short List*

A list of mediators is held by the Society of Mediators[79], the CMC[80], the National Mediator[81] and Trust Mediation[82] (amongst other) databases. Personal contact works well. Describe your case to a mediator and ask, "Other than yourself, who are the most skilled mediators in this kind of case?"

Talk to people who have been in a mediation with the mediator (you can ask the mediator for names of former clients who are willing to provide feedback). What was their case about and what were their impressions of the mediator?

2.10.4 *Evaluate Written Materials.*

Call or email several mediators on your list and ask them to send you their promotional materials, resume, references and a sample of their written work. Or drill down on their web links. These materials should cover most of the following topics.

   a. Mediation Training. How was the mediator trained? Some medi-
      ators receive formal classroom-style training. Some participate in

---

79 Email or call the charity for option – +44(0) 207 353 3936 or SOM@218S-trand.com

80 For example in the format: http://www.civilmediation.org/member/dingle-frsa-jonathan/1266/

81 Again, for example: http://www.clerksroom.com/profile?type=mediators&fl=S&pid=773

82 See: https://www.trustmediation.org.uk/about-us/clinical-negligence-mediators/

apprenticeships or in mentoring programs. While training alone does not guarantee a competent mediator, most professional mediators have had some type of formal training. How many hours of training has this mediator had[83]? How recent was the training[84]?

b. Experience. Evaluate the mediator's type and amount of experience (number of years of mediation, number of mediations conducted, types of mediations conducted). How many cases similar to yours has the mediator handled? A mediator's experience is particularly important if there is limited formal training. Conversely, excellent training, observations and pro-bono work can make a relative novice an excellent choice especially if money is limited.

c. Written Work. Some mediators are authors of books (!), blogs, articles, active Twitter accounts, or have their own promotional materials. Websites may also be personal rather than corporate. Any sample of the mediator's work should be clear, well organized, and use neutral language. Evidence of an active, curious, and analytical mind, which is thoughtful about the process, is to be welcomed by most consumers.

d. Orientation Session. Some mediators offer an introductory or orientation session after which the parties decide whether they wish to continue. If so is it offered at no cost, reduced cost, or otherwise? Other mediators prepare videos showing the process which are online on their website or YouTube These are worth considering for assurance but perhaps not as primary sources.

e. Cost. It is important to understand the provider's fee structure. Does the mediator charge by the hour or the day? How much per hour/day? Is there overtime and travel included – and is VAT

---

83 Civil Mediation Council rules require 40 hours of contact time with assessed role play mediations, followed by three observations. The Society of Mediators requires a written examination in addition and annual CPD.

84 Annual CPD should be demonstrated with a minimum of six hours of contact time mediation related work.

charged? What are the cancellation or adjournment/postpone-
ment policies and charges?

f. Other Considerations. Find out whether the mediator carries
professional liability insurance which specifically covers mediation[85]. Is the mediator certified or accredited, and if so by whom?
While certification usually shows the mediator has completed a
specific amount of training or education, training and education
do not guarantee competence. Do ask to see certificates – one
organization whose website still exists in England asserts that its
mediators have been practicing since 2000 when, to the author's
knowledge, the two principals trained in 2010 and 2011. If in
doubt ask the CMC or SOM.

g. Does the mediator belong to a national or local mediation organization, and is the mediator a practicing or general member? Cost
may prevent some competent mediators from joining organizations, becoming certified, or carrying liability insurance.
Membership does not guarantee standing or much more than
basic insurance and CPD checks have been conducted – but an
absence of any memberships might be worth questioning.

2.10.5 *Interview the Mediators.*

Talk to the mediators in person, by Facetime, Skype, or by phone.
During the interview, observe the mediator's interpersonal and professional skills. It can be telling.

As discussed above, qualities often found in effective mediators include
neutrality, emotional stability and maturity, integrity, and sensitivity.
Look also for good interviewing skills, verbal and nonverbal communication, ability to listen, ability to define and clarify issues, neutrality,
some evidence of a problem-solving ability, and organisation. During

---

85 Most providers require £1 million in insurance and the mediator should be able to
produce a certificate. Insurance, due to almost no claims, is available to mediators
for less than £100 per annum through Oxygen and Towergate according to colleagues of the authors. Other providers are available.

the conversation, consider questions about matters covered in the written materials and other topics, eg:

a. Training, Knowledge and Experience. Ask the mediator,

"How has your education and experience prepared you to help us work out this specific dispute?" If the mediator had formal training, but few mediations since, ask if it included role play and observations of skilled mediators? And – "Do you participate in continuing education, on-going supervision, or consultation?" Many professional mediation organizations encourage or require their members to participate in ongoing education or other professional development.

b. Expertise. Ask:

"Do you think subject-matter expertise is necessary for this dispute, and why or why not?" In some cases, the parties may prefer a mediator with no special knowledge of the subject. Benefits of this approach include avoiding a mediator's preconceived notions of what a settlement should look like and letting the parties come up with unique or creative alternatives. In complex cases, a mediator who comes to the table with some substantive knowledge could help the parties focus, save time with a cultural or technical issue, or simply have confidence in the language used.

c. Style. Ask:

"What values and goals do you emphasize in your practice?" For example, does the mediator encourage the parties to communicate directly with each other, or control the interchanges? The mediator should be able to describe their style of mediation and perceived role in the mediation process. Different mediators may practice their craft in different ways, and some mediators change their style to suit specific needs.

d. Ethics. Ask:

"Which ethical standards or Code of Conduct will you follow?" (You may ask for a copy of the standards). All mediators should be able to show or explain their ethical standards to you. If the mediator is a lawyer or other professional, ask what parts of the professional code of ethics will apply to the mediator's services. Ask the mediator too: "Do you have a prior relationship with any of the parties or their attorneys?" The mediator should reveal any prior relationship or bias which would affect his or her performance, and any financial interest that may affect the case.

e. Confidentiality. Ask:

"Do you take notes – and if so what becomes of them?"

"How do ensure Data Protection compliance? What is your ICO number?"

f. Cost. Ask:

"How would you estimate costs for this case?; How can we keep costs down?" Are there any other charges associated with the mediation? Does the mediator perform any *pro bono* (free) services[86] or work on a sliding fee scale? If more than one mediator attends the session, must the parties pay for both? Does the mediator charge separately for mediation preparation time and the actual mediation?

4.1.6 *Evaluate information and make the decision.*

During the interview(s), consumers probably observed the mediators' skills and abilities at several important tasks. These tasks, which mediators perform in almost all mediations, include:

---

86 See for example the Free Mediation Project: http://www.218strand.com/page/free-mediation-project/91/

- gathering background information,

- communicating with the parties and helping the parties communicate,

- referring the parties to other people or programs where appropriate,

- analysing information,

- helping the parties agree,

- managing cases, and

- familiarity with administration.

Consumers should ask which of the mediators best demonstrated these skills. Did the mediator understand the problem? Did they understand the questions and answer them clearly? Did the mediator convey respect and neutrality? Did the mediator appear trustworthy? Did the mediator refer to other helpful sources of information?

Finally, consumers should review the other questions on this checklist and make sure that the mediator's cost and availability coincide with your resources and timeframe. The other parties to the mediation must agree to work with this person, too. To that end, consumers may want to suggest two or three acceptable mediators so that one can be agreed.

But, whoever they chose, the common thread will be the ethical behavior mediators must demonstrate. It those issues the next Part of this work addresses.

PART THREE –
ON ETHICS

3.1   Basic Ethical Norms

Acting ethically is mandatory. It is what a mediator does. Many practicing mediators have come from the legal profession as ADR has gained prominence. Those professions have their Codes of Conduct which will still govern practitioners even when undertaking mediation duties. So too do other professions.

In the United States recognition of the need for ethical codes appeared by 1980 and was being actively adopted by 1992[1].

Chris Honeyman reported[2] in 2013 that the ethics of dispute resolution are the rules and codes of behaviour by which acceptable practice is defined. Both rules and codes of practice vary according to the subject matter of the dispute, the type of process that is being used, the role of the person governed by the rule or code, and the location (or culture).

Thus, ethical rules and codes for divorce mediators in Mississippi may be very different than for commercial arbitrators in Manhattan, let alone any kind of mediator in Mumbai.

For mediators in the United Kingdom not members of regulatory bodies there is (as of 2017/18) no formal regulation. Nor does Parliamentary time seem likely to be given up to the expense and perceived low need for regulation. The authors understand there to have been still very few complaints and no effective legal actions against UK mediators. Regulation is not, then, seen as necessary.

---

1   See, for example: Bush, Robert A. Baruch. *The Dilemmas of Mediation Practice: A Study of Ethical Dilemmas and Policy Implications.* A report on a Study for The National Institute For Dispute Resolution. NIDR, 1992. http://www.beyondintractability.org/bksum/bush-dilemmas

2   See: http://www.beyondintractability.org/coreknowledge/dispute-resolution-ethics

There is the European Code of Conduct for Mediators (reproduced at Annex E) which offers a useful voluntary framework.

Furthermore, membership of such organisations as the Society of Mediators (SoM) and the Civil Mediation Council (CMC[3]) provides strong guidance and advice. Whichever code is adopted, the ethical mediator will act with sensitivity, equality, and honesty and integrity, whilst respecting and adhering to confidentiality.

There are a number of challenges regularly faced by mediators – lies and potential money laundering issues, dramatic power imbalances, and sharp behaviours. The balance of this section is intended to offer outline guidance but as has been indicated earlier, reputable organisations engaged in training or mediation provision will have mentors and a helpline to support their members.

The starting point, counter-intuitively, is when a mediation should be terminated. For it is this question that many of the ethical questions about mediation fall to be considered.

3.1.1   *When should a mediator terminate process?*

But first 'Termination' needs to be placed in context. Termination is an extremely rare event indeed. Neither of the authors have terminated a mediation of their own initiative in over 40 years of combined experience.

If, however, fates conspire – then the starting point is (as with so many other matters) the Agreement to Mediate, the contractual basis that governs the relationship between all participants and the mediator. The mediation agreement will contain reference to termination with a statement such as:

> *"At any time during the Mediation, if the Mediator in his/her absolute discretion decides it should be terminated in which case the*

---

3   www.civilmediation.org

*Parties agree they shall not challenge that decision nor shall the
Mediator give or be asked for a reason for the termination."*

So, for example, if when mediating the mediator:

(a) suspects that there is fraudulent activity taking place;

(b) suspects that there is an activity proscribed under the Proceeds
of Crime Act[4];

(c) sees or hears that there has been a threat to a person in terms of
violence or worse;

(d) considers that that there is a child protection issue;

(e) considers that there is an irremediable equality or discrimination
issue;

(f) has been the subject of a bribe or improper approach;

(g) realises that there is some oppression making it inappropriate to
continue; or

(h) the mediation is taking a course that is outside of the mediator's
values to such an extent that their own ethical position is
compromised

then it may be appropriate to terminate the mediation. Each of these
scenarios is discussed in a more detail below with the observation that
they apply equally to co-mediations as they do to a mediation by one
mediator.

(a)   <u>A suspicion of fraud</u>

If the mediator suspects that there is fraudulent activity taking place
then this is plainly not a place for the integrity and neutrality of a medi-

---

4 Useful guidance on POCA and the perceived duties of regulated and unregulated
mediators is to be found on the CMC site at http://www.civilmediation.org/down-
loads-get?id=117 and from the Chartered Institute of Arbitrators at
www.ciarb.org/docs/.../proceedsofcrimeact2012.pdf though mediators should seek
advice.

ator to be exercised. But what is a suspicion? And what is fraud? A very experienced mediator, formerly a senior High Court judge, contacted the authors one day to say that he suspected fraud. There were three sets of books, all with different VAT rates, being referred to in the mediation. Should the mediation be terminated?

The authors, having the immense benefit of not being so close to the trees, asked what were the three sets of books for? Later that day, when the mediator was encountered for mentoring and reflection, he expressed gratitude at the authors sight of the woods. The books were for the then three sets of VAT rates that applied – 17.%, 20% and 0% and were perfectly maintained.

The first point that arises, is that a mediator, however experienced, should never be afraid to consult colleagues before reaching a decision on how to act in an ethical question. Nor should they be afraid to ask questions, and to probe, provided it is permissible to do so in the context. Any of these approaches may well dispose of the question.

If they do not, then the mediator has to ask the rhetorical question – is it right for me to continue? Most participants do not disclose fraud and most participants do not actively seek to use a mediation as a vehicle for fraud. But some might and will. If there are legal representatives present it might be worth breaking the general rule of not speaking to lawyers away from their clients to discuss what is troubling the mediator.

If the legal representatives are seemingly engaged in a ruse or activity that appears to raise a suspicion of fraud, the mediator might, with delicacy, enquire in private of the lawyer how that action is compatible with their duty to the Court or their regulator's Code of Conduct. Care needs to be taken, however, and this area is one where, as has been stated, discussion with a mentor may offer a better perspective on what is inevitably a fact sensitive situation.

That said, if the suspicion remains, and there is no more than that, then a mediator should terminate the mediation. If there is more than a suspicion, the answer is clear cut. Either may, however, lead to a decision under (b) below.

(b)   A suspicion of an activity proscribed under the Proceeds of Crime Act[5];

This is a complex area legally. The authors do not offer legal advice here or in mediations. Mediators should take careful counsel of their professional bodies if they are in this situation and are regulated professionals. That said, the conclusions of the CMC and CIArb panels that looked at the problem are that:

"34. It would seem clear from this that the Regulations apply to legal professionals, such as barristers and solicitors, when they participate in financial or real property transactions but not when they act for clients in connection with actual or potential legal proceedings.

35. It is therefore concluded:

(a) that mediators and arbitrators who are not lawyers fall outside the regulated sector.

(b) that a legal professional does not —participate‖ in a financial or real property transaction when he acts as mediator, arbitrator or other third-party neutral and so likewise falls outside the regulated sector when performing those functions."

If that is right, and there has not been a challenge to this that the authors have encountered then this gives some reassurance on the duty to report to the National Crime Agency – and the liability to prosecution.

Lawyers, acting as legal advisers at mediation, have clear duties as do other regulated professionals. Mediators are not regulated professionals and are not providing advice. It seems that there is unlikely to be a duty

---

5   Useful guidance on POCA and the perceived duties of regulated and unregulated mediators is to be found on the CMC site at http://www.civilmediation.org/downloads-get?id=117 and from the Chartered Institute of Arbitrators at www.ciarb.org/docs/.../proceedsofcrimeact2012.pdf though mediators should seek advice.

to report, but there is, in the opinion of the authors a clear duty to terminate a mediation if there is a suspicion or more of one or more of the participants being concerned in the making of an arrangement for the disposal of the proceeds of crime.

(c)   Sees or hears that there has been a threat to a person in terms of violence or worse

This certainly, in the authors' minds, mandates termination. Than can be no proper consent to process under a threat of violence or worse. The mediator cannot continue to act. There may also be a duty to report the matter to police as discussed below.

There have been actual instances of this reported to the authors. One contained threats to demolish part of a house, and threats to kill. The mediator did not terminate but later, on advice, reported the matter to police who took the matter seriously and attended the scene. Cautions were issued to those engaged in the threats.

The reason why the mediator sought advice and did not call police was because the mediator was concerned that this would represent a breach of confidentiality on the part of the mediator – the Agreement to Mediate requiring there to be confidentiality. Advice was given that there was an implied term of that Agreement that there would be no criminal activities engaged in by the participants under the veil of confidentiality and that once threats to kill were made the participant uttering them unilateral terminated the contract. There could be no complaint of breach our client contract.

In another instance, and one which is equally instructive, a mediator saw a spouse hit the other spouse in a private (caucus) session in the presence of their lawyer, when the victim spouse refused to agree to an offer that the violent spouse wished to accept. The mediator in this instance decided to call the police. It was a nasty little assault with red marks on the face and the lawyer was prepared to give evidence even if the victim was not. The mediation could not continue and mediator considered that there was a duty of care.

Some mediators might not have acted in the last case in the way that the mediator in question did. The authors support the practical approach taken on the facts known. These questions are always difficult, and most mediation courses debate the questions for half a day with practical examples based on deception, violence and collateral threats. There is much to learn and consider on the facts in every instance.

(d)   The mediator considers that that there is a child protection issue

This should present no problems in deciding to terminate – the only real question being which authorities to contact depending on whether it is an immediate or slightly more medium term threat to the welfare of a child. Guidance can be obtained from professional bodies or the police. There is useful help on the internet[6].

(e)   The mediator considers that there is an irremediable equality or discrimination issue

These issues need to be treated with care and context-based sensitivity. If the mediation is about this subject then the threshold may be higher than if one participant (or indeed a third party) begins to behave in a manner that is unacceptable under equality or discrimination law. Guidance can be taken from professional bodies or from the internet[7].

In the authors' view, it will be an unusual case where it remains appro-priate to mediate in the face of illegal or in appropriate behaviours of this kind. There might be ways of managing the situation but generally the mediator's role is not to transform behaviours. Terminate.

---

6   https://www.nspcc.org.uk/preventing-abuse/child-protection-system/england/reporting-your-concerns/ gives guidance from the NSPCC or https://www.gov.uk/report-child-abuse from the government websight.

7   The Equality and Human Rights Commission publishes guidance on the internet relevant to the UK at https://www.equalityhumanrights.com/en/multipage-guide/responding-questions-discrimination-workplace

(f)   The mediator as been the subject of a bribe or improper approach

Obvious bribes require action to terminate and potentially under the Bribery Act or other legislation. But not all bribes are obvious. What if a participant runs a garage and offers, "after this is all over" to service the mediator's car for a good discount if a settlement is reached. What if a cup of coffee from Starbucks is offered (with or without a bun)? Mediators need to be alive to the spectrum of threats to their neutrality and how to respond – if the offer is innocent it can declined and the mediation proceeded with provided that the other participants are told about it so that everyone knows what is happening. But if the offer is more loaded, and attempt to suborn, then the authors suggest that the mediator should take advice before, probably, terminating.

Other improper approaches happen. A number of mediators of all genders report that lay participants have invited them out "for a drink" or more after the mediation is over. Great care must be taken in these circumstances. The mediator must assess what has taken place and how it can be dealt with neutrally. If the mediator considers that their neutrality is impeached, then the matter must lead to termination.

(g)   The mediator realises that there is some oppression taking place

Mediators will be alive to the fact that many mediations will be stressful places for some or all participants. Many may feel under pressure which some may describe as oppressive, however skilled, patient, and gentle paced the mediator. The feeling of oppression may come from the facts, from financial difficulties, or the risk of a court hearing which may be lost.

These pressures are perhaps the normal and unfortunate consequences of disputes, and should not of themselves lead to the termination of a mediation – unless perhaps an unrepresented individual is incapable as a result of those pressures of conducting the matter. But where the conduct, behaviour, and legal process threats of the other participant go beyond the norm, then the mediator needs to act with care. The mediator is neutral, and has a duty to ensure that there is an ethical context for the mediation. Whilst the mediator cannot criticise legitimate comment, there should not be wrongful oppressive behaviour designed to force the other participant to succumb. This is irrespective of the merits of the case.

(h)   Other ethical problems

It may come to pass that whilst the participants behave honourably within their own spectrum of values, and no crime is committed, the mediation takes a course that is outside of the mediator's values to such an extent that their own ethical position is compromised. The authors are aware of one case where the mediator withdrew because the outcome would have been an affront to their religious beliefs and would have been incompatible with the teachings of their faith leader. These cases will be rare, and unfortunate, but a mediator should not abandon their own ethical principles in order to assist in a resolution of a dispute.

That said, mediators should be careful when it comes to the use of non-business language. They should try not to be too sensitive. One mediator did successfully reduce the flow of invective and expletives which none of the participants minded, by asking politely if they could cease using the F and C words as it was distracting him from assisting them to the fullest of his abilities. That level of honesty paid off, the participants christened the mediator "the Vicar" and used that humour as the basis to find common ground and a resolution.

3.1.2   *How to terminate*

In, what the authors trust, is the unlikely event that termination becomes necessary during the course of the mediation, the mediator should quietly take a break and gather any papers in the normal manner without alerting the participants. The mediator might then take a short while to collect any thoughts and consult with their mentor or panel by telephone.

If there is an immediate child protection issue, or a threat of violence, or actual violence, then rapid consideration should be given to contacting the relevant police or other authority and taking guidance on the immediate actions required in accordance with the notes above.

If no one else is to be involved then, having decided to terminate, the mediator should call the participants, or at the very least their representatives, to the plenary room and announce as follows:

> *"You will recall from the Mediation Agreement that as the mediator I can terminate this mediation without being asked for and without giving a reason for doing so if in my absolute discretion I consider that appropriate. That time has arrived. I can assist you no further. This mediation is over and I shall now depart. Good morning / good afternoon."*

Thereafter, the mediator should walk out of the room and leave the building. It is suggested that standing by a doorway to the room so that a quick unhindered departure can be made is appropriate. There should be no need to run, just be appropriately assertive and do not engage in discussion. The mediator's role is over.

If the mediator has made any notes or holds any papers these should be destroyed and the only document kept being the Agreement to Mediate unless a POCA report[8] is required.

3.1.3   *When should a mediator intervene?*

As described above in the process there are many ways in which the mediator can intervene using a variety of skills, while allowing the participants to talk. At other times it is necessary to protect the mediation process and to intervene, for ethical reasons.

These occasions fall short of termination but are far more common. They contrast in manner and style to the soft skill "intervention points" which were discussed in Part Two when specific skills are used such as:

---

8   To the National Crime Agency in the UK – see http://www.nationalcrimeagency.-gov.uk/about-us/what-we-do/economic-crime/ukfiu/legal-basis-for-reporting

- Summarising what has been said and discussed;

- Reflecting back to the participant(s) a particular aspect;

- Being curious about something that has been said;

- Probing further and not letting a particular thread of the conversation go; and

- Testing the reality of a particular circumstance or offer.

The above are part of the routine craft of the mediator and should and will happen as part of normal course.

However, intervention might be necessary at other times on ethical grounds such as in the event of participants venting anger. This is understandable and during the opening "ground rules" will have been formed including that of politeness and not talking over each other.

Participants can be forgiven here and as we have discussed venting is sometimes necessary; but there is a point at which the mediator would need to intervene to restore the equilibrium. Other times when it is appropriate to intervene are:

- As events unfold inviting the participant to consider whether they may wish to enter a private session;

- On noticing fatigue, inviting that the participants consider a break in the process; and

- As time passes perhaps identifying the fact and encouraging progress before the end of the day by reminding that although there is provision for extra time it will incur costs.

3.2 Why a Mediator Must Be Independent, Neutral and Impartial

In becoming a mediator an individual is assumes a significant responsibility. Through the principles of mediation confidentiality and that of without prejudice mediators are gifted with highly confidential and sensitive information. Thus, a mediator has the potential to either directly influence or be perceived to influence whether a settlement takes place or not. Clearly this is not a position in which mediators would wish to find themselves.

In the broadest terms mediators must act in a manner that is both professional and ethical of which independence, impartiality and neutrality form part.

3.2.1 The European Code of Conduct

In 2004 the European Code of Conduct for Mediators was established and many organisations adhere to that code although they are under obligation to do so. Concerning Independence and Neutrality – the following text is taken directly from the European Code of Conduct for Mediators.

"The mediator must not act, or, having started to do so, continue to act, before having disclosed any circumstances that may, or may be seen to, affect his or her independence or conflict of interests. The duty to disclose is a continuing obligation throughout the process. Such circumstances shall include:

- Any personal or business relationship with one of the parties,

- any financial or other interest, direct or indirect, in the outcome of the mediation, or

- the mediator, or a member of his or her firm, having acted in any capacity other than mediator for one of the parties.

In such cases the mediator may only accept or continue the mediation provided that he/she is certain of being able to carry out the mediation with full independence and neutrality in order to guarantee full impartiality and that the parties explicitly consent."

The following text relates to impartiality in the European Code of Conduct for Mediators

> *"The mediator shall at all times act, and endeavour to be seen to act, with impartiality towards the parties and be committed to serve all parties equally with respect to the process of mediation."*

3.2.2 *Communicating the neutrality*

The mediator's independence, neutrality and impartiality are emphasised throughout the mediation process from the initial email of introduction, in the Agreement to Mediate, and orally in the opening of the mediation itself. There should be no doubt in participant's mind as to the role and neutrality of the mediator. Advice can never be offered.

3.2.3 *Responding to requests for advice*

And yet, almost always during some phase of the mediation, this neutrality will be put at risk. A participant or an adviser will seek the mediator's advice. If the request is about process then the Agreement to Mediate and the Rules specifically permit such advice to be given.

But if the request goes to the substance of the mediation, or very often the size or scope of an offer, then that is a different matter. Such advice is expressly not permitted for that would not only usurp the role of any adviser or representative but, more importantly, would lead the mediator to become aligned with the participant and thereby risk accusations of bias.

Why are such requests made? It may be that a participant has genuinely forgotten or perhaps misunderstood this principle. Or the participant may want to suborn the process and the neutrality of the mediator.

It matters not – the request cannot be granted. But should it be bluntly rejected?

The authors submit not. It is their belief that for the mediator the request for advice may present a great opportunity for working with a participant. Whilst it would be natural for the mediator simply to decline to answer and reinforce their role by reference to the Agreement to Mediate, that would be a lost chance. The better response is surely on the lines of:

> "I am flattered you have asked me for advice. I will deal with your request in a moment. First though, tell me what troubles you?"

The mediator can then open up the conversation through open questions, finding out why the participant feels they need advice, what they would do it that advice were 'x' or 'y', and what are presently their priorities.

At no point will the mediator actually give advice. If pressed, later in the dialogue, the mediator can say something like:

> "Were I in the other room just now, with all I know and am keeping confidential, and they asked me for advice, what you would expect me to do – and why?"

By using the techniques of asking the questioner to stand in the shoes of their opponent, the mediator can make progress without ever declining and with the gain of letting the participant work the matter out for themselves.

And having got the participant thinking about what is happening in the other room, the mediator can broaden out the subject – by asking for example:

"What do you think is preventing (the other participant) from giving you closer to what you tell me you are seeking? What do they need to move closer? How can that be delivered?"

It follows that in a circumstance that might seem unpromising, with the mediator's neutrality being threatened, rather than batting away the request and being unhelpful, the mediator can seize an initiative, add value, and use the challenge as a golden thread to tug and maybe to unravel a level or two of fibres holding back the conversation.

3.2.4   *Summary of this Part*

Mediation codes of ethics all require the mediator to be neutral and impartial, to avoid conflicts of interest, to obtain informed consent for their involvement from the parties, to maintain confidentiality, to reject cases which are beyond their expertise, and to be truthful in advertising their services and fees. Even without a professed code, mediators should so act.

Yet within the ethical spectrum there is much to be learned and gained about how participants are thinking. Provided the mediator is alive to every opportunity, and has finely honed soft skills, the application and enforcement of ethics can really open up dialogue and reflection.

3.3 Afterword – Ethical Issues From Texas

The authors were passed the following ethical questions[9] assembled by Texan mediators: they may not seem to be directly relevant to most readers, but they offer a useful refresher on ethical principles and the application of the Agreement to Mediate in some bizarre situations.

3.3.1 *Experience counts – or does it?*

You have been asked to mediate a federal court employment dispute based on a Title VII case because you once clerked for the federal judge who will hear the case. A summary judgment motion is pending. Both parties want to know your "best guess" on the likelihood of success of the motion for summary judgment so they can determine the value of the case. What do you do?

3.3.2 *Attorney's little helper?*

You are serving as a mediator in an age discrimination case. Expert designation deadlines are looming, but both parties want the deadlines to be extended so they can keep costs down and further discuss settlement in the mediation. However, both parties are not from your jurisdiction, and do not know the most expeditious manner in which to move the deadline with the certainty needed to resolve the mediation. You have offered to call the court coordinator, because you know her and know that the issue will be resolved quickly. Now that you have offered, you have second thoughts because you are fearful you might be treading on dangerous ethical waters. Should you proceed or not? If so, how should you proceed?

---

9 The authors' summary answers follow: readers may compare their own and see how, if at all, they differ.

3.3.3   Desperate lawyer

You are a mediator in federal employee discrimination case. The employee's attorney pulls you aside prior to the mediation and says, "my lady is crazy and I need your help to settle this case." What do you do when you are told this? Should you proceed? Should you tell the client?

3.3.4   In Mediators we trust

You have been mediating an employment case all day. The attorney for the plaintiff has begged his client to settle the case and agreed to cut his fee. The plaintiff finally tells her room that she believes in God: since God has brought her to mediation and that God has also brought you she will trust in your judgment. What do you do?

3.3.5   Packing heat

You are mediating a hotly contested employee case with two opposing individuals that are both permitted to carry firearms in their profession. You discover after the mediation starts that they are both packing "heat".

3.3.6   Christians v Witches

You are mediating a case concerning Christian employees vs. a self claimed witch in a coven that supervises the Christians. The witch says in a caucus…do you believe in witches or are you a Christian? You look down at your ring and it has a cross on it.

3.3.7   The handshake deal (or no deal) that is the question

You have been asked to mediated a pre-lawsuit employment wrongful discharge case. Neither the employee nor the company are represented by attorneys. The statute of limitations period is only a week away. The parties reach an agreement. They shake hands and state they have a deal. Do you offer to draft the agreement; suggest the parties draft the agreement; or let the handshake deal stand?

3.3.8   *Odd man out*

From the outset of the mediation it is apparent that everyone involved in the process except one has an instant connection because of some factor. It is equally apparent that the "odd man out" is very uncomfortable. What do you do to achieve a balance or perception of neutrality? What if you as the mediator are the "odd man out??

3.3.9   *Going it alone*

An attorney is late to the mediation, and she suggests that you go over your opening session in caucus with each party. He gives you permission to generally go over your opening session without her being present because she knows your spiel. Assuming all parties have previously requested that they do not want an opening joint session, and you have agreed, should you proceed to give your opening statement in caucus without the attorney present?

3.3.10 *Suggested summary answers to the Texan questions*

q1   Politely refer to the Agreement to Mediate: unless you are contracted to evaluate, then decline to do so. If you are so contracted, then adopt the agreed structure.

q2   Mediators can (under the Agreement to Mediate) assist with mediation process but not with litigation. Give the attorneys the court coordinators name and number and invite them to call her directly if they wish.

q3   Assuming crazy does not mean that she lacks capacity, in which case you should not proceed, you must stress your neutrality and your role under the Agreement to Mediate. You might also ask the lawyer what their Code of Conduct requires them to do. There is no separate obligation to tell the client what their lawyer has said.

q4   Politely thank her for her trust but decline to advise: review the options in private and ask them if they have any reason to suppose that a better deal with be available today, in the future, or after a hearing.

q5   There is no right answer: if the mediator feels the situation is safe and is comfortable the authors imagine that the matter could proceed. For their part, the authors would almost certainly wait until the weapons were locked in a safe place. That said, Maria Arpa of the Centre for Peaceful Solutions[10], reports mediating with armed gang members as being a focussing experience.

q6   This is a classic: in a divorce case, the authors have been asked whether they have been divorced, and in a lemon car case whether they have driven or own the defective model. The first point is that the mediator should seek to avoid conflict before the mediation begins by declaring anything that reasonably give rise to perceptions of bias. That does not mean removing the crossed ring for the duration but being open.

If, however, the point is raised in the mediation for the first time, then the first question a mediator might ask is – as I am neutral, and am not here to decide anything, how would any answer I might give affect you? The authors would in any event decline to answer the question but if the participant insisted that they would not proceed if the mediator did not state (for

---

10 https://www.centreforpeacefulsolutions.org/staff/maria-arpa/ – Maria is an inspiring mediator and campaigner whose Charity offers mediation observations and really effective courses in community and ;oca; business mediation skills. The authors thoroughly recommend the Centre's work and training.

example) to all participants that they believed in witchcraft, then termination might be the only option.

q7   Refer (as part of your permitted advice on process role) to the Agreement to Mediate which states that deals made in mediation are only binding if they are put in writing and signed by the parties. Ask them if they wish to make some form of written record. If they decline the authors would annotate their copy of ATM to that effect.

q8   Odd participant: ask questions in a private session to find out what is wrong and see if this negates the process being a safe haven. Being isolated as the mediator is quite normal initially and a spur to building rapport.

q9   Provided the client has agreed this with her attorney and there are no capacity issues, and you have permission to tell the other participants that this is what you are doing, then if there are no objections you could do so.

3.3.11 *Another example*

Honeyman cites[11] a further Texan hypothetical example, much beloved of ethical regulators in the United States. It concerns a mediator, employed by a Texas state agency, who is assigned to mediate a dispute between a would-be truck driver and a truck driving training school, when the driver refused to pay the school fees, claiming that the practice trucks were unsafe. The mediator, operating under typical confidentiality rules, helps the parties reach a settlement, but later gets a phone call from the chair of the Texas State Assembly's (fictional) Committee on Highway Safety. This powerful state legislator, whose jurisdiction also includes the budget of the agency the mediator works for, demands to know what was said in the mediation about the safety of the trucks — and wants the information quickly.

---

11 *Ibid:* http://www.beyondintractability.org/coreknowledge/dispute-resolution-ethics

While acknowledging the uncomfortable (or even, potentially, career-ending) dilemma presented to the mediator, mediator groups have been virtually unanimous in arguing that the mediator must refuse to provide the requested information.

Ethical problems, says Honeyman, are presented differently according to circumstance and role. For this reason, ethics codes and rules tend to address quite different problems for neutrals than for parties and their advocates. While the specific concerns of these rules can vary quite widely, a common theme of ethics codes for parties and their negotiators is to demand negotiation in good faith, a concept which includes prohibiting dragging out the negotiations unnecessarily, sending representatives who have no authority to conclude an agreement, and other forms of conduct which tend to make an honest search for mutual agreement impossible.

For neutrals, the concerns are different, and may include prohibitions on accepting business in another context from someone who is a party in a case before that neutral; requirements to keep matters discussed in the negotiations confidential; and requirements to disclose friendships and other relationships which might cause concern to either party as to whether the neutral really is neutral.

PART FOUR –
ON CO-MEDIATION

4.1 Introducing Co-Mediation

Co-mediation[1] has been described[2] as an intricate dance. Performed well it is like an expert foxtrot, smooth as silk, with both mediators taking turns leading and following, two moving as one, making the supremely difficult look effortless. When is not done well it can resemble a memorable Strictly Come Dancing fail, each person doing their own thing, trying very hard, but lacking in synchronicity. This Part of the book is intended to give co-mediators sufficient to look back, and say, as the late host[3] might have done, "didn't we do well?"

4.1.1 *Why co-mediation?*

Co-mediation is a mediation that uses two or more mediators. The mediators are trained to work as a team to assist the participants in resolving their conflict. Co-mediation as a model of mediation process can be a very effective and practical option in a wide variety of circumstances. Some would argue co-mediation is the best practice model while others would say it is usually unnecessary to involve two mediators. In community mediation[4] it is generally used to ensure protection and safety for the mediators, and to ensure that the participants, who are generally unrepresented, are neutrally and appropriately supported.

Co-mediation is reported to be beneficial in a number of situations. In complex mediations, across a wide variety of contexts, from international conflict to large costs cases, sometimes two or more heads are

---

1   Where two or more mediators work together in what is generally a single mediation process

2   by Keryn Foley, Australian Mediator 2016 – see: http://www.mediationconference.com.au/wp-content/uploads/2016/07/Poster-Presentation-Ms-Keryn-Foley.pdf

3   Sir Bruce Forsyth (1928-2017)

4   See section 5.5, below

better than one. This can not only be for assimilating information but also for case management. The authors are engaged in preparing for a co-mediation in Africa which may involve 10,000 participants, and several teams of co-mediators over some time. It is inconceivable that a single mediator could, in any reasonable timescale, manage or deal with such number.

In mediations with many participants, two mediators provide more attention to each individual. As a result, the participants may experience a greater feeling of being heard. Further a participant is more likely to develop trust with at least one of the mediators. It is important, however, to make sure that the participants do not feel that one of the mediators is "their" mediator and biased in their favour[5].

Even in smaller mediations, one mediator can, for example, listen and observe while the other mediator asks questions. Or, one mediator can focus on the details, while the other focuses on the big picture. Further, having two mediators who can divide tasks may also accelerate the process. For example, each mediator can caucus (meet individually) with one of the participants at the same time, making the mediation more efficient.

Two mediators may also be beneficial when the mediators have varying skills. For example, the participants may want one mediator who is an expert in one particular field and another mediator that is an expert in a different field.

Sometimes, to feel comfortable, participants need their differing ethnicities, genders or ages represented in the mediators. For example, in family law mediations, it sometimes makes the participants more comfortable to have mediators of both genders present. A male participant may otherwise feel that a female mediator would favour his wife, or vice versa. In a mediation involving discrimination issues, it may make a difference to have mediators of different ethnicities or ages.

---

5 See: Keys, Bianca (2009) "Co-mediation: positives, pitfalls and lessons learned," ADR Bulletin: Vol. 11: No. 4, Article 3. Available at http://epublications.bond.e-du.au/cgi/viewcontent.cgi?article=1474&context=adr

4.1.2 *Co-mediation skills*

Co-mediation demands a high degree of cooperative work, refined listening skills, and a willingness to pace matters appropriately. The fundamental skills are those set out in Parts One and Two above, with the ethical requirements being the same as those in Part Three. But co-mediators need also to consider the particular needs of unrepresented participants who often have a need or desire to seeks affirmation or advice. The approach offered in Section 3.2.3 above which can be especially effective with unrepresented participants.

The essence of effective co-mediation is the combination of careful planning and skillful execution. Time spent planning a co-mediation is never wasted.

4.1.3 *What co-mediators consider when planning the process*

A positive dynamic between co-mediators is therefore an essential aspect of working together in a complimentary manner. This will not be possible for all pairings; however good preparation and a firm understanding of who is responsible for what tasks, or aspects of the discussions, will enhance effective team-work. Above all, mutual respect will set the tone for a meeting where differences do not inhibit constructive discussion and healthy debate.

Inside The Caucus Room

The following are some important points for co-mediators to consider prior to the mediation meeting:

- Will one mediator lead, or will the mediators share direction equally?

- Seating arrangements – will the mediators sit opposite to maintain eye contact or will they work alongside each other and, if necessary, use visual clues?

- Introductions – who will give the introduction and begin the mediation in the opening session? Will this task be shared?

- Together or apart – will the mediators both stay in the same room at all times, as is recommended and required in most community mediations; or work in parallel rooms as may be appropriate in complex commercial co-mediations?

- Interrupting – what are the protocols for a mediator who wants to interrupt the other's dialogue?

- Handling emotions – who will go to check on a party who storms out or appears overwrought?

- Unscheduled breaks – how and when to use and to suggest them.

- Handovers – how to hand over to each other.

- How to ask for help – agreed signals, verbal or physical.

- How to bring each other into the discussion.

- How to discuss the matters that have been heard in a co-mediator caucus

- How to close the session.

- How to adjourn and reconvene sessions.

The authors' typical approach to each of these questions is set out below.

4.2　Recommended Approach to a Typical Co-Mediation

By recommended, the authors hasten immediately to caution that every co-mediation is different, and there are factors in civil and commercial co-mediations, as distinct from the special demands of workplace or community co-mediations, that may necessitate a variation. As is also the case, mediation is structured but flexible and flexibility is certainly appreciated in co-mediation.

4.2.1　<u>Will one mediator lead, or will the mediators share direction equally?</u>

If both co-mediators are experienced in the art, and are comfortable with the options, then they may decide wither that one should lead, and the other support. Alternatively, they may decide that it will be made clear to the participants that the co-mediators are in every way carrying out the same roles and neither one is the leader.

Whichever approach is taken, it is vital (unless one is present solely as a trainee) that the participants are told that the co-mediators are equal in status however much one might talk and the other listen. This can be explained in information provided before the mediation, as well as in the opening brief in the plenary session. It can and must also be made clear by the body language and compliments that pass between the mediators.

If it is planned that the co-mediators will stay together throughout the process, then there is no question of one mediator appearing to be less significant than the other and participants both wanting the apparently more senior mediator. In that circumstance the authors tend to prefer a lead mediator role and a support mediator role – albeit that both roles are equally important to process (and equally paid).

If it is planned that the co-mediators will conduct parallel private sessions (caucuses) whereby one mediator is with one set of participants, whilst at the same time the other mediator is with another set of participants, then it is preferable that from the outset equal prominence in terms of speaking and leading is given to both mediators. This is to ensure that one mediator is not seen as preferable or senior to the other, and a participant does not feel aggrieved through being asked to caucus with a mediator of lower perceived status.

The question whether to stay together or work in parallel is discussed in Section 4.2.4 below.

Whichever approach – sole leadership or direction-sharing – is decided upon the authors emphasise that the division of labour is carefully planned. Co-mediators must aim for a seamless partnership and there is no substitute for time spent together, both formally planning the mediation and informally learning to appreciate respective styles, language, and skills.

4.2.2   <u>Seating arrangements</u>

The topography of mediation with a sole mediator can be of significance but, as indicated in Section 2, the authors are increasingly relaxed about this when working on their own. Whilst some mediators go to great lengths[6] to arrange seating plans, the important principle when there is a sole mediator is that the mediator can see everyone from a neutral position. Indeed, the authors find that walking around a room when mediating in plenary or caucus sessions can assist change the dynamic, or even give the mediator a moment to reflect.

But in co-mediations, greater thought needs to be given to the use of the room available.

---

6   Inspirational mediator and friend Steven C Jones (now a pastor in Jackson, Michigan) tells a story of the mediator who sought to control seating by placing writing implements in different places in the room. Two pencils, two biros, and two more expensive looking pens would be obtained. The pencils would be placed on a legal pad where the mediator wished the clients to sit. The biros placed on a pad where the mediator wished solicitors to sit, and the pens where it was preferred that the barristers would sit. It was said to be such an effective *ruse de guerre* that no words needed to be spoken to achieve the envisaged seating.

The co-mediators will need to decide if they sit opposite each other to maintain eye contact, or will work alongside each other and use verbal or some other visual cues. Sometimes, of course, especially in home scenarios in community mediations, there is little option. But where there is a choice, the factors to be decided considered will include:

(a) the first decision[7] for one mediator to lead – or for direction to be shared: if the direction is shared then it is preferable for the co-mediators to be in a place where they both observe and engage with the participants equally: but if there is to be single leader the more significant factor will be the ability of the second mediator to observe the process as a whole and gently make eye contact with the lead mediator;

(b) the number of participants are there: if there are a significant number then it may be more important for the co-mediators to sit somewhere where they can jointly survey or watch the whole room; and

(c) the sophistication or otherwise of the co-mediators system for signalling to each other the need to interject, interrupt, take time outs and so forth.

On a practical level, the authors' preference is that inferred in (a) above – if there is a single leader then seats should be chosen to afford maximum observation opportunities to the support mediator as well as eye contact between the mediators; but if there is to be shared direction then both mediators should sit where they can most easily engage with the participants first of all and work out a suitable communications protocol between themselves.

4.2.3 Introductions – in private rooms and in the opening session

The question of who will commence introductions, both in the private rooms before the mediation (if there are any) and in the plenary session can be on much the same principles as the decision in Section 4.2.2 as

---

7 (Section 4.2.1)

to the seating arrangements It should slow from whether the co-mediators are jointly directing process, or whether one mediator is taking the lead.

If it is the former course, then care should be taken to work out a balanced opening, both in the private rooms of the participants and the opening session in the plenary room. This balance extends to the email to be sent to the participants before the mediation. They should be addressed from both mediators and everything done to ensure that the participants, correctly, assume that the mediators are on an equal status.

If the latter situation is in play, then the 'lead mediator' will ordinarily do just that – although it is usually helpful for the support mediator to introduce themselves and describe the role that they will be playing. Naturally, this part of the process benefits from careful planning and rehearsal – it is surprising what a difference a slick handover between sections of the opening or introductions makes to the overall presentation of the mediation.

4.2.4   Together or apart

As has been suggested in Section 4.2.1, there are two main options for co-mediators once the plenary section has completed and private (caucus) sections commence, either the mediators both stay in the same room at all times, as is recommended and required in most community mediations; or for each mediator to work in parallel rooms as may be appropriate in complex commercial co-mediations.

Experienced North American mediator Lynn Duryee[8] reported in June 2017 in favour of co-mediators, and of them staying together. She wrote:

> *"The high-conflict, emotional case can also benefit by two neutrals. If there's a participant who needs a ton of attention or handholding, one neutral can be assigned that task while the co-mediator works on*

---

8   http://www.mediate.com/articles/DuryeeL20170630.cfm

other matters; in that way, the needy party has her day in court, does not feel ignored or unimportant, and, perhaps most significantly to other participants, doesn't hold up progress. Other difficult cases may involve a litigant who is suspicious of the process or unwilling to work with the agreed-upon neutral. In such a case, a co-mediator can be paired with that litigant and progress can be achieved.

...

With two heads, we find that we are better able to assist participants in generating options for resolution. While listening to the parties, if one of us misses a key concept or clue to settlement, the other one will have captured it ... If one neutral shows signs of impatience, the other can gently kick her partner under the table.

The name of the game in mediation is overcoming impasse and achieving resolution. Here too, co-mediators can be effective in supercharging momentum. Whether working together in the same room or apart in separate caucuses, co-mediators can create a convincing chorus of optimism. If energy and enthusiasm begin to wane, one or both neutrals can swoop to the rescue to remind participants that progress has been made, that parties really do want to settle (despite the loud grumbling), and that we are so very close to the finish line that giving up is not an option."

The authors take the view that where the co-mediators are one experienced mediator, and one novice or trainee, it is mandatory to stay together. Obviously where the policies of any parent organisation require the co-mediators to stay to together then this must be done.

Where the participants are unrepresented it is again, regardless of the experience of the mediators, strongly recommended that the co-mediators work together at all times. There are so many potential pitfalls[9] in community mediation with unrepresented participants that if there is an option (as there will be definition be with co-mediators) to work together it should be taken. The additional time taken by having two

---

9 See Section 5.4.5 below

people together is generally more than compensated for by the quality of the sessions and the reduction of risk.

Where participants are represented, where there are no risks identified, and where but for the numbers of complexity a sole mediator might have been appointed, then it seems to the authors that there may sometimes be advantages in running parallel caucuses. If this step is taken, however, the co-mediators will need to have careful protocols in place for interruptions, breaks, differing emotions, and handovers. They will also need to be mindful of the risk of inadvertent confidentiality breach.

Thus, with parallel caucus sessions, a keen eye must be kept on the time spent in the private rooms. These sessions must be followed by co-mediator discussions which permit the co-mediators to catch up.

To facilitate these co-mediator discussions it is necessary for the co-mediators to obtain the participants' agreement that anything said to one mediator is to be treated as said to both for the purposes of one co-mediator being able to share it with the other. When co-mediators do share information they need to be clear whether any of it can be passed to the other participants. This risk of breach of confidentiality is high unless the co-mediators are absolutely sure on what basis one was told something.

Finally, co-mediators must be clear with the participants that they cannot ask one mediator to withhold something they have been told from the other co-mediator. If the mediators are not free to share with each other then the basis of trust in the mediation process is no longer present and the mediation will need to end.

4.2.5 Interrupting and stepping into a caucus

Sometimes one mediator will want to interrupt during the open (plenary) session. This may be whether the mediator is the support mediator or in a joint role, but at that point silent. On other occasions, one mediator may have reached a critical stage in a parallel caucus when the other mediator wishes to enter the room, potentially with nothing more than trivial information or potentially with a key time-limited offer. Co-mediators must devise protocols for such eventualities.

Where the co-mediators are working together, this is relatively easy. Some form of signalling, eye contact, movement of a pen, or direct spoken gambit can work. Mediators should consider different protocols for different degrees of perceived urgency and also methods by which the co-mediator might politely decline to be interrupted.

The situation is more difficult in cases where parallel caucuses are held. Some mediators have a code of knocks, one for routine, two for urgent to indicate the degree of significance. Others send texts that buzz a number of times in their co-mediator's pocket. Others, and this is the authors' preferred approach for this situation, automatically invite the co-mediator in but, depending on the point reached in the session, ask whether they might delay their information for a moment or is there something that needs immediate attention.

There is never a right answer here, and it is one of the risks of parallel caucuses that interruptions may end up making real problems for either of the co-mediators. It is another reason why the authors prefer to stay together throughout the mediation.

4.2.6   Handling emotions

The matters that come into play here range from the mundane, the offering of tissues or a glass of water, to the relatively fraught – who will go to check on a party who storms out or appears overwrought? Co-mediators may identify particular skills that each has in such a situation and should allocate their resources accordingly. This will flow naturally on the day but is another matter that benefits from careful planning.

In the case of the runaway participant, if one mediator initially leaves the room, however, then it is preferable that the other does not carry on with substantive discussions, but probably (after settling the remaining participants) goes to find the other co-mediator. No progress can be made until it has been established what has become of the runaway and there is a risk of inappropriate matters being said. Further, the co-mediator going after the overwrought participant may well need assistance.

Co-mediators should not hurry anyone back into session. Time is often the best nurse.

4.2.7   Unscheduled breaks

Co-mediators will, when working together in plenary or caucus sessions, often find that there are moments when they need to have an unscheduled break to consider how to respond to what they have just heard. Co-mediators should not simply press on hoping that matters become clearer but instead be sufficiently confident to say to each other that they would value a conversation to discuss options for getting the most out of the time that remains, or some such similar wording.

Safe words

It may also be appropriate, here or in more urgent cases, to have a safe word that sounds innocuous but means that the other co-mediator should finish immediately and discuss matters outside of the earshot of participants. Examples of safe words or phrases have varied from a reference to "Mrs Thatcher" and "I think I heard Lord Harvey say that" to "Can we just go and check something on my iPad?"

Co-mediators should select something that works for them and there may be scope for different words or phrases for differing degrees of urgency.

4.2.8   Handovers – how to hand over to each other

This sounds trite but it is remarkable how unprofessional some co-mediators can be in talking over each other, failing to let the other speak or complete a sentence, or leaping in to ask that burning question. Rather as in Section 4.2.5, co-mediators will want to devise smooth protocols for handovers in plenary sessions or in caucuses.

The authors have found that, unless there is a perceived need to interrupt, as set out above, then one mediator should, when they are ready, look at their co-mediator and say words to the effect of, "What would you like to add or ask?" – an open question – rather than the more obvious "Is there anything you would like to ask?".

Sometimes they will say: "In a moment I am going to go round the room and see what anyone else would like to say, but right now – [co-mediator's name]." And leave it hanging.

4.2.9   How to ask for help – agreed signals, verbal or physical

As indicated above, signalling (or mediator to mediator non-verbal communication) is an important part of the co-mediator's toolkit. It is suggested that co-mediators write down their agreed signs or signals or cues, so that there is no room for ambiguity. It is also recommended that co-mediators rehearse them so that there is a naturalness about the whole process. It may seem odd, or amusing, to do so without partici-pants, but it is better that so that providing clues or cues to the co-mediator can pass smoothly when in the mediation.

4.2.10 How to close or adjourn the session.

Co-mediators will want to agree in advance that save in exceptional circumstances neither mediator will terminate the mediation without discussing it with the other. That much is trite. The means by which co-mediators come to close, adjourn and reconvene open or private sessions is a little more spontaneous – it should be a natural break but there must also be a weather eye on the time.

It is suggested that a co-mediator who feels that the moment has come to end a session says to the other, following protocols, if it is intended to come back – words to the effect of,

"I wonder if it would be sensible to pause there for a moment and for us to take stock? I would value a comfort break/cup of coffee and we can see what is happening in the other room. Shall we say five minutes?"

Similar phrases can be developed for closing a session. Closed questions can assist at this point.

4.3 Summary

Co-mediation is no dark art but it does, as indicated, have pitfalls for the unwary or overbold mediator. With preparation, these can be transformed into a safe process that can be rewarding and effective for mediators and participants alike. The watchword, however, is preparation following effective training. There is no substitute.

PART FIVE –
ON SPECIALISMS

5.1 Overview

The authors consider it appropriate to introduce a number of specialist areas of mediating. These include (as an example of a scheme) the NHS Resolutions Clinical Negligence introduced after a pilot and evaluation in January 2017, workplace and employment mediation, and community mediation.

This work does not cover family mediation[1], although there is a great deal of this work now happening (even in the face of financial cuts and the removal of Legal Aid in many cases). Family mediation in England and Wales – including the residence and contact arrangements for children, and the financial consequences of divorce is closely regulated and subject to judicial scrutiny[2].

---

1 The Family Mediation Council:
https://www.familymediationcouncil.org.uk/family-mediation/ offers considerable guidance as to the process and is recommended to those interested in this work.

2 See: https://www.familymediationcouncil.org.uk/family-mediation/mediation-meetings-sessions/

Mediation Information and Assessment Meetings (MIAMs[3]) are used to see whether the parents or spouses could benefit from mediation. Its ambit is outside the scope of this text but its influence (or potential influence if fully funded) should not be underestimated.

Wills and probate, and disputes about the future of family estates, which are closely allied to family matters, are in contrast frequently mediated by mediators various and very much follow the processes set out in Parts One, Two and Three above. Participants do not generally need to seek the approval of the Court for any settlement unless there are children or persons lacking in capacity in the mediation[4]. There is considerable sensitivity in those cases and some degree of knowledge of TOLATA[5] and the 1975 Act[6] can be of assistance – hence there can be a level of specialism in these cases.

Evaluative mediation (see Section 1.1.8 above for the CADR scheme) is also a specialist area but the authors believe that this area of work requires very precise training. There are, as is discussed in that Section, numerous difficulties that need precise thought and engagement. Whilst many mediators in practice may stray towards some form of evaluation the authors strongly recommend that mediators consider the difference between evaluating and reality resting, and what they are authorised to do within the scope of the Agreement to Mediate.

---

3 See: https://www.familymediationcouncil.org.uk/family-mediation/assessment-meeting-miam/

4 See CPR Part 21.10 https://www.justice.gov.uk/courts/procedure-rules/civil/rules/part21#21.10

5 A useful guide dated 11th May 2017 is at http://www.familylaw.co.uk/news_and_comment/everything-you-always-wanted-to-know-about-tolata#.WaxBetJ0zMA but is no substitute for actual learning

6 The Inheritance (Provision for Family and Dependants) Act 1975 www.legislation.gov.uk/ukpga/1975/63

5.2   The NHS Resolution Clinical Negligence Scheme

The NHS is one of jewels of post-Second World War Britain but it is widely known to have difficulties. One of those areas is how it responds to the inevitable or avoidable medical accidents, mistakes, or clinical negligence that happen.

As such, the authors hold that it is rather a litmus test of where the United Kingdom may be going in terms of mediation, at least at a governmental level.

5.2.1   *The context*

Negligence generally means[7] substandard care and is discussed below in more detail. A mistake is not necessarily negligence and does not of itself give rise to compensation.

But mistakes and sub-standard care are expensive. In the UK, the National Health Service sets aside (2014/2017) around £2 Billion ($3 Billion) annually to pay for the consequences of medical mistakes. The NHS is already allocating and ring-fencing funds for claims until the end of the century.

Much will go to the accidently injured patients but around 20% is reportedly paid to the lawyers involved in pursuing or defending the actions. It is, by anyone's analysis, an enormous drain on public resources in a time of austerity.

Yet, intriguingly for all those interested in conflict resolution, surveys in many different jurisdictions of the victims of medical accidents consistently demonstrate that they think of compensation last. Their prime concerns on learning of, or suspecting, a medical mistake are:

---

7 In the USA, negligence generally means conduct that falls below the standards of behaviour established by law for the protection of others against unreasonable risk of harm.

(1) to get better and have the mistake remedied

(2) to have an honest explanation

(3) to have an apology

(4) to see that no one else suffers as they have done

(5) to see that the medical staff learn for the incident

Equally consistently, the mechanisms deployed by health providers in many countries have frustrated most if not all of these ambitions. A culture of openness is a rare blessing but the attempts to introduce a duty of candour into the NHS in isolation have been fraught with difficulty.

Yet research in countries as diverse as the United States, Australia, and Scotland also shows that where there is openness, and these five principles of patient participation are adopted, claims and compensation are reduced, and satisfaction increases. There is even evidence that medical standards increase with candour where the culture permits.

5.2.2 *What is clinical negligence?*

Clinical Negligence is a tort – a civil wrong. It shares with all other civil wrongs (from road accidents to tripping over in Tesco) certain elements and principles. Negligence, as has been observed above, does not mean simply a mistake or "carelessness".

There are three key legal aspects:

(a) The existence of a duty of care – usually not disputed

(b) A breach of the duty of dare – very often disputed, sometimes passionately, illogically, or expensively for a range of reasons.

(c) Causation of damage by the breach of the duty of dare – sometimes the most difficult part of any case.

A duty of care can arise in a number of ways in tort – under statute, regulations, or at common law – the basic law of this and many other countries created by judicial decisions and principles. For a doctor or a dentist there is a duty to the patient whether they be a NHS or private patient. In addition, there is a contractual relationship with the private patient.

Put at its most basic, there is a duty not to injure a patient by incorrect treatment or by a failure to deliver correct treatment. That duty can be extensive and can include for a health authority or trust, practice or consultant, and vicarious responsibility for employees. This can include assistant dentists, nurses, receptionists and so forth.

There is a duty to ensure competence and to delegate appropriately. There is a duty to identify other medical conditions. There is a duty to protect the patient for example form physical or sexual abuse. There is even a duty to non-patients and visitors – to avoid, for example, infection, harm and injury. The duty is accordingly wide – or even very wide. Lawyers are forever seeking to broaden that duty.

But to be actionable, and to attract lawyers, there must be a breach of the duty of care. The question of breach may fall under private contractual or NHS terms of service. Dentists, for example, have to provide "appropriate dental services" and to offer "all necessary and appropriate personal dental services of the type usually provided by general dental practitioners." Other professionals may only need to supply adequate care.

The lies at the heart of English law in considering adequate care. It comes from a case now more than sixty years old, that of <u>Bolam v Friern Hospital Management Committee</u> (1957). The key passage to understand for mediators is in the decision of McNair J who said (to a jury in words that were very much of their time):

"a doctor is not guilty of negligence if he has acted in accordance with a practice accepted as proper by a responsible body of medical men skilled in that particular art...."

Putting it the other way round, a doctor is not negligent if he is acting in accordance with such a practice, merely because there is a body of opinion that takes a contrary view."

This is the legal standard of care. The test is whether the doctor has behaved in accordance with what is regarded as acceptable by a responsible body of practitioners at the time, judging the doctor by the then prevailing standards and knowledge.

This test has been refined over time by a range of cases, and perhaps (except in the area of consenting) most importantly by a case called *Bolitho* where it was suggested that the test is what is "rightly" regarded as proper by a responsible body of opinion. <u>Bolitho v. City and Hackney Health Authority</u> [1997] 4 All ER 771. Importing this word into the test means that it would be the Court which would decide objectively whether the views held by a body of opinion were in fact justified. It will call upon a doctor or dentist defending a claim to produce evidence to show that a body of opinion and a prevailing clinical practice is justified.

This might be seen as importing evidence-based medicine or dentistry into the test of medical negligence. A body of opinion may be disregarded if the Court considers it to be *"unreasonable, irresponsible, or illogical."*

This is also influenced by guidance from bodies such as the National Institute for Clinical Excellence (NICE). Generally expert witnesses must give their now carefully regulated opinions as to whether a doctor or dentist complied with the applicable standard. It follows that a judge in clinical negligence cases cannot prefer one treatment to another. Lord Scarman made this clear in <u>Maynard v West Midlands Regional H.A.</u> in 1985. He said:

"In the realm of diagnosis and treatment, negligence is not established by preferring one respectable body of professional opinion to another. Failure to exercise the ordinary skill of a doctor (in the appropriate specialty if he is a specialist) is necessary."

If there is a breach of the duty of care, or a breach of contract, that is far from the end of the matter. The question in almost all clinical negligence cases will be – did the breach cause damage, or would the patient have been in the same condition in any event? Breach and causation are put in the context of the cases of the now leading cases of <u>Montgomery v Lanarkshire Health Board</u>[8] and <u>Chester v Afshar</u>[9].

In effect, the question put harshly is – was the patient doomed in any event?

5.2.3 *The NHS Response*

It is against this background that the devolved management structures of the NHS (known as 'Trusts') and training organisations (known as 'Deaneries') began over the last decade in different ways to explore the use of mediation in medical mistakes. Enlightened chief executives, directors, and deans had been making mediation part of the training for clinical and administrative staff for some years and the lessons learned were fascinating.

The key principles – of rapport and trust, of being neutral and non-judgmental, of confidentiality and curiosity, are universal. But applying them to a person who has had the wrong leg amputated, or whose baby has died in a maternity suite, or who has not had breast cancer identified in time, presents unique challenges.

The NHS Litigation Authority (now rebranded as "NHS Resolution" or NHSR) announced[10] in late 2016 that following a successful pilot scheme it had launched its new mediation service. The scheme was (and

---

8 [2015] EWSC 11 – which has sometimes been taken to suggest that *Bolam* is dead: that is not a correct propostion although *Bolam* now has little relevance to the question of consent.

9 The but for test and what would have happened on a different day in spinal surgery [2004] 4 All ER 507

10 See (still in September 2017, the old website) http://www.nhsla.com/Claims/Pages/Handling.aspx

is) intended to provide injured claimants with a possible resolution of their claim without the need to litigate the claim through the courts.

Contracts were awarded to four panels of mediators. CEDR and Trust Mediation operate the Clinical Negligence panel and are involved in the Personal Injury panel. CADR operate the costs mediation panel.

Claimant solicitors had long thought (and in the main argued) that mediation was an ideal way of resolving disputes in Clinical Negligence claims. One of the authors, writing the ADR section of the standard work on Clinical Negligence in 2008[11] promoted the same and there were signs that it might happen. Like much else in the growth of mediation in these islands, it took a decade longer than it should. Nevertheless it has been much welcomed in 2017 as a major step in the right direction.

Helen Vernon of NHS Resolution said about the scheme at its launch:

> *"Mediation is an excellent forum for dispute resolution and provides injured patients and their families with an opportunity for face to face explanations and apologies when things go wrong and reducing the need for unnecessary litigation."*

Claimant lawyers report[12] that they are often told by clients that one of the most important things they hope to gain by bringing an action is an explanation and answers to their questions about what went wrong with their treatment. Freeths said that their clients often sought an apology where appropriate, which was usually not achieved via formal litigation. Freeths said that if mediation could provide these things as well as compensation then it would be something to be very enthusiastic about.

Like many firms, Freeths were concerned that this was not a step towards removing lawyers from the process of compensation. The firm argued that it remained essential that a Claimant in a Clinical Negligence action had access to skilled, specialist lawyers to analyse evidence

---

11 http://www.waterstonesmarketplace.com/Powers-and-Harris-Clinical-Negligence/book/145255 Powers & Harris (2008)

12 Eg: Freeths – http://www.freeths.co.uk/blog/clinicalnegligence/?p=416

and secure fair compensation. They also felt that it was important to realise that mediation should be used at an appropriate time in a case. That would usually be after expert medical evidence had been gathered to assess the injury and to allow the appropriate level damages to be calculated.

5.2.4   The Scheme in operation

The scheme is at the time of writing less than a year old. Yet there have been numerous mediations. One of the authors is a panel member and can report that in the first six months of instructions, 90% of his mediations settled on the day and one a few weeks later. One was adjourned. These were all complex matters with fraught issues, often with breach of duty and causation denied, or substantially in dispute.

They resolved through the skills and excellence of the lawyers involved, the realism of the NHSR representatives, and the overall cathartic effect the process has for the lay participants. In one case, a bereaved parent came physically to embrace a treating consultant, the pair in tears. In another, a seemingly divided family became united and able to move forward.

The numbers that can be attested to at this stage are, of course, too small to be anything other than anecdotal. But they do conform to the general expectations of complex mediations well run and taking place at the correct moment – most cases are capable of settlement if:

(a) sufficient care is taken in preparing for the mediation;

(b) sufficient time is allowed;

(c) the participants are allowed to vent and have their "day in court"

(d) there is strong story-telling, rapport building, reality testing, and probing; and

(e) the mediator is curious, interested, and does not pressurise participants.

5.2.5 Lessons of general application

The NHS Clinical Negligence mediation scheme is likely to be deemed a success. It is not expensive to run and offers much quicker resolutions, at much lower costs, on a legitimate and principled basis, whilst affording a real human recognition to the disasters that befall families and patients when well-meaning professionals err.

It is reasonable to extrapolate the potential to other Departments of State. Claims against the Ministry of Defence by injured service personnel are numerous and often fought long and hard in seemingly unpromising circumstances for the armed services. Costs become substantial in cases where, in the very large part, Courts recognise that most injured service personnel are honest and straight-forward people who have lost a vocation serving the Country. It is a curious fact that very few – the authors can personally recall a very unscientific and dubious statistic of two cases in twenty years – involving the Ministry of Defence are mediated. Yet, if the benefits that the NHS is achieving can be replicated this should be an important area.

Outside Government, and returning to the medical arena, the medical defence unions are actively looking at mediation processes. Private medicine, and general practitioners, as well as cases involving dentists, are likely to see similar opportunities for mediators in the next few years. The authors welcome this growth and only note that it remains many years astern of the progress in the United States and Canada, which are in theory much more litigious societies.

5.3   Workplace and Employment Mediation

"Every workplace generates chronic conflicts, yet few organizations have rethought the way they work, or used conflict resolution skills and ideas to prevent and transform chronic conflicts at their sources, or examined their organizational communications and conflict cultures to discover how these conflicts are generated and reduce their re-occurrence.[13]"

In those words, Kenneth Cloke seeks to capture the realty of the workplace, such that where there are people spending considerable time together, who are subject to organisational requirements, and are at times, under considerable pressure there will undoubtedly be conflict. Diversity is often not recognised and stresses emerge at every level of management.

"Next up on the agenda...diversity."

Furthermore, it is evident in the literature that although in past years workplace conflict has been possibly overlooked, with arguably a past attitude that employees perhaps just have to "get on with it"; as a result of initiatives from government, Trade Unions and professional organisations over the past 10 or so years there is now much positive movement in this area.

Encouragingly, it is the experience of the authors more organisations are now seeking to redress what Cloke identified in 2013.

13 Kenneth Cloke (2013)

This represents opportunity for the workplace mediator, whether working internally as a suitably trained and qualified employee in an organisation or being brought in as an external mediator for a particular mediation.

In this section the authors focus on a number of aspects of the workplace to assist the workplace mediator in developing their practice. Later, this section will explore the workplace mediation process. Just as an appropriately experience mediator might be sought to mediate a dispute over say, an insurance matter, those with HR and leadership & management experience in organisation might be better placed to mediate in the workplace. Thus, an appreciation of current topics is invaluable for the mediator setting out to establish him or herself in this interesting mediation niche.

These include: the context of the contemporary workplace and how it is changing; the sort of issues that give rise to often deep-seated conflict; how government has moved to develop resolution strategies; how people react to conflict in the workplace; what is important to the employer in achieving appositive outcome; and who is involved in a workplace mediation.

The section also includes comment on well-established psychological knowledge from the work of Maslow and Hertzberg, as well as the psychological contract and its importance. It is the intention of the authors not to convey mastery of such topics, as there is much separate literature available for the more curious, but to provide an awareness of such topics to enhance the mediation process.

It should be noted that those who seek workplace mediators would more than likely be HR professionals who will, as their profession requires, have knowledge of such subjects. Finally, to close this section aspects of Employment Mediation will be considered to bring out the important differences between that and Workplace Mediation.

5.3.1   Definitions of Workplace and Employment Mediation

It is important to understand the differences between these two types of mediation. Clive Lewis in his excellent book, "The Definitive Guide to Workplace Mediation" states what are the generally accepted definitions:

- Workplace Mediation is conducted when there is an ongoing employment relationship; and

- Employment Mediation is conducted when an employee has left the employer.[14]

The Employment Mediation definition in the experience of the authors may be extended to include a person in transition from an organisation when the decision to leave has been made and the mediation is used to establish the terms of the leaving.

5.3.2   The Context of Workplace Mediation

Globalisation, the pace of change, and the financial crisis are changing both the business landscape and the shape of organisations. Competition in the private sector is increasing and the public sector has adopted practices of the former to make scarce resources go further. This puts pressure on the whole of society. In the United Kingdom workplace conflict is estimated to cost the economy a staggering £24bn per year. Arguably poor management and leadership have contributed to epidemic levels of bullying, as has been shown in surveys by the Chartered Management Institute (CMI)[15].

---

14 Clive Lewis (2006)

15 Woodman,P, & Cook, P. (2005) Bullying at Work: The Experience of Managers. CMI, UNISON & ACAS; and Woodman,P, & Kumar, V. (2008) Bullying at Work 2008: The Experience of Managers. CMI, UNISON & ACAS.

In a survey conducted by the consultancy firm OPP[16], in 2008, it was estimated that in the UK Workplace the average employee spends 2 hours per week dealing with conflict that results in 370 million lost days per year. Significant numbers of employees believe that they could do a better job than their current manager and would be prepared to take a pay cut in order to work with a better manager. Employee attitudes are characterised by decreasing loyalty and an increased awareness of statutory rights, coupled with a willingness to seek re-dress. All of this points to a workplace that is either rife with or has the potential to generate conflict in an instant.

As a result, in 2009 ACAS published a Code Of Conduct for the resolution of Workplace Conflict. Around this time during the financial crisis, press announcements indicated a significant increase in suicide rates in many countries, with speculation that the deaths were likely to be attributable to the global recession and the pressure of the everyday – a tragic situation.

The workplace is constantly evolving and more recently a number of trends are emerging such as, the use of what are termed Zero Hours Contracts where employees have no actual contracted hours and can be called upon when required by the employer. These have attracted much media attention, mainly negative but for some employees they work well.

The cost of employment to the employer is rising and that in part has induced the formation of the so-called "Gig Economy." In the "Gig Economy" workers are paid for specific jobs and pieces of work rather than working for a single employer. This style of working has been central in a number of recent employment disputes. The facets that make up the contemporary workplace include:

- Change
- Corporate scandals
- Leadership

---

16 OPP (2008) Fight, flight or face it? Celebrating the effective management of conflict at work. OPP in association with the CIPD

- Globalisation
- Increasing technology and artificial intelligence
- Employee flexibility
- Diversity
- Health and well-being
- Immigration
- Inequality
- Bureaucracy
- Financial considerations (resources and crises)
- Rising cost of living
- Insecurity
- Communication
- Political uncertainty and change – including Brexit and minority government

More recently mental health is becoming a topic that was very much "a taboo" but with high profile figures such as Duke and Duchess of Cambridge and Prince Harry at the forefront of the charity "Heads Together[17]" there is a step-change occurring. On the charity's home page it states: "Through our work with young people, emergency response, homeless charities, and with veterans, we have seen time and time again that unresolved mental health problems lie at the heart of some of our greatest social challenges.

Too often, people feel afraid to admit that they are struggling with their mental health. This fear of prejudice and judgment stops people from getting help and can destroy families and end lives. Heads Together wants to help people feel much more comfortable with their everyday mental wellbeing and have the practical tools to support their friends and family." Interestingly, Hertzberg to whom the authors refer to later held the belief in the 1950s that "mental health is the core issue of our times."

---

17 www.headstogether.org.uk

However, there is also evidence to suggest that trust is at an all time low across society and more globally. Trust is an essential ingredient in relationships, in that it creates order in society and is needed to ensure business relationships develop and in turn deliver prosperity. It allows innovation to thrive and where there are high levels of trust people and individuals can accept risk.

Those workplaces that have high levels of trust are seen to cope with, and adapt to change better than those with low levels of trust. Trust fosters cooperation, teamwork and allows partnerships to develop and entrepreneurial ventures to grow.

It is at the heart of a flourishing society.

5.3.3 The impact of a loss of trust

In the workplace if trust breaks down the impact will be significant and research at the University of Bath (2012-2014)[18] identified the following impacts of low levels of trust. There is likely to be a growth in feelings of vulnerability amongst staff that leads to unwillingness to invest in relationship building. A silo mentality emerges with the resultant loss of information sharing and poor communication. Innovation and initiative suffer, as people feel unsafe and unprotected.

There is a much reduced willingness to take risks. Eventually behaviours may become disruptive as anxiety and stress increase with a resultant fall in morale and loss of commitment across the organisation.

A chronic situation across an organisation like that just described will present considerable challenge for a mediator. At that point it is very much focusing on the task in hand and assisting those participants who have come to mediation, although being mindful that the conflict may be wider across the organisation.

---

18 CIPD, Research Report (Reference 5746), Where has all the trust gone? March 2012; CIPD & University of Bath, Research Report (Reference 6525), Cultivating trustworthy leaders, April 2014; and CIPD & University of Bath, Research Report (Reference 6701), Experiencing Trustworthy Leadership, September 2014.

5.3.4   *The Role of Government*

Employment Law and associated statutes continually evolve and over the last 10 – 15 years dispute resolution has featured within carious Acts of Parliament. In brief the Employment Act 2002 (1 October 2004) was introduced to reduce the number of grievances although the opposite happened.

In 2007 the Gibbons Review reported on employment dispute resolution in Britain.

ACAS, Trade Unions, employer organisations and others have produced a range of guidance to assist employers and employees. More recently the UK government introduced the Equality Act 2010 with its Employment Statutory Code of Practice and more recently the Enterprise and Regulatory Reform Act 2013 emerged.

Of interest and note, specifically the department for Business Enterprise and Regulatory Reform (BERR) offered the principle that:

> *"Employers and employees should always try to resolve problems in the workplace at the earliest possible opportunity and usually with the least formality."*

And the key points of the ACAS Code in 2009 were:

- Employers and employees should raise and deal with issues promptly and should not unreasonably delay meetings, decisions and confirmation of these decisions;

- Employers and employees should act consistently;

- Employers should carry out any necessary investigations, to establish the facts of the case;

- Employers should inform employees of the basis of the problem and give them an opportunity to put their case in response before any decisions are made;

- Employers should allow employees to be accompanied at any disciplinary or grievance hearing;

- Employers should allow an employee to appeal against any formal decision made.

Workplace mediators may well find themselves instructed at anytime during a dispute. Unfortunately, in the authors' experience it tends to be once grievance and disciplinary processes have been followed, whereas intervention at an earlier stage and thus "nipping it in the bud" may have proved more beneficial to all. A workplace mediator definitely does not have to be an employment law specialist just as the authors have described previously for more general civil and commercial mediators. Indeed such is the complexity of workplace and employment law, and more so with the repeal legislation and regulations flowing from Brexit, that it is a specialist area for lawyers in their own right. Nevertheless it is useful to be aware of what guidance to employers emerges following interpretation of the law.

5.3.5 *Causes of Conflict in the Workplace*

Several causes of conflict in the United Kingdom were identified by ACAS in a study taken in 2011[19] that reported as indicated in Table 4:

Table 4 – Causes of Workplace Conflict found by ACAS	
Cause	
Personality clashes and warring egos	49%
Stress	34%
Heavy workloads and inadequate resources	33%
Poor leadership from the top	29%
Lack of honesty and openness	26%
Poor line management	23%
Lack of role clarity	22%
Lack of clarity about accountability	21%
Clash of values	18%
Poor selection and pairing of teams	16%
Taboo subjects e.g. office affairs	15%
Poor performance management	14%
Bullying and harassment	13%
Perceived discrimination	10%

The Equality Act 2010 states that harassment is unwanted conduct related to a relevant protected characteristic, which has the purpose or effect of violating an individual's dignity or creating an intimidating, hostile, degrading, humiliating or offensive environment for that indi-

19 ACAS (2011) Thematic Review of Workplace Mediation

vidual. Bullying may be characterised as offensive, intimidating, malicious or insulting behaviour, an abuse or misuse of power through means that undermine, humiliate, denigrate or injure the recipient. Both bullying and harassment form major parts of workplace mediators' caseloads, yet appears to be underreported to ACAS. ACAS provide a useful pamphlet on the topic of Bullying and Harassment.[20]

A more recent study in 2015 by the CIPD[21] revealed the following as the key issues that might lead to workplace conflict at Table 5.

Table 5 – Issues leading to conflict: CIPD 2015	
Issue	
Difference in personality and style of working	44%
Individual competence and performance	33%
Level of support or resource	23%
Agreeing deliverables or setting targets	18%
Contracts of Employment or Terms & Conditions	10%
Absence or absence management	8%
Promotion	4%
Other	18%

The authors consider that for the workplace mediator having a sound awareness of what is causing workplace conflicts allows a greater insight when working with people who have been impacted by such events to understand better their reality and appreciate how they may be feeling.

---

20 ACAS (2014). Bullying and Harassment: A Guide for Employers.

21 CIPD (2015) Getting under the skin of workplace conflict.

5.3.6   Ill-treatment in the workplace

Of increasing concern is represented in a striking piece of research from Cardiff University[22] through the Economic and Social Research Council over ill-treatment in the workplace. The authors raise this sensitive issue to forewarn that it may well be encountered in workplace mediation. Depending upon the severity of the ill-treatment it may be that the issues needs the input of other professions such as occupational health physicians, psychotherapist or others to ensure an appropriate outcome. For the mediator that will require deft handling bearing in mind the confidentiality. In the authors' experience it may well be a "cry for help" and that the mediator is well placed to raise the issue with others with the agreement of the participant. The Cardiff University research defined workplace ill-treatment as falling into three distinct categories:

- *"Just under half the British workforce experience unreasonable treatment at work over a two year period. Some of the more common forms of unreasonable treatment are experienced by nearly one in three, or one in four, British employees. Most unreasonable treatment originates with their managers and supervisors."*

- *"Forty percent of employees experience incivility or disrespect over a two year period. Managers and supervisors are the most important source of incivility and disrespect but more of this kind of ill-treatment is meted out by co-workers, and by customers and clients. The most common forms of incivility and disrespect are experienced by one in five employees."*

- *"Violence and injury is less common than other types of ill treatment but is still experienced by the equivalent of over one million British workers. Actual physical violence, and injury as a result of aggressive and violent acts, are primarily perpetrated by non-employees."*

---

22 Feve, R., Lewis, D., Robinson, A., & Jones, T. (2011) <u>Insight into ill-treatment in the workplace: patters, causes and solutions.</u> Cardiff University & Economic and Social Research Council.

5.3.7 *The "workplace relationship" – the needs of both employer and employee*

Classical Human Resource theory is that employers want to buy the skills and competencies of potential employees for as minimal cost as possible, whereas employees wish to sell their skills and competencies for as higher a sum as possible. That is a relatively simplistic stance but serves as starting point and over the years employee relations has evolved as the workplace had developed. The authors consider that it is worthwhile that the workplace mediator has an awareness of a number of areas of contemporary employment practice. These are: Contracts of Employment; Annual Appraisals; Job Descriptions; The Psychological Contract; Employee Engagement; and Culture, Ethos and Values.

a. Contracts of Employment – Express Terms and Implicit Terms. The express terms include such points as hours worked, starting and finishing times, annual holiday, and amount of pay. There are also terms that are implied and are implicit. For example a contract might include a section on working attire, stating the term "Business Dress." The employer might consider that means a business suit, crisp white shirt and toe for men and the equivalent for women.

    The employee might consider that to be a more relaxed jacket, no tie and a pair of chinos with a neat pair of brown shoes or equivalent for women. The phrase "equivalent for women" is interesting in terns of what does it actually mean? Such hangovers from a previous era are commonplace and divisive. Mediators are sometimes called to mediate such issues but it may be that specific issue such as business attire is hiding the real crus of the conflict. So, once again be curious and probe with respect and empathy.

b. Annual Appraisals. A vital tool in employee relations and engagement of people annual appraisals serve to recognise achievement and identify areas for development. All employees across any business should receive an annual appraisal; and furthermore, ongoing dialogue with a line manager throughout the year should ensure that there are no surprises. However, in the experience of the author this at times fails to happen. Appraisals serve to build trust and understanding and they are an opportunity to foster a positive relationship between employer and employee.

c. Job Descriptions. These outline what an employee is to do in their job and might be called "Terms of Reference." There will probably be a primary purpose supported by secondary purpose or purposes and thereafter a range of specific tasks that the employee is required to do in the course of their job. The latter might include specific reference to meetings attended. It is good practice that a job description is updated annually and an ideal time is at the annual appraisal linking to objectives both business and personal.

d. The Psychological Contract. This can be defined as "…. the perceptions of the two parties, employee and employer, of what their mutual obligations are towards each other." Guest identified that:

- the extent to which employers adopt people management practices will influence the state of the psychological contract;

- the contract is based on employees' sense of fairness and trust and their belief that the employer is honouring a "deal" between them;

- where the psychological contract is positive, increased employee commitment and satisfaction will have a positive impact on business performance.

If the contact breaks there is negative impact on:

- Job satisfaction;

- Employee commitment; and

- Employee Engagement.

In mediation it is well worthwhile asking questions upon these three issues, as the answers will reveal where the participant is in relation to their organisation. It also opens out the opportunity for self-reflection and thus the chance to develop potential solutions.

e. Employee Engagement. MacLeod and Clarke (2009)[23] in a report to the UK Government wrote extensively on the topic and although they stated that there were many definitions they cited the following as example:

"Engagement is about creating opportunities for employees to connect with their colleagues, managers and wider organisation. It is also about creating an environment where employees are motivated to want to connect with their work and really care about doing a good job. It is a concept that places flexibility, change and continuous improvement at the heart of what it means to be an employee and an employer in a twenty-first century workplace." (Professor Katie Truss[24])

"A positive attitude held by the employee towards the organisation and its values. An engaged employee is aware of the business context, and works with colleagues to improve performance within the job for the benefit of the organisation. The organisation must work to develop and nurture engagement, which requires a two-way relationship between employee and employer." (Institute of Employment Studies[25])

"A set of positive attitudes and behaviours enabling high job performance of a kind which are in tune with the organisation's mission." (Professor John Storey[26])

---

23 McLeod, D., & Clarke, N., (2009). Engaging for Success: Enhancing Performance Through Employee Engagement. Department of Business Innovation & Skills, HM Government.

24 Gatenby, M., Rees, C., Soane, E. and Truss, C (2009) Employee engagement in context. London: Chartered Institute of Personnel and Development.

25 Robinson, D., Perryman S., & Hayday, S. (2004). The drivers of employee engagement. IES Report 408.

26 Storey, J., Wright, PM., & Ulrich, D,. eds. (2008). The Routledge Companion to Strategic Human Resource Management.

It can be that in workplace mediation participants will be met who are at a very low ebb. Enquiry and empathetic questioning may well reveal a psychological contract that is broken and a lack of engagement, although there may well be an underlying desire to recover. The mediation is the point at which that recovery and transformation can start.

f. Culture, ethos and values. The culture of an organisation might be described as "The way we get things done around here." The ethos and values of an organisation may stem from a well-defined vision statement or mission that increasingly organisations are headlining in their documentation and at times through digital media and overtly within their buildings.

A brief internet search can reveal much about the Code of Values published by a company and documentation in the public domain describing a firm's culture. Potential employees are attracted to an organisation by reading such information and equating their own values with that of a prospective employer. There are many excellent examples and it would be invidious to cite just one or two. There is considerable best practice in this area and in selection interviewing there is now emphasis amongst many employers of undertaking demonstrable analysis, such as through psychometric testing, in the process to ensure that there is as feasible as possible a "good cultural fit" between employer and employee.

For the workplace mediator it is well worth being mindful of the culture, ethos and values of an organisation he or she might be instructed to mediate within. Not only to ensure that the best possible mediation practice is delivered but in terms of one's own values. Quite simply, a reasonable question to ask oneself is, "Am I comfortable working within a particular organisation?" Often when talking with participants in a workplace mediation it might be revealed that the cultural fit they had previously has waned, or perhaps it was never truly there in the first place. If it has waned there is opportunity to explore why that might be so and work to restore the situation. If it was never there in the first place it might be that the participant is reaching a point of considering alternative options. This latter point does not necessarily mean the mediation has been unsuccessful – to the contrary, it is an outcome that may well be positive for both employee and employer and is delivered in a mutually respectful and considerate way.

Culture, ethos and values in organisation development are now centre stage and need to be acknowledged and brought out when appropriate in the workplace mediation process.

5.3.8   *How people respond to conflict and the impact of change*

A fundamental piece of work by the psychologist Elisabeth Kubler-Ross is her book, On Death and Dying (1969). Kubler-Ross, a Swiss doctor studied the reactions of people who were given the news that they were terminally ill. In her work she explored the link between emotional state and time that is broadly represented in the Transition Curve below. The axis representing emotion might be considered as representing a sense of "positive" feeling about a situation, hence "denial" giving rise to more positive feelings through ignoring the issue, i.e. "When I think about it I get depressed."

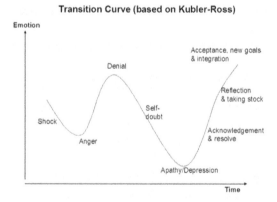

The time is an interesting aspect in that for some when dealing with "significant" events the passage to acceptance, new goals and integration can be relatively quick but for others it can take some time. It is in the experience of the authors that those experiencing workplace conflict are thus, "on a journey."

As a mediator in the workplace it is always worthwhile considering and assessing where the participants may lie on this curve. Questions such as "Could you explain to me how you feel about what is happening at the moment," followed by, "How is that compared to when you first experienced what happened to you?" In asking these questions listen carefully to the responses, what words does the participant use and what does their body language convey.

The above is also called the "Change Curve" as it illustrates how a person might react to being advised of major change, such as redundancy, structural change in an organisation, or an unwanted relocation. It is the impact of change that may well be a cause of conflict in its own right and people respond differently in terms of emotions and reactions.

Some individuals will:

- Feel threatened
- Feel a loss of status, territory and comfort zone.

If the above do not receive time and effort from management, conflict may result. In contrast some individuals will:

- Be enthusiastic;
- See opportunity.

This may cause conflict unless harnessed positively, for example using change ambassadors.

5.3.9 *Psychology in Workplace Mediation*

There is much in the field of psychology and organisational behaviour that can be accessed to enable the workplace mediator to enhance their skills. Mediation is all about individuals and groups meeting their needs, especially in the workplace. It is well worth drawing on the work of Abraham Maslow[27] in the 1940s and 50s. Maslow introduced a hierarchy of needs as a motivational theory in psychology that comprised a five-tier model of human needs as follows:

Self-Actualisation (Highest need)
Esteem
Love and Belonging
Safety and Security
Physiological and Physical Survival (Lowest need)

Maslow suggested that people are motivated to achieve certain needs and that some needs take precedence over others. Our most basic need is for physical survival, and this will be the first thing that motivates behaviour. Once that level is fulfilled the next level up is what motivates us, and so on.

Later, Professor Herzberg developed his Hygiene-Motivation Theory[28] by asking a sample of 200 engineers and accountants what pleased and displeased them about their jobs. He concluded that humans have two sets of needs:

- Lower level needs as an animal to avoid pain and deprivation; and
- Higher level needs as a human being to grow psychologically.

Some factors in the workplace will satisfy the first set of needs but not the second and vice versa. The first set is called "Hygiene factors" and includes:

- Company policy and administration
- Supervision
- Working relationships
- Status and security

---

27 Maslow, A,. (1943). <u>A Theory of Human Motivation</u>. Psychology Review.

28 Herzberg, F., Mausner, B., & Bloch-Snyderman, B. (1959). <u>The Motivation to Work, 2nd Edition</u>. John Wiley, New York.

The "Hygiene factors" on their own do not promote job satisfaction, but serve to prevent job dissatisfaction.

The second set is called "Motivators" and includes:

- Achievement
- Recognition
- Work itself
- Responsibility
- Advancement and growth

The "Motivators" relate to what the person does at work, rather than the context in which it is done.

Herzberg opined that the "Hygiene factors" and the "Motivators" are not opposites and that they are separate and distinct, being concerned with two independent sets of needs.

For the workplace mediator the work of both Maslow and Herzberg can be used to gain a picture of where the participant(s) might be in terms of needs. Questioning and being curious, mindful of this work can reveal what is in the power of the individual participant to solve and perhaps what needs input from others in an organisation to ensure a sustainable outcome going forward. Furthermore, mediators can develop their own question bank around the above factors that suits their personal mediation style.

5.3.10 *The Participants in Workplace Mediations*

In civil and commercial mediations there are present the participants (the Claimant and Defendant), their legal representatives, or advisors, and the mediator or mediators.

In contrast, in a workplace mediation at the point of mediation there may be just the complainant and the respondent working with a mediator. Getting to the mediation day, however, may well involve input from many people and throughout the process they are potentially involved to a lesser or greater degree:

- Complainant
- Respondent
- Human Resource professionals
- Union representatives
- Line manager and other managers
- Colleagues
- Occupational Health and other medical professionals

It is probable that initial contact with an external mediator is made via a member of the Human Resource department who may well have the mediator "on their books" or have been recommended to the mediator. Thereafter, the involvement of others increases, which will be explored below.

5.3.11 *The Agreement to Mediate and Confidentiality*

As in civil and commercial mediations, the Agreement to Mediate is a vital part of the process and is the only document that survives the mediation. Clive Lewis (2009) provides an excellent example of a straightforward and pragmatic format that can be adapted as appropriate. The Chartered Institute for Personnel and Development have useful guidance on confidentiality and the authors have incorporated this advice into the sample workplace mediation agreement that is as Annex D. In addition, at Annex E there is a sample confidentiality agreement that can be used if others join the mediation who were not originally signatories to the Agreement to Mediate.

Thus, if the mediation is conducted over several short sessions rather than a full day it might be that a participant on one session wishes to bring a friend for comfort of they are anxious or stressed. Provided the other participant agrees a simple and quick way to maintain confidentiality is for the mediator to meet with the attendee and discuss the confidential aspects of the process and request that they sign the Confidentiality Agreement.

In workplace mediation participants are invariably anxious, exhibiting degrees of stress and are often highly cautious of signing anything. The author will discuss pre-meeting below and this is the point at which following explanation the participants are invited to sign the mediation agreement or consider it and sign at their convenience ahead of the mediation itself. In may ways the mediation agreement contains administrative details that are more focused upon the instructing authority so there is a reasonable approach to having the participants perhaps just sign the confidentiality agreement? There is no right or wrong here other than for the authors it is paramount that the mediator has in their hand a signed mediation agreement – it is for the mediator's protection and to do otherwise is fool hardy.

5.3.12 *The Workplace Mediation Sequence*

Workplace mediation typically takes place over more than a single day. It is more a sequence of events perhaps over a number of weeks. There are a number of stages.

a. Initial meetings with client.

As described above the instruction authority (the client) will make contact with the mediator and perhaps over the telephone describe the situation. It might be that a meeting with the client is face-to-face – that is matter of choice, taking into account geography and diaries of those concerned.

During this conversation stakeholders are identified and dates are considered when pre-meetings might take place. There may well be considerable juggling of dairies at this stage.

b. Pre-meetings with stakeholders. Pre-meetings herald the start of the true mediation itself. They are the point when trust is built between the mediator and the participants in particular and others involved. If possible a series of meetings are booked with say: Human Resources; Line Management; Complainant and Respondent. Timings vary but usually it is best to allow an hour and a half with participants as often much is talked.

It can be exhausting for the mediator especially of it is team mediation involving several people. The pre-meeting often reveals a great deal. It will depend upon the mediator's style and approach. It is probably worthwhile pointing out that mediating workplace dispute is not to everyone's liking and for may one considering entering the workplace field they would be well advised to consider observing. That said, many organisations are cautious about having observers. It is not necessarily right to be prescriptive but the advice of the author would be for a potential workplace mediator to perhaps be thorough in their consideration for doing such work. A genuine interest in people and a willingness to assist people is required, whilst acknowledging the needs of the organisation and awareness of people and organisational behaviour.

In the pre-meeting the mediation process is considered and explained, as people will often need putting at ease. The psychology that emerges is fascinating and if trust is achieved mediators should be prepared to perhaps being taken outside of the easy comfort zone. Mediators should remember not to judge although they will recognised that what happens in workplace conflict may not match their own values.

When plaintiffs' counsel opened, the mediator sensed she was going to have a difficult time toning down expectations.

Once the mediator has talked with the first participant they will have a picture in the mediator's mind of the person that is just about to walk through the door who is in conflict. At this point mediators have to guard against the transference of their feelings to the next person – body language, facial expression and words will be running at a pace through your mind.

At the end of each pre-meeting is an ideal time to sign the Mediation Agreement. However, some participants may ask to think it over. Do explain that it is a 'must" but perhaps they just need time to rationalise what is happening. On rare occasions in the authors' experience mediators may face a person who is not prepared to sign it – and on some occasions participants might want to change the content. That may be fine but it will involve collective work between appropriate stakeholders to reach a satisfactory conclusion. A refusal to sign will mean that the mediation cannot proceed.

It follows that the Pre-Meetings stage is conducted in "good faith." The key point is not to enter the defined formal mediation without a signed agreement.

c. The actual mediation. There is no difference here to any other mediation in that there is an opening, plenary and private sessions as appropriate, and an agreement. It may well be caustic and there may well be a desire to vent anger and more likely than not there will be tears. Some may go into particularly "dark places" in their minds. Above all take your time and treat people in a way that is how you would wish to be treated. If a respondent witnesses deep emotion, it may elicit the response "Gosh I never knew you felt like that." Be kindly and "listen, listen, listen." Much of the mediation is about defining reality and each participant beginning to understand the other's perspective and what is common to both. It may take time and emerge over a number of weeks.

The authors normally set aside a day from 1000-1600 with the caveat that if by early afternoon there has been so much emotional release it may well be better to adjourn to another day.

This can work in two ways. Firstly, it loses momentum and secondly more positively it allows of intervening reflection. Talk it through with the participants: it is their mediation so do find out what they would like to do.

If all goes well and in the main it will, there comes a point when an agreement needs to be produced. Mediation best practice is that it is for the participant to write down and sign. That document will then be binding under English Law. It may however be that after a lengthy time in conflict and not having been able to bear the sight of each other they agree to meet once a week for a tea or coffee.

It is very much a case of doing what is right for the participants. An approach that can work well is to invite the line management or HR professional into the final stage of defining the agreement.

The latter have no need to be apprised of the detail but it gives the participants an opportunity for discussion with their colleagues who can then help then take forward their outcome from the mediation.

The workplace mediator will have to show flexibility and agility at this point.

d. Follow up. In other mediations once a resolution is achieved the participant may well go their separate ways. However, in workplace mediation that may not be the case as it is all about restoring relationships. Thus, talking with stakeholders and in the author's experience participants on occasions request a follow up session say in 2-3 months following the mediation.

5.3.13 *Transformative Mediation in the Workplace.*

The authors have covered Facilitative Mediation in earlier sections. The unique feature of workplace mediation is that in it is more than likely that the participants will remain in contact with each other perhaps on a daily basis there is therefore a need to transform relationships and change behaviours. The early shoots of transformative mediation emerged in the 1970s and in 1994 Bush & Folger published, "The Promise of Mediation." A definition of transformative mediation can be found in The Jackson ADR Handbook[29] as follows:

> *"Transformative mediation tends to focus on improving the relation-ship and communication between the parties rather than having the settlement of the dispute as its primary focus. Transformative media-tors aim to help the parties to improve their communication so that they can resolve their own dispute. The parties themselves will control the nature of discussions, with the mediator primarily providing a reflective role. Whilst some mediators will display some aspects of a transformative mediation style during the course of a mediation, most will also use elements of a facilitative or an evaluative approach."*

As a consequence, if this approach is adopted the "outcome" of work-place mediation may well involve the mediator working with HR and Line Managers, within the agreed confidentiality to identify a need for:

- Coaching
- Psychotherapy
- Mentoring
- Training & Development
- Counseling
- Occupational Health

Clearly other professionals will be involved and the approach will be holistic. Thus, as mentioned earlier workplace mediators may well, depending upon their skills be involved in follow-up sessions as an inte-gral part of the process. The participants as stated earlier will be on an emotional journey and new issues may well emerge that will require a multi-stakeholder approach. Some employers are moving towards this style of resolving disputes as it indicates investment and commitment to

---

29 Blake, S., Browne, J., & Sime, S. (2013). The Jackson ADR Handbook, Oxford University Press, paragraphs 14.17 & 14.18.

their employees and is part of the "overall package" of employment, taking us back to the work of Maslow and Herzberg of years ago.

The authors are most positive in their view of these developments.

5.3.14 *Employment Mediation*

As defined above Employment Mediation is conducted when an employee has left the employer. In the experience of the author this definition may be extended to include those employees who may be in the process of leading an organisation and the process of Employment Mediation is used to foster a positive outcome, i.e. a settlement agreement.

A fundamental principle of Employment Mediation is that if an agreement is reached in the absence of legal advice a participant must present that agreement to a lawyer for a review. Therefore, when conducting employment mediation it is important to consider interaction with lawyers; and legal costs.

As with a Workplace Agreement to Mediate, the Employment Agreement to Mediation may include specifics on:

- Confidentiality;
- Privilege;
- Fees; and
- Location.

In terms of a Settlement Agreement, taking a statement from a typical mediation agreement that, "Any settlement reached in the mediation will not be binding until it has been reduced to writing and signed by each of the participants" a number of points emerge as follows:

- Signing on the day often compromised by deep emotion and time may be needed to reflect;

- As emphasised above a participant is strongly advised to seek legal advice over the content of his or her Settlement Agreement;

- The may be continued involvement of others stakeholders such as line managers or HR representatives, in effect perhaps undertaking a "duty of care" until the individual finally leaves the organisation; and

- There may be a need to have a subsequent session to finalise the Settlement Agreement prior to signature following independent legal advice.

Settlement Agreements are gaining in popularity in particular when terminating employment and they are valuable in allowing people to move on in an ordered and as amicable manner as is possible. Typical uses include:

- To remove an employee for poor performance;

- To aid reorganisation and restructuring;

- To remove an employee who will not accept the outcome of a grievance process;

- To remove individuals who do not share the organisation's ethos, values and work ethic; and

- Where the relationship between employee and employer has broken down irrevocably.

For the mediator it is important remain flexible throughout such a process and work methodically and steadily with all stakeholders and it is often the case that "more haste means less speed."

5.3.15 *Employment Tribunals*

To close this chapter it is worthwhile mentioning Employment Tribunals. In 2013 HM Government introduced a system of charging those who wished to bring a claim to an ET that might amount to as much as £1,200. As a result, there was staggering 70% reduction in claim to ETs. On 26 July 2017 in what a number of commentators described as a shock judgement The Supreme Court ruled that tribunal fees were unlawful and must be scrapped. The consequence being that those who have paid to bring a case over the past four years will be refunded amounting to a total bill of some £27M.

In their unanimous judgement by seven Supreme Court judges it was noted that employment tribunals "are intended to provide a forum for the enforcement of employment rights by employees and workers, including the low paid, those who have recently lost their jobs and those who a vulnerable to long-term unemployment". The judges concluded that the fees levied were preventing access to justice.

The coming months will reveal if the number of claims returns to previous levels. For employers, there is opinion forming that they will need to assess the risk when approaching an ET, as it is well known that reputation can be adversely affected, let alone the costs that might be incurred. Thus, in the resolution of workplace conflict, mediation whether performed by internal or external mediators is a ready alternative to attendance at an ET. Leading players in this field from the management organisations such as the CIPD through to many of the Unions support the use of timely mediation in the resolution of workplace disputes.

5.4   Mediation in the Community

Research into community mediation across the United Kingdom reveals many mediation organisations that offer mediation at a local level. At present there is no umbrella organisation that draws together community mediation services. A number of years ago a company known as "Mediation UK" sought to fulfil that role but it went into liquidation a few years ago. Years on, the picture still presents as a large number of independent organisations, generally with charitable status that provide "free at the point of use" or for a moderate sum, mediation within a defined locality. The Society of Mediators will in 2018 be joining this picture following a successful pilot, with its Free Mediation Project.

5.4.1   *A definition of Community Mediation*

Community mediation can be defined either by inclusion or exclusion, but before that is explored in more detail in general terms community mediation can be defined as covering three areas:

- Victim-Offender mediation;
- Peer mediation / conflict resolution work in schools; and
- Neighbourhood mediation between households and residents.

In terms of inclusivity, the meaning here is that community mediation means just that with the emphasis on the word "community." Members of that community, usually volunteers, provide the mediation.

It is important to be aware that there is a cultural message here with mediation often being used to resolve disputes and differences across social groupings and culture in order to build a stronger community that has a deeper understanding of itself. In terms of exclusivity the definition becomes somewhat academic in that as mediation has developed in the UK, family and commercial mediation evolved separate national bodies and the community was left to focus on the three areas as indicated in the bullet points above.

5.4.2 *How it is made to work?*

The majority of community mediation is delivered by one of two models:

a. Model 1 – An independent charity registered with the Charity Commissioners is established and managed by a board of trustees. The trustees will come from a variety of backgrounds such as, representatives from local funding bodies, referral organisations, people with a genuine interest in their community, and mediators. The charity might fund raise within the local community and seek funding from local bodies active in the community, or realistically a combination of both. Governance of the charity is achieved through regular trustee meetings and an Annual General Meeting.

   An administrative assistant might provide administrative support to the trustees and that supporting element may be a small team of volunteers working on a rota basis or a combination. Some community mediation organisations may have an established premises or office, funded by the charity or potentially provided by the community perhaps associated with a church or community hall. This is probably the most popular model.

b. Model 2 – This involves an agency-managed service and might be provided through a local authority. Volunteer mediators are still used to deliver the mediation but staff may be employees of the local authority and are line managed. A small number of organisations work through this model.

5.4.3 *Hybrids*

Over recent years the pressures on charity mediation providers have increased with constrains on all-round funding and community mediation organisations are seeking ways to maintain their service through Hybrid Models such as combining with like-minded organisations;

working with local solicitors; and linking with Citizens Advice Bureaus and other neighbourhood support groups.

With the steady growth more widely in mediation and increasing awareness of its advantages a trend to community mediators offering more commercially orientated services is emerging This often captures workplace and employment or within schools the mediation of Special Educational Needs provision between the parents/guardians and the provider. In addition, depending upon the make up of the mediation cadre of a community organisation, some are offering conflict resolution training within organisations in the community.

As a result of the above some organisations are now paying mediators, although the range of payment will vary considerably. For more commercially orientated work this allows the mediator to receive a fair payment and also for the charity to perhaps gain a benefit for enhancing the provision of the core community work.

5.4.4 *What types of cases do community mediation organisations deal with?*

In 2001, the then "Mediation UK" conducted a survey with the following results. In terms of sources of work, those organisations referring were as follows:

- Housing Departments   39%;
- Self-referrals   30%
- Police   9%;
- Others[30]   12%

The subject matters that community mediators were asked to mediate were:

---

30 'Others' included: Environmental Health Departments; Advice Centres; Local Councillors; Other Council departments; and legal professionals.

Issue	Percentage[31]
Noise	45
Abusive behaviour and threats	20
Children's behaviour	17
Boundary and property disputes	17
Anti-social behaviour	15
Cars, parking, vehicle repairs	6
Untidiness, gardens, rubbish, smells	5
Animals including domestic pets	5
Racial harassment	2
DIY and building work	2
Family or relationship issues	2
Mental health / care in the community	<1
Other issues including litter, landlord-tenant and small debts	7

5.4.5 *The conduct of community mediations*

In general terms the approach to community mediation follows the classical facilitative method with variations depending upon circumstances. From the outset it is worthwhile noting that community mediation is usually delivered through co-mediation[32], that is using two mediators, a "lead mediator" and a "support mediator." Typically a community mediation enquiry might be progressed through to a conclusion thus:

    a. Step 1 – Enquiry / referral is received by the administrator. Lead and support mediators are identified and contacted to determine if they are content to proceed on the matter. In addition, a Super-

---

31 The percentage column adds up to over 100%. That is because many community disputes result in a mediation being over more than one issue and neighbours often have differing views as to what the dispute is all about. This variety makes community work both challenging and exciting for the mediator, as it is never quite known what is going to ensue. It is certainly a good training ground for newly qualified mediators.

32 See Part Four of this work, above

vising Mediator might be nominated, depending on the size and practice of the organisation who is available for discussion and advice.

b. Step 2 – The lead mediator with the assistance from the adminis-trator makes contact with the participants and arranges initial visits. Most community mediation organisations have a list of suitable venues but more than likely the meeting will be in a participant's home. The administrator provides the paperwork and agreements.

c. Step 3 – The mediators visit the first participant ("the claimant" / aggrieved party) and discuss the situation, having explained the mediation process and what will happen and how mediation can help and assist. It might be that the matter des not progress further and is "dropped." If this is the case the office is informed and brief case notes completed and returned to the administrative officer.

d. Step 4 – Mediators visit the second participant and talk through the situation and the process. Practice might vary but the decision to go ahead and involve the second participant may rest with the first participant. If the second participant decides not to proceed once again brief case notes are made and returned to the office.

e. Step 5 – If all are content to proceed a meeting date is agreed. Depending upon the nature of the dispute and how the parti-cipants feel it may be that the mediation is either face-to-face or through a "shuttle" process. The latter is when the participants just cannot face each other but viable and successful mediation can be achieved through the mediator shuttling between the participants. It may be by simply exchanging messages through to passing written agreements. Flexibility is key here and being patient and taking time will assist.

f. Step 6 – In either a positive outcome or if the mediation does not proceed it is usual that brief case notes are returned to the office and any administrative paperwork. Feedback forms are left with the participants and are in many cases returned with positive comment. If agreement is reached it can be recorded in writing as is best practice or it may remain as a verbal agreement. The Jackson ADR Handbook[33] advises that in either case it is unlikely to be legally binding on the participants.

5.4.6   *How effective is community mediation?*

Community mediation is conducted in a potentially tough user-environment and positive outcomes are sometimes hard to define. Often it is about improving communication and allowing people to see a different perspective and the mediation serves to "open the door" so that they are able to re-build a relationship on their own devices.

It is difficult to generalise but probably about 30-40% of cases achieve either an agreement or partial agreement on all issues. Mediators report this level of agreement is because the participants often differ on what is the actual issue. Further, participants are often living the problem on a recurring daily basis and whilst communication may have been improved, the underlying causes have not been removed.

5.4.7   *Limits on mediation casework*

As a tool for intervention in situations of individual conflict, mediation can uncover practical solutions, demonstrate more positive forms of communication, reframe contentious issues into shared problems, and often give disputants a different perspective on the actions of themselves and their immediate neighbours. This in itself will have an impact on the general well being of communities – less individual conflict means more energy is available for other things, as people who are under the immediate pressure of such conflicts are often unlikely to be able to look further than their back fence.

---

33 Blake, S., Browne, J., & Sime, S. (2013) The Jackson ADR Handbook, Oxford University Press, paragraph 16.49

In recent years, however, Scottish community mediation services (for example[34]) have increasingly realised that individual casework is only a part of the answer to the incidence of destructive conflict in our communities, and can very often get bogged down in treating the symptoms rather than the causes. For people with little power or status, living in poverty and in poor housing conditions, the problem with their neighbour may be low in their list of priorities, something they can afford to expend only limited energy on.

Of course the dispute may exacerbate their other problems considerably, but its resolution is unlikely to remove them. In such situations mediation can play a useful, if limited, role given the opportunity, but it should surprise no one if the disputants are unable to summon the considerable effort involved in constructively resolving the dispute.

Some critics of community mediation have accused the process of failing to right injustices by perpetuating the status quo. In this argument community mediation is seen as being an instrument by which the oppressed are encouraged to accept situations which should not be tolerated, and to come up with compromises which simply serve to legitimise power imbalances.

In the case of council tenants on an estate where the soundproofing is completely inadequate, these critics would hold that to assist neighbours to come to agreement about their respective levels of living noise is not only failing to identify and deal with the real problem, it is hindering any effective action by focussing the issue on the behaviour of the individuals rather than the responsibilities of the landlord.

One counter to this argument is, of course, the one previously mentioned – less individual conflict means more energy is available for other things, as people who are under the immediate pressure of unresolved conflicts are often unlikely to be able to look further than their back fence. It can be argued, however, that this only frees community mediation from part of the criticism – as long as mediation focuses

---

34 See: http://www.scmc.sacro.org.uk/sites/default/files/resource/COMMUNITY%20MEDIATION%206.pdf

exclusively on individual issues, it can not be said to be assisting in the development of strong, positive and equitable communities[35].

5.4.8 *Practice points to consider in the community*

Community mediation may be similar to civil mediation, albeit that co-mediators work together, but there are practical considerations. The following are offered for reflection:

- Planning is essential – co-mediators will want to work through all their protocols for opening the mediation, questioning, engagement, movement, private sessions, plenary sessions, interventions, and timing in advance

- Co-mediators should agree safe words for various circumstances including the need to break into private mediator discussion

- Mediators will need to ensure that there is adequate information and an Agreement to Mediate that is accessible and readily understood

- The need for interpreters or translators may need to be considered

- Home visits are common and may well be challenging places in which to work. There may be many distractions; children and young adults may be curious as to what is happening, unexpected visitors, pets, the television may compete and seating arrangements can be ad hoc. Community mediators need to adapt and improvise.

- Some domestic locations may be not be smoke free and can challenge allergies

- Timely arrival is always important even if participants may not share the same precision

---

35 cf: Linda Baron: https://www.nottingham.ac.uk/research/groups...community-mediation.pdf

- Consistency and fulfilment of commitments by mediators are crucial to trust

- Mediators should say what they are going to do and be very clear of what they cannot do

- Mediators will need to respect their environment, be discrete, and build rapport quickly

- Other family members may give their view whether invited or not

- Mediators may be offered hospitality, a drink or food and will have to decide on how they wish to deal with that situation; it may not be as easy as just saying "no."

- Co-mediators should liaise and consider their attire: some find formal business attire inappropriate but others find it is a useful distinguishing feature.

- Travel and transport arrangement will need to be considered.

- In some cases mediators will need to be self-aware and ensure personal safety

- Having a withdrawal plan is sensible

- Avoiding personal identification may be necessary – most community organisations issue ID cards without a surname: the ID will have the organisations contact details.

5.4.9 Training and continuous professional development in community mediation

In the experience of the authors' community mediation organisations do provide excellent training for their mediators and hold training development evenings. At these events experiences are shared and best practice is discussed and mediators are often invited to present on a topic of interest for collective learning.

Consequently joining a community mediation group is a great way not only to enhance well-defined existing skills and competencies but also to establish oneself as mediator. The co-mediator approach is an excellent form of working, enabling an exchange of ideas and inevitably mediators of whatever experience find they learn from each other.

In the community setting the co-mediation practice serves also to go some way to ensure personal safety throughout the process.

5.4.10 *Summary*

Community mediation groups do some remarkable things and are properly celebrated. They can be found on the internet and by approaching to such organisations as the Citizens Advice Bureau and local councils. They are an established yet continuously evolving part of mediation and the work is varied and challenging. The authors commend their use and membership.

Joining a community mediation group should not, however, be taken as a given or viewed lightly, as many involved with the organisation will have a deep knowledge of the communities which the serve. Mediators may well be interviewed thoroughly on wishing to join, including consideration of their personal drivers are and values.

It is important that mediators are culturally aligned with the ethos and values of any community mediation organisation and can work effectively with co-mediators, the organisation and community.

Finally, learning to work as a co-mediator, and seeing at close quarters a skilled lead in action, is a very significant fillip to a new mediator's practice. The reverse is also true – an experienced mediator, working with a colleague in co-mediation, can be constantly refreshed and renewed by the experience.

Both also benefit from candid reflective conversations after the mediation is over and can adopt effective mentoring and peer review gains. There are technical challenges with co-mediation, as set out in Section

5.5.7 above, but these are part of its strength once learned. Community mediation is therefore a very practical place to deliver the benefits of mediation and to develop vocational and professional skills.

5.5   Mediation and Coaching

In the experience of the authors there is an evolving and strengthening linkage between the two skill sets of mediation and coaching, and that there is opportunity to deploy coaching skills within mediation and that at times the need for mediation emerges from within the coaching setting.

Before exploring in more detail, historically it is recognised that the Phoenicians used mediation to solve disputes over trade. Similarly, for coaching there is evidence in cave paintings suggesting that coaching might have been used to impart the skills needed to hunt and gather food. So, mediation and coaching are not new, but they have undergone an evolution, or perhaps even a revolution over the last 30 years.

Mediation is now an increasingly integral part of Law School curriculums and is arguably moving towards being a mandated part of the legal process in a number of jurisdictions.

Coaching has "gone mainstream" and business or executive coaching in particular is now a key component in the development of leaders across sectors. There is a recognition that leadership skills need to be enhanced and not only at the top of an organisation but across an organisation. Leadership is equally important on the "shop floor" as it is in the "boardroom." Traditionally training courses have fulfilled the development of leaders but with coaching much can be covered in the workplace, with the coachee being able to continue their daily tasks around the coaching and in fact relate their workplace experience to their personal development.

The growth of coaching over the last 10-15 years has been rapid and it withstood the shocks of the financial crisis in the mid to late "noughties," during which its value was widely recognised in the financial and legal sectors. The business case for coaching continues to strengthen[36] as it does equally for mediation. Coaching is beginning to

---

36 For selected studies and reports see the following: www.meylercampbell.com; www.sherpacoaching.com; *'What can coaches do for you?'*, Harvard Business Review, January 2009 (Reprint No. R0901H), for the full *HBR* research report see www.-

niche, with coaches specialising in areas, such as career development, lifestyle and of course, leadership development.

Coaching can be used as a highly focused instrument with just a few sessions being offered to meet a need or perhaps more of a medium term approach over a year or so, with the coach working regularly with client. What coaches might experience, is that as they work with a client the coaching can uncover conflict. And that conflict might take many forms, revealing disputes within the client's workplace or perhaps in their personal lives. If encountered such conflicts may well need careful handling. It may be that in raising a dispute within the coaching framework that it is a classic "cry for help" from the client.

Coaches are often highly experienced at working with their clients to contextualize a conflict and will hopefully have the skills to work with others in an organisation in a discreet way to engage other professionals to provide appropriate input to resolve issues. As the contemporary world becomes more intense mental health issues are on the rise and therefore conflict both internally for people and with others is increasing. Fortunately, organisations with human resource departments are developing and publishing as part of their grievance policies specific guidance on using mediation within the organisation.

In mediations participants can often become stuck and unable to think in a way to allow them to move forward. This can happen in the civil and commercial forum in which participants may be so engrossed in their dispute that they have lost sight of the outcome that they might wish to achieve. This often happens in workplace mediations in which there may be compounding other factors, such as anxiety and stress causing ill health. Private sessions can assist here but time may be short and it is well worth think about how coaching might assist. The confidentially can be overcome with an appropriate agreement and in doing so a specialist coach brought in to work with the participants to explore what is causing the problem and develop participant based solutions.

---

carolkauffman.com; EFMD 'Corporate Coaching' special supplement to Global Focus, Vol 03 Issue 03 2009; and www.frank-bresser-consulting.com.

At the end of a workplace mediation in which the participants may well be going back into the same place of work coaching can be used to develop the achievements made in the mediation and embed changes in behaviour between the participants. This is when mediation becomes truly transformational.

With the continual evolution of technology the world continues to change dramatically, with communications and the media constantly shaping the business and social landscape.

The change agenda is apparent across all sectors and pervades people's personal lives and therefore, conflict and dispute are never far away. But there are emerging techniques available that can overcome difficulties and if deployed early can "nip things in the bud." Let's now look at the linkage between coaching and mediation in more detail and explore how it might be used to advantage.

5.5.1   *Mediation and Coaching – Defining the linkage*

To establish the linkage it is worthwhile studying a few of the many definitions of mediation and coaching. The Arbitration Conciliation and Advisory Service, states that,

> *"Mediation is based on the principle of collaborative problem solving, with a focus on the future and rebuilding relationships, rather than apportioning blame."*

In the world of coaching the ubiquitous Sir John Whitmore writes,

> *"Coaching focuses on future possibilities, not past mistakes."*

A similarity is readily apparent in that mediation and coaching are both about looking ahead rather than dwelling on the past. So, 'How is that future-look achieved? Clift in 2006[37] wrote,

---

37 Clift, R., (2006) Introduction to Alternative Dispute Resolution: A Comparison Between Arbitration and Mediation, Hill Dickenson.

"... a neutral third party, the mediator, assists the parties to settle their disputes. The mediator is a catalyst. The presence of an independent third party is the key distinguishing feature of the process."

And finally from Jenny Rogers[38] who defines coaching as,

"The coach work[ing] with clients to achieve speedy, increased and sustainable effectiveness in their lives and careers through focused learning. The coach's sole aim is to work with the client to achieve all of the clients' potential – as defined by the client".

Furthermore, Jenny Rogers advocates that the role of the coach is not to give advice, in that to do so leads to client dependency. The direct parallel in mediation is that if a mediator gives advice or suggests a way ahead; the solution is taken from the participant(s) and ownership of the solution transferred to the mediator, with potentially disastrous consequences. The role of the coach is to ask questions, to take the client into new areas, to allow the client to build their own resourcefulness, confidence and ownership. And once again to be directive would shift the relationship, alter the dynamic and extinguish the client's resourcefulness. Thus, there are intrinsic parallels between mediation and coaching, in that they are both:

- non-directive;
- they both involve a third or neutral party as the catalyst,
- they are both future focused; and
- they do not attribute blame nor invoke un-necessary negative reflection.

As a consequence of the above, outlined below are three coaching techniques that have direct applicability in a mediation and of course vice versa, these are: the GROW Model; the Thinking Environment; and Perceptual Positions.

---

38 Rogers, J., (2008) <u>Coaching Skills: A Handbook, 2nd Edition</u>, Open University Press.

5.5.2   *The GROW Model*

Just as in mediation where the mediator is the captain or guardian of the process and maintains that during the mediation, in coaching a coach often follows a model or sequence to achieve an outcome with a client.

The classical coaching model, which is both well documented and well acknowledged is the GROW model. The meanings of the G, R, O & W are stated below, along with styles of questions a coach might ask at each stage, which of course could be easily adapted to the mediation setting.

(G) GOAL – A clear vision is key and one that can be articulated.

- We have an hour so what would you want to achieve at the end of our session?
- How does that contribute to your overall work?
- By achieving that what do you think it will feel like?
- How will you / we know that you have succeeded?
- Is that the only thing you want to talk about today?

(R) REALITY – Creating a greater awareness at this stage, opening out to broaden the perspective and gain insight. Drilling down to find something concrete, the crux of the issue.

- Talk me through the key facts as you see them?
- What's the history behind this?
- Is anything else relevant or you think may have relevance?
- How are you really feeling about this issue?

(O) OPTIONS – Broaden out further and consider possibilities, distilling to a manageable number.

- What have you already done or considered?

- What else could or have not done?

- If you had a magic wand what would you do?

- What are the upsides and downsides?

(W) WILL – Seeking a positive closure if possible, with a defined and agreed commitment.

- So what will you do when and how?

- What could get in the way or you should be aware of?

- Who else do you think can help you to deliver this?

- Commitment to deliver scale 1 to 10

The above has so much in common with three great opening mediation questions to the participants of:

- What has brought us here today?

- What impact is this dispute having upon you?

- What would you like to achieve here today in order to move forward in a positive way?

5.5.3 *The Thinking Environment*[39]

Mediation is all about encouraging the participants to "think" about how things might be done differently and seeking positive outcomes that belong to them. Once again in coaching much the same is done and it is worthwhile acknowledging and drawing on the work of Nancy Kline in her book "Time to Think." In her book, Kline introduced the notion of the "Thinking Environment" and has gone onto develop many techniques and approaches that the reader is encouraged to review. Kline defined the "Thinking Environment" as having ten

---

39 Kline, N., (1999) *Time to Think*, Cassell Illustrated

components that are reproduced below, along with a brief description of each. What is striking about the ten components is that they chime so well with what a mediator will be doing in a mediation – not in every mediation and certainly not in sequence, but drawing on these components when appropriate. The authors have added a note in each of the ten components to enable the reader to consider further the mediation parallel.

1.   Attention – Listening with respect, interest and fascination.

Mediation's golden rule: "Listen, listen, listen and don't make matters worse."

2.   Incisive Questions – Removing assumptions that limit ideas.

In mediation: Using open questions, not judging, being curious asking why.

3.   Equality – Treating others as thinking peers.

- Giving equal turns and attention.
- Keeping agreements and boundaries.

In mediation: Setting the scene, agreeing ground rules, managing the process fairly and equitably especially with private sessions.

4.   Appreciation – Practicing a five-to-one ratio of appreciation to criticism.

In mediation: Neither a coach nor a mediator would of course be critical as that conveys judgment but appreciating the participants for what they are achieving through empathy and encouragement (see below) to move the mediation forward is entirely appropriate.

5.   <u>Ease</u> – Offering freedom from rush or urgency.

In mediation: Allowing time to consider through the process and for the mediator being the guardian of that process, to ensure reality is fully defined as is possible.

6.   <u>Encouragement</u> – Moving beyond competition.

In mediation: The mediator is using his or her skills to place each participant centre stage such that they define a solution that is theirs.

7.   <u>Feelings</u> – Allowing sufficient emotional release to restore thinking.

In mediation: Upset and emotion will happen at time and it is important the in a mediation it is expressed in safe way with respect for all.

8.   <u>Information</u> – Providing a full and accurate picture of reality.

In mediation: Using questions to allow the participants to define their own reality.

9.   <u>Place</u> – Creating a physical environment that says back to people, "You matter".

In mediation: Ensuring that the mediation space is acceptable to all, it might not be perfect but taking care with room layout, presentation, refreshments and timings go a long way to allow the participants the opportunity to deliver a positive outcome.

10.   <u>Diversity</u> – Adding quality because of the differences between us.

In mediation: Allowing participants to recognise their differences in a positive way and encouraging an awareness of what each participant's strengths are and what they offer the mediation.

5.5.4 *Perceptual Positions*

The authors have approached this in other sections and it is all about encouraging the participant to "walk in the other person's shoes". This piece brings together the work of several authors and is used by Business Coaches but is equally applicable in the field of mediation. It is recognised that and individual's learning from a situation or experience is enhanced when an individual has access to as many different points of view as possible. These points of view in effect give different representations of the reality of a situation. It is accepted that individuals cannot function on just one representation of reality and that at least two are needed. One representation takes in the information and a second interprets that information in a different way.

The way a person perceives the world will depend on such as culture, upbringing, and habits. People may for whatever reasons have "thinking" that causes poor perception of a situation. Thus, if a person can train himself or herself to see the world from another perspective then poor perception can be overcome.

There is a wonderful quote from the Greek Philosopher, Epictetus, 55-135 AD that is so applicable in both coaching and mediation and is:

> *"Man is not influenced by events themselves but by the view he takes of them."*

Research by Ginder and DeLozier identified the First, Second and Third Perceptual Positions. Examining each in turn reveals the following"

The First Position. In the First Position an individual looks at the situation from entirely their own point of view or perspective and thus takes no account of any other point of view. The result is that they view the situation from their own reality.

The Second Position. This is when an individual looks at a situation through the eyes of another individual and appreciates that situation from the other person's perspective, i.e. "How would it appear to them?" A person they are connected with by some means, such as partner, friend or business colleague.

The Third Position. This position views the situation from the point of view of a completely different person, i.e. an independent observer. In effect this is "How would it look to someone who is not involved?" This gives the objective viewpoint.

All three positions are equally important and for the most part we use them either consciously or sub-consciously daily to define our reality of events and happenings. However, if a person becomes stuck in the First Position it might be that their view of events could be described as egotistical and self-centred. In contrast, if a person is stuck in the Second Position and constantly looks at life from another person's perspective they may become overly influenced by the views of others. If on the other hand an individual is stuck in the Third Position they will be a detached observer of life.

So how can Perceptual Positions assist in mediation?

People in conflict are more than likely to be stuck in the First Position and thus, they are just viewing the dispute from their own perspective. So, in terms of practice consider when in private session having three chairs in a triangle shape. Invite the participant to sit in one of the chairs and ask them, "How do you personally view the conflict situation you are currently in?" Once they have explained to you, and perhaps you have explored their reality with additional questions, invite them to physically move to the next chair. When they are comfortable ask them "How would the other person involved in the dispute view the conflict or prevailing situation." Once again ask questions and explore that perceived reality. Finally, invite the participant to move to the third chair. When they are ready ask them, "How do you think someone totally outside of their conflict might describe the situation." Once again, ask questions to clarify understanding. Perhaps, at the end of the exercise ask the participant to summarise or you might prefer to do that.

The result of the above can be surprising and revealing.

Often the process might lead to a better understanding by in effect resetting the participant to be able to think more rationally across the three positions. There may be an acceptance that the whole situation appears stupid and futile – but of course that may well depend on the nature of the dispute.

5.5.5   *In conclusion*

So, where to from here? The authors are not advocating that mediators all 'dash-off' to train as coaches or vice versa, more an approach where mediators and coaches perhaps work together on particular cases. What is important from the outset is to apply the right technique, at the right time, and in the right way. Coaching and mediation are natural partners. Mediators are in effect using coaching techniques and coaches are perhaps at times being mediators – both perhaps without knowing they are doing so. Each professional has a wealth of documented knowledge and experience upon which to draw to improve and enhance their practice. Thus, enabling both participants and clients to reach solutions through the development of original thinking with ownership, leading to a sustainable and enduring reconciliation, all through a neutral third party or parties.

5.6   Mediation As a Life Skill

5.6.1   *Time for reflection*

We live in an interconnected world. Casting back just 50 years reveals huge advances in communications and associated technologies. Information now flows across the world in seconds and the expression "near real time" has emerged in our vocabulary, along with 24/7. Data is available in an instant and there is now the reality of what is termed "Big Data." There are upsides of great benefit, yet there are downsides too.

A lot of time and effort is being spent on "pushing data and information out" but perhaps less effort and understanding of how to process and what to do with it when we get it, right down to how we communicate. As we have discussed elsewhere in this book the stresses, strains and overloading of modern life can, and do give rise to conflict. Not that these didn't happen in days gone by. It is not unusual for coaches and mediators to hear the expression, "I feel as though I am on a hamster wheel."

There is arguably more intervention into people's lives nowadays from numerous sources that cascade down to everyday activity, such as making purchases in a supermarket and withdrawing money from a cashpoint. All perhaps with the right sentiment but perhaps the ability of people to make heir own decisions and pre-determine what they wish to do is being compromised? We will all have our own views on this.

Thus, to quote Friedrick Nietzsche, "The world is deep; deeper than day can comprehend."

Thus, Mediation as a Life Skill – or perhaps more specifically using mediation skills and competencies in the day-to-day, to enhance communication, bringing people together, to create an environment for thinking, and look at different ways of doing things is a way of looking at life through a different lens. Mediating techniques can be used to distinct advantage.

Mediation places the participants centre stage and it acknowledges them as people and in being human they can be self-determining. Generally, people do not want or wish to be told and mediation respects that by allowing time and space for people to explore their reality and define solutions that will work for them.

We can probably all think of an encounter, whether at work or in our private lives that when having spoken with someone we walk away and reflect, thinking to ourselves,

"That could have gone so much better!"

The authors would simply wish to invite the reader to consider how the techniques of mediation could be used to enhance everyday conversation to achieve better results in business and professional life, as well as enriching personal lives.

5.6.2 *Transactional Analysis*

Before doing so, the authors consider that it would be worthwhile to explore a well established subject known as Transactional Analysis that can readily show us how things can go wrong and the psychology behind why that might be so. There is much literature on this subject and the following notes provide an introduction. As there is much complexity to explore in this subject here is a brief overview.

The father of Transactional Analysis is considered to be a Dr Eric Berne[40] who in the 1950s defined the following:

- A transaction – the fundamental unit of social intercourse; and

- A stroke – the fundamental unit of social action.

Berne went onto say that:

---

40 Berne, E., (1961). <u>Transactional Analysis in Psychotherapy</u>. Grove Press, Inc., New York.

"The unit of social intercourse is called a transaction. If two or more people encounter each other... sooner or later one of them will speak, or give some other indication of acknowledging the presence of the others. This is called transactional stimulus. Another person will then say or do something which is in some way related to the stimulus, and that is called the transactional response."

So, Transactional Analysis is the method for studying interactions between individuals. We will come onto "Strokes" later in this chapter.

Berne defined three ego states and an ego state being "a consistent pattern of feeling and experience directly related to a corresponding consistent pattern of behaviour."

Berne's three ego states are:

- Parent;
- Adult; and
- Child.

It should be noted that the descriptions of these ego states do not necessarily correspond to their common definitions as used the English language. In a little more detail each ego state can be defined as follows:

The "Parent" ego state represents a massive collection of recordings in the human brain of thousands upon thousands of external events experienced or perceived in approximately the first five years of life, by the child observing the actions of a parent or someone operating in a parental role.

The "Child" ego state represents the recordings in the brain of internal events associated with external events that the child perceives; or explained in another way, stored in the "Child" ego state are the emotions or feelings, associated with external events. For example a recording in the "Child" ego state might be:

"As the car went past, the noise really frightened me"

The "Adult" ego state is when, as a child at about one year of age gross motor activity starts to emerge. For example, the child learns that he or she can control a cup from which to drink, that he or she can grab a toy. In social settings, the child can play such games as "peek-a-boo." This is the beginning of the development of the "Adult" ego state in the small child. "Adult" ego state data grows out of the child's ability to see what is different than what he or she observed when developing the "Parent" or felt when developing the "Child." In other words, the "Adult" allows the young person to evaluate and validate "Child" and "Parental" data. Berne opined that the "Adult" ego state is that of being:

"Principally concerned with transforming stimuli into pieces of information, and processing and filing that information on the basis of previous experience."

One of the key functions of the "Adult" ego state is to validate data in the "Parent." An example is:

"Wow. It really is true that pot handles should always be turned into the stove," said Sally, as she saw her brother burn himself when he grabbed a pot handle sticking out from the stove.

In this example, Sally's "Adult" ego state has reached the conclusion that data in her "Parent" ego state was valid. Her "Parent" ego state had been taught, "Always turn pot handles into the stove, otherwise you could get burned." And with her analysis of her brother's experience, her "Adult" ego state concluded that this was indeed correct.

So how does Transactional Analysis work? When two people communicate, one person initiates a transaction with a transactional stimulus. The person at whom the stimulus is directed will respond with the transactional response. Simple Transactional Analysis involves identifying which ego state directed the stimulus and which ego state in the other person executed the response.

The simplest transactions are between "Adult" ego states and perhaps "Child" or "Parent." But not all transactions proceed in this manner. Some transactions involve ego states other than the "Adult."

The structural diagram below represents the complete personality of any individual. It includes the "Parent", "Adult", and "Child" ego states, are all separate and distinct from each other.

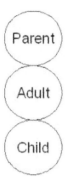

Thus for a "Child" interacting with a "Parent" the following structural diagram can be drawn showing a transactional response.

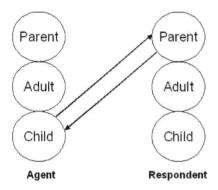

Thus, a complementary transaction is achieved, in which the response must go back from the receiving ego state to the sending ego state. These transactions are healthy and represent normal human interactions.

However, not all transactions between humans are healthy or normal. In those cases, the transaction is classified as a crossed transaction, in which, an ego state different than the ego state, which received the stimuli is the one that responds. The diagram below shows a typical crossed transaction.

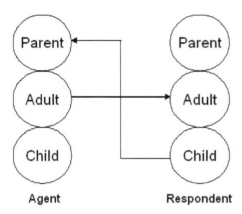

So, "How might this sound?"

Agent's Adult: "Do you know where my car keys are?" (Note that this stimulus is directed at the Respondent's "Adult").

Respondent's Child: "You always blame me for everything!"

Instead of the Respondent's "Adult" responding with "I think they're on the desk", it is the Respondent's "Child" that responds back.

Therefore, one must look beyond what is being said and to how the words are being delivered with accents on particular words, changes in tone, and volume, as well as the non-verbal signs accompanying those words with body language and facial expressions.

5.6.3 Strokes

At the time of developing his theories on Transactional Analysis, Berne considered the research work of Rene Spitz on child development. Spitz had observed that infants that were deprived of handling were more prone to emotional and physical difficulties. These infants lacked the cuddling, touching, and handling that most other infants received and

Berne considered the handling to be a "stroke," which he defined as the: "fundamental unit of social action".

Thus, for Berne a stroke is unit of recognition, when one person recognises another person either verbally or non-verbally. He identified that as adults we all respond to a smile, hand gesture or facial expression. Furthermore, he concluded that any stroke, whether it be positive or negative is better than no stroke at all.

For example, if one morning, you are walking in front of your house and you see your neighbour, you may well smile and say "Good morning." Your neighbour will likely say "hello" back. This is an example of a positive stroke. Your neighbour could also frown at you and say nothing, which is an example of a negative stroke. But either case is better than no stroke at all, such as, if your neighbour ignored you completely.

In many ways in the interconnected world of today perhaps Transactional Analysis is under pressure since we don't receive full feedback when we communicate, such as in an email or a text when we lack facial expressions and tone.

So, bearing in mind Transactional Analysis, let's recap on what skills mediation can bring to everyday life. In the earlier chapters at the very heart of the mediation process were such soft skills as:

- Creating rapport;
- Building trust;
- Listening actively to understand and not just to respond;
- Questioning both in an open way and a closed way;
- Probing and being curious;
- Reflecting; and
- Summarising.

All of those can be absorbed into our communication in everyday life, at whatever level and in whatever context.

5.6.4 *Non-Violent Communication*

It is well worthwhile considering the work of Marshall Rossenberg,[41] an American Clinical Psychologist, on Non-Violent Communication. Much of human communication forms in judgement and makes assumptions about what is being said and rapidly draws to conclusions that are perhaps often, at times either incorrect or wide of the mark.

Consider the expression in response to hearing a work colleague (in Transactional Analysis terms "the agent," explaining something and "the respondent" saying:

"What you told me was …."

The first observation is that the respondent is assuming that they have heard what they were being told exactly as was said;

Secondly, it assumes much; and

Thirdly, it has no acknowledgment of feelings or emotion. It does not attempt to build rapport and depending upon your point of view it could be considered aggressive, especially when presented with such a tone.

In contrast if the respondent were to say something like,

> *"Thank you for taking the time to explain that issue to me. What I heard you tell me is ……"*

and then for the respondent to go onto give a brief summary of what was said.

The respondent would then pause using a silence to give the agent thinking time and then the agent might explain some more about the issue as they reflect.

---

41 Rossenberg, M., (2003) Non-Violent Communication: A Language of Life. Second Edition, Encinitas CA: PuddleDancer Press

Thereafter, the respondent might say,

"Okay – what I have heard you tell me now is that ... "

a further summary follows from the respondent that would include key point from the summary given earlier.

This shows to the agent that the respondent is listening and building a picture; and in a way sharing the agent's reality. These steps can be repeated as many times as needed, until a point is reached when the respondent might say.

"Thank you once again for all that you have explained to me – might I just ask you a question?"

The agent is unlikely to say "no." Also, in seeking permission the respondent has very much taken the conversation to that of the "Adult"-"Adult" ego state level.

This then opens the door for the respondent to start to probe and to be curious and start to reality test and build towards considering options.

It may be seen that this is time consuming but it is not, as it saves time in the longer term, whilst building rapport, trust and understanding. It is a way of entering a person's world and seeing the situation from their perspective and much more.

5.6.5 Reflection

Mediation is very much a life skill that can be learned and applied in a practical manner. It offers insights and learning, and even a business model. It should be treasured.

PART SIX –
ZEN AND THE ART OF
PRACTICAL MEDIATION

The authors should offer an immediate confession[1]: this concluding section is no place to learn about Zen. Nor do they know how mediation will develop or what the future of mediation holds[2]. They suspect that very few people do. Lord Palmerston said this of his age's version of Brexit "The Schleswig-Holstein question is so complicated, only three men in Europe have ever understood it. One was Prince Albert, who is dead. The second was a German professor who became mad. I am the third and I have forgotten all about it." Much the same can be said about dispute resolution in ten years' time.

The mediator had them all tethered for their own safety
during their inflated opening statements.

The authors still cannot believe that Donald Trump, or before him Ronald Reagan, was elected President, so they have no illusions about their ability to predict the future. And when it comes to mediation, that is a good thing. If mediators learn only one thing from complexity science, it ought to be that no matter how much people analyse, study, reflect, and dissect, humans live in a chaotic world where their systems

---

1 With due deference to Robert Pirsig.

2 …although with incorrigible hubris they attempt to describe future mediation training at Annex H below.

are complex and nonlinear. Assessing the future, or knowing the exact (or even general) impact of different decisions that may be taken, or moves that will be made, is impossible.

The authors' goal therefore ought to be to offer an art of mediation that is structure yet flexible, one that is practical and adaptable to a wide range of possible futures.

6.1   The Challenges for Practical Mediators

The challenge faced by being adaptable, and thereby practical,[3] is still to be focused and effective. To run this gauntlet, mediators need six talismen:

(a) to remain clear about their fundamental purpose,

(b) to keep working on refining their skills through continuing professional development,

(c) to use reflective learning,

(d) to enhance the range of toolkit skills available to achieving those purposes,

(e) to commit to diversifying the profession; and

(f) to maintain a clear hold on our values and ethical principles.

Bernard Mayer suggested[4] in October 2016 that:

> *".. the biggest trap (mediators) can fall into that will interfere with our adaptability is to limit our purpose or goals to a particular approach, format, or set of tactical moves (however much "in vogue" this approach might be). We may be drawn to an evaluative, transformative, facilitative, or narrative approach. We may choose to focus on a particular role in conflict – perhaps as mediators, coaches, system designers, or evaluators. We may believe that we should always caucus, never caucus, offer substantive recommendations, or refrain from such recommendations at all costs. But if we think these preferences or choices define our essential professional identity, then we have lost the plot. And if we think that the choices we make about tactics or specific approaches on such matters are not simply that—our choices—and instead view them as morally superior or particularly well grounded in reality, than we are deluding ourselves to the detriment of both our practice and profession."*

---

3   Or as the Fat Controller might have said "Really Useful Mediators"

4   https://www.mediate.com/articles/MayerFutures.cfm

Returning to Professor Hawking's 2012 paralympic theme, mediators must be curious. They must look up at the stars and not down at their feet. They must wonder, why? Different circumstances, different players, and especially the interactional dynamics of players and circumstances determine what is possible, what works, and what is ethical.

Mayer suggests that the better able mediators are to recognise and the more flexible mediators are in adapting to these interactional dynamics, the more successful they will be over time, and more to the point – the more useful a service they will provide. It follows then that this Zen requires a consideration of the six talisman.

6.2 The Fundamental Purpose of a Practical Mediator

Bill Potapchuk once asked: "If mediation is our position, what is our interest?" Every mediator may answer differently, which is probably good, but it is also interesting. Some would describe their interest as wanting to help people deal with conflict more constructively, which may be to say more courageously, wisely, and with a long-term view.

Some might want to transform lives, including their own, or to earn a living, or to smarten up their local community. Others are motivated by the goal of settling disputes outside of court, or reaching as many agreements as possible, or generally being effective. Some want to right injustice or prevent wrongs, or be the equalizer. Yet others enjoy the human challenge.

Some disputes, however, need a judge. Some need a strike. Some need a change in the law or some deserve someone to lose.

It seems to the authors that while finding a resolution where agreement is possible and valuable may be an important part of what mediators do, it is not what mediators actually do, – or should seek to do. For mediation is a process that belongs to the participants and the mediator a facilitator of process. The mediator is not contracted to produce results but to offer a means of empowerment, of self-determination, and progression, should the participants so desire.

The authors believe there is much in the analogy of a taxi driver. In London, black cab (hackney carriage) drivers train for years[5] to obtain "the knowledge" of the capital's streets.

That knowledge is not truly knowledge of lasting relevance to the fares that the cab driver may pick up. It is a knowledge of streets and byways, traffic flows and obstructions, options and possibilities, structures and practicalities that may help the fare get to where they want to go with the minimum of risks, delay and difficulty. The fare by then reach their chosen destination to catch a train or get married, gain a job or lose a fortune, blessed or troubled by the conversations that have gone on in

---

5 As opposed to Uber drivers who need only buy a Prius and an iPhone

the privacy of the cab. The driver and the fare will have interacted with others, and driver will have from time to time guided process, but ultimately the fare will have decided where and when to get out – and will likely promptly forget the driver who had no stake in the destination.

Is that not a pretty summary of a mediator? And just as with a taxi driver so with a mediator – as has been discussed, the harder or quicker a mediator pushes participants towards a destination, the longer and more difficult it a journey it is likely to be.

Mediation like the taxi cab is a means to an end, and that end is to help people deal with the conflict in their lives that they choose to bring to mediator, productively, wisely, effectively and ethically. Mediation, however, is also like a cab ride in that it is generally a short term intervention. It is not the destination and mediators must be aware of the context.

Mediators are offering one process to society. It is probably going to be important, for the survival and growth of that process, that the Practical Mediator offers a range of approaches in the future.

6.3   The Practical Mediators' Guide to the Galaxy

The answer to Practical Mediation's future, is unlikely to be 42[6]. That said, the adaptability of mediation in some ways replicates the supreme utility of the towel in intergalactic travel. Adams wrote of the towel:

> "...it has great practical value – you can wrap it around you for warmth as you bound across the cold moons of Jaglan Beta; you can lie on it on the brilliant marble-sanded beaches of Santraginus V, inhaling the heady sea vapours; you can sleep under it beneath the stars which shine so redly on the desert world of Kakrafoon; use it to sail a mini raft down the slow heavy river Moth; wet it for use in hand-to-hand-combat; wrap it round your head to ward off noxious fumes or to avoid the gaze of the Ravenous Bugblatter Beast of Traal (a mindboggingly stupid animal, it assumes that if you can't see it, it can't see you – daft as a brush, but very, very ravenous); you can wave your towel in emergencies as a distress signal, and of course dry yourself off with it if it still seems to be clean enough."

The diversity of approaches to mediation that are being practiced, refined, and taught suggest that there is a towel here to be treasured. The spectrum is more than transformative through facilitative to evaluative approaches. As indicated in Part Five of this work there is narrative, therapeutic, restorative, hybrid, med-arb, insight, systems mediation, and coaching, as well as life skill applications

There are many variations and combinations of each of these approaches although it is improbable that any one mediator can practice across this entire range. But in combination mediators can (without even mediating dangerously) push the boundaries of personal practice to increase our capacity to respond to a greater range of conflicts.

The significant growth in mediation-related activities that have been nourished by the growth of mediation – and that in turn have enhanced the practice of mediation. For example: restorative justice, public conversations, civic engagement, world cafes, on-line dispute resolution, ombudsman services, family group conferencing, policy dialogues, and

---

6   Douglas Adams.

moderated debates. When even heavily criticized former prime ministers appear as Middle East mediators, it is clear that something substantial is happening.

But mediators, especially Practical Mediators, should not be too optimistic or self satisfied with what has been accomplished. Mayer refers to "important caveats and warning signs" and finds that "it is not clear that this proliferation in services has led to a significant positive change in the culture of conflict and decision making in general or even in the organisations who have most embraced these efforts."

In other words, just as the availability of Band Aids and sticking plasters did not stop children from fighting over toys or towels, or mean that cooks paid closer attention to their sharp knives, so too has mediation failed to reduce the level of conflict. And some would argue that the rise in the number of people anxious to offer mediation has not been matched by the willingness of individuals to embrace it – at least in some fields of activity.

Another criticism that Practical Mediators will need to address is that the broadening of the field of mediation has not necessarily been matched by its deepening. The development of the mediator's knowledge base, educational programmes, and professional development processes has been very much a secondary process. This is addressed in Annex H below.

6.4 Practical Mediation Must Become Diverse and Inclusive

A recent study found that that most civil and commercial mediators were older white males (like the authors). Many of these older white males have a legal background. Family and community mediators are more likely to be female. Court mediators are a more diverse group, but are mostly female. Private mediators are mostly white. Most dispute resolution conferences look largely white and increasingly old. While there are many reasons to be concerned about this, one clear consequence of the lack of diversity is a diminished ability to adapt to an uncertain future. The less diverse, the less adaptable and the less relevant we are.

The Society of Mediators has an effective policy of diversity and inclusion. This applies both in the training programmes it runs and the Free Mediation Project. But mediators overall do not appear to be growing as a field. Those regularly selected are aging. They are not very diverse. This is not a good sign for the profession's capacity to adapt to an uncertain future or to serve a broad cross section of the public.

6.5   Practical Mediators Need Conceptual Skills

Mediators tend, says Mayer, to think of skills in very practical, behavioural terms—e.g., framing, active listening, creating a safe negotiating atmosphere, responding to power plays, or identifying underlying interests. But there are at least two other kinds of skills that are critical to intervention capacity – emotional and conceptual skills. Mediation tends to be more attuned to the importance of emotional skills (e.g., emotional intelligence, knowing our button pushers, comfort with emotionality in others) than to enhancing our conceptual and analytical skills, but these too are critical to effectiveness and adaptability.

There has been little empirical research, and no real analysis of reflective practice. Nor has there been a systematic evaluation of mediators' most cherished frameworks and beliefs.

The problems with training, a decade a go and now, are addressed in the essay at Annex H. There has still been no real and persuasive research on what training is really needed, and what skills or concepts have to be taught and learned. There is a substantial anecdotal and experience base, but these offer perhaps only marginally more than a priori assumptions about what makes a good mediator. Mayer observes that that the basic tenets of mediators' practices remain those articulated 30 years ago by Fisher and Ury in *Getting to Yes*.

The authors agree that while this good work still provides (as this book has shown) some solid practical advice, it is not a powerful or sophisticated enough conceptual framework (for example, in relation to the impact of identity, gender, cultures, and ethnicity) to provide the foundation for a substantive and adaptable field of practice. This lack of conceptual framework has been the reason why this book is entitled Practical Mediation – and not, following Machiavelli, the Art of Mediation. There is plenty on which to base a practical guide for practical mediators, but not enough to offer anything more substantive.

Returning to the cab driver analogy – the shape of a taxi, and the way it is operated largely remained unchanged for decades. Until Uber, with protective sanctions against minicabs, there was an effective framework that appeared to offer enough. That hegemony looks increasingly insecure with the rise of AI meaning that driverless cabs will surely replace both black cabs and Ubers. Knowledge of streets is not enough. AI and algorithms can purport at least to understand transport desires.

For mediators, a framework has offered a means for tactical intervention, which has for the last fifty years in the West been enough. But that framework has so far failed to offer to mediators the ability to understand the nature of conflict and the dynamics of intervention. The new science of Practical Mediation needs to draw on neuroscience, evolutionary biology, political science, economics, systems theory, game theory, psychology, sociology, law, organisational development, and even Luke Rhinehart's dice theory to increase the sophistication of mediator's body of knowledge and conceptual skills.

Mayer argues that developing what the authors have termed the new science of Practical Mediation may provide the greatest challenge to mediators' capacity to adapt, but perhaps is at the same time mediation's greatest opportunity.

6.6   Conclusion – Zen and the Art of Practical Mediation

Zen can be taken to mean taken to mean learning or enlightenment based on meditation and intuition rather than ritual. Mediators, like devotees of differing churches of reason, need certain rituals, or perhaps structures or frameworks. But they must be flexible and capable of adopting evidence-based thought and ethics.

It is to the credit of mediators that professional and personal values, and ethical commitments have defined the identity of a profession of neutrals. The embracing of the European Code of Conduct and all that it says about empowerment, self-determination, and fairness strong indices for a successful profession. The success of mediators in turning those values into a daily reality in mediations great and small makes mediators effective and relevant. Practical Mediation needs an ethical core of committed individuals.

Superficially, government programmes also offer hope – but whilst NHS Clinical Negligence scheme is potentially an exception, there are concerns expressed over time limited small claims mediation schemes. The more that a lack of resources limit the time and skills available for mediation, the greater the risk that pressure is applied to create agreements. Mayer also observes that the domination of the legal profession in many arenas of mediation risks enshrining a rights-based, settlement conference orientation, despite the fact that this narrow focus may contradict mediations espoused values (such as client empowerment).

Mediation will not be alone in being engaged in a tension between practical issues such as funding and instant expectations, and core values such as neutrality and considered empowerment. Practical Mediation, the authors argue, needs a scientific base and artistic freedom. Zen might, through suitable contemplation deliver the combination of art and science that the profession, the public, and society needs. It is work that must now progress.

In the meantime, the authors dare to welcome Practical Mediators to this rich world of their choosing. If a towel is not the ideal companion it is hoped that this book can be a worthy substitute – a guide, philosopher, and friend in which Professor Glanville Williams would have delighted. And if 42 is not the answer, the message to mediators must surely be: Don't Panic.

ANNEXES

ANNEX A – MEDIATION OPENING BRIEF AND CHECKLIST 2017/18

Please remember that this is a general guide and not intended to be a script.

- Meet all participants outside the plenary room: and check,
    - o the location of washrooms, fire-exits and fire-alarm drill;
    - o who is present and that they have authority;
    - o that the Agreement to Mediate has been signed by the participants;
    - o that any non-participants and/or un-regulated representatives are agreed;
    - o that any such people have signed the confidentiality undertaking;
    - o that everyone knows where the facilities are and health and safety issues;
    - o Check chairs: invite all participants into the main room to sit where they wish;
    - o Introduce yourself – and ask everyone around the table to do so (make your table map)

- State that you have (seen) the signed mediation agreement and that you will be working under its terms and rules in what is of course a confidential and without prejudice process.

- Thank advisers (or the participants) for the papers you have received – confirm what you have read. Mention some uncontroversial rapport details seen in your reading.

- State that today is about looking forward rather than back – therefore no need to go over the papers that you have read from your perspective.

- Say that from what you have read you are confident that the process will be of benefit.

- Remind people that your role is to facilitate discussion not to provide any advice or to recommend any particular solution – you are here to help negotiations but not to judge.

- Say that if any one needs legal advice they are free to break at any time – just ask.

- Remind people that you may work in open session or in private – and what is said in any private session to you will remain absolutely confidential unless you are asked to transmit it to the other participants – so please do not ask me what happened in these sessions.

- Say that sometimes it helps if in private sessions you can have permission to play the devil's advocate – to ask questions that may probe or challenge: no one has to answer your questions but this can assist in the facilitation process. Is that OK?

- State the time available and check that is OK. If so, remind people that they are free to leave at any time but if in the unlikely event they want to go: ask for the five minute rule.

- Say that before you start you would just like to find out a little more about everyone – once you have done that then you will invite people to suggest a structure for the day.

- Say experience suggests that a rule that only one person speaks at once works well, so you can focus on the speaker. Would that be appropriate? Who would like to begin?

ANNEX B – SAMPLE[1] AGREEMENT TO MEDIATE 2018

Name of Case: ....
Reference: 2018/001/

BETWEEN:

Party 1 ....

AND

Party 2 ....

The parties and the Representatives, signing this Agreement, agree as follows:

1. The Mediator(s) for this dispute is/are
   (1) .... (2) ....
   of FreeMed,   (Address and Contact Number)

2. The mediation will be held on .... 2018, commencing at ....

3. The Parties listed in the Schedule and their Representatives agree to attempt in good faith to resolve their dispute at the Mediation, and that the provisions of FreeMed's Pro Bono Mediation Rules 2018 Edition ("The Rules") attached hereto, shall apply to this mediation.

4. The Parties authorise the Mediator to conduct the mediation using the procedures set out in the Rules.

---

1 NB: This Sample Agreement to Mediate (and the Rules) are for training and education purposes only. It is not warranted or certified for real cases. Live Agreements to Mediate and Rules may be found via Google

5. The Parties and their Representatives in signing this Agreement confirm that they specifically acknowledge and understand that the Mediator has accepted their invitation to mediate this matter on the sole basis that by virtue of the Rules and the intrinsic nature of mediation, the Parties agree that no liability shall arise or accrue against the Mediator or FreeMed as a result of the conduct of the Mediation by the Mediator or as a result of the administration of the Mediation.

I have read, understand and agree the provisions of this Agreement and the attached Rules.

Signed: _____ for and on behalf of Party 1 and its Representatives

Signed: _____ for and on behalf of Party 2 and its Representatives

Signed: _____ Mediator (who also signs for FreeMed)

Dated this _____ day of _____ 2018

<u>SCHEDULE</u>

PARTIES AND REPRESENTATIVES

Party 1

Name _____

Address _____
_____
_____
_____

Representative _____

Firm _____

DX _____

Telephone _____

Email _____

Party 2

Name _____

Address _____
_____
_____
_____

Representative _____

Firm _____

DX _____

Telephone _____

Email _____

FREEMED'S PRO BONO MEDIATION
RULES – 2018 EDITION

1.   INTERPRETATION

1(1)   In these Rules, the following terms shall have the following meanings:

(a)   "Mediator" means a member of FreeMed's panel of mediators appointed by the Parties as a neutral to conduct the mediation. The Mediator is an independent contractor chosen by or agreed to by the Parties with whom they contract for services rendered. The Mediator is not an employee of FreeMed. The Mediator is not a person who will provide legal or professional advice to the Parties or their Representatives or who will give a judgment or an award. References to the Mediator include both Mediators where there is a Co-Mediation conducted by two Mediators.

(b)   "Agreement to Mediate" means a legally-binding contract to mediate, prepared by FreeMed for the Parties, their Representatives, the Mediator and any Non-Parties attending the Mediation, to be executed prior to the commencement of the Mediation, containing various provisions relating to the process of Mediation, confidentiality, privilege, liability, and the duties and obligations of the Parties to each other, to the Mediator and FreeMed. The Agreement to Mediate requires agreement to and compliance with these Rules.

(c)   "Party" means a Party to a dispute, controversy, or legal action who is a participant in the mediation or who is represented by a participant in the mediation.

(d)   "Representative" means the lawyer, counsel, attorney, or other authorised representative of the Party.

(e)   "Evaluative Mediation" shall mean a process of mediation in which the Parties jointly invite the Mediator to comment on the merits or substance of the case, and/or to provide a non-binding evaluation: the Mediator may in his or her absolute discretion defer accepting, or decline, any such invitation without being asked for or giving a reason. FreeMed does not offer Evaluative Mediation.

(f) "Facilitative Mediation" shall mean a process of mediation in which the Mediator offers no comment on the merits or substance of the case, nor provides any evaluation but instead assists the Parties to an agreement using principled negotiation: the Mediator may in his or her absolute discretion comment on the use of the process of the Mediation if such comment is likely to assist the Parties.

(e) "Settlement Agreement" means a document signed by the Parties or their Representatives before the conclusion of the Mediation, setting forth agreed terms of settlement between the Parties which are intended by them to be legally binding

1(2) These Rules shall be interpreted in such a way as to provide the Parties with an efficient and effective Mediation.

2. AGREEMENT OF PARTIES

2(1) These Rules, and all amendments to them, shall be deemed to be part of the Agreement to Mediate which provides for Mediation with the Mediator.

2(2) Subject to the agreement of the Mediator, these Rules may be varied at any time by written amendment signed by the Parties or their Representatives.

3. PRIVACY AND CONFIDENTIALITY OF MEDIATION

3(1) The Mediation is private and confidential.

3(2) A person who is not a Party or a Representative may only attend the Mediation with the consent of all of the Parties and of the

Mediator: every such person shall sign Schedule 1 before the Mediation.

3(3) Every Party and Representative agrees that all offers, promises and proposals, whether oral or written, actions, determinations, representations and statements (including but not limited to admissions) made in the course of the Mediation by any of the Parties, their agents, employees, experts, Representatives and all statements, comments, or observations made or relayed, by the Mediator, and all notes, documents and reports prepared or exchanged during the Mediation are "without prejudice" and for the purpose of negotiation only.

3(4) The Parties agree that any such offers, promises, proposals, conduct, statements, notes, documents, and reports shall not be disclosed to any third party and they shall not be offered as evidence in any arbitration, judicial or other proceeding, at any time.

3(5) Notwithstanding Rule 3(4), the parties acknowledge that evidence that is otherwise admissible shall not be rendered inadmissible because it has been used in a Mediation.

3(6) Neither the Mediator, nor any person present observing the Mediation nor any of FreeMed's staff shall be invited or compelled by the Parties, jointly or severally, to appear as a witness in any pending or future adversarial or judicial proceeding involving any one or more of the Parties or relating in any way to the subject matter of the Mediation.

3(7) The Parties agree that they shall not jointly or severally seek to summons the Mediator or any person observing the mediation or any of FreeMed's staff.

3(8) Any notes made by the Mediator are confidential to the Mediator and shall not be available to the Parties at any time, nor subject to subpoena for production as evidence in any arbitration, judicial or other proceeding. The Mediator undertakes that he/she shall in any event destroy any notes.

4.   BASIC PRINCIPLES

4(1)   The Parties and their Representatives agree that each Party shall attend the Mediation with full authority to settle.

4(2)   At the Mediation, the Parties agree that they will be prepared to make a brief oral statement explaining what they wish to achieve from the process and acknowledge that they are expected to participate in good faith in the process conducted with the assistance of the Mediator.

4(3)   The Parties agree where reasonably practicable to make available to the Mediator such copies of documents or materials as are likely to be needed in order effectively to negotiate.

4(4)   The Parties agree that the Mediator may meet (caucus) privately with each Party and its Representative during the Mediation if he or she considers that it will assist the process. Any Party and Representative may request a private caucus with the Mediator at any time.

4(5)   The Parties agree that there shall be no electronic recording by any means of the mediation, nor any verbatim stenographic record taken of the Mediation. Parties may make notes but these must not be shown to any person and are not admissible in any court, arbitration or other proceedings.

5.   MEDIATION PROCEDURE

5(1)   The Mediator will conduct the Mediation using Facilitative Mediation as defined in Rule 1(1)(f). The Mediator will conduct process non-judgmentally by exploring the interests, needs and concerns of the Parties allowing them to generate options for a mutually agreed resolution.

5(2)   The Mediator will not advise any person, nor comment or offer legal or professional opinions. The Parties will rely on their own counsel or Representatives for legal or professional advice.

5(3)   The Mediator will not propose a settlement nor draft any offers or settlement. Parties must attend the Mediation ready, willing, and able to write or draft any offers or settlement.

5(4)   The Mediator will continue to use Facilitative Mediation techniques until a settlement is reached, or the Mediation is adjourned or terminated as set out below.

Evaluative Mediation

5(5)   Evaluative Mediation is not offered by FreeMed. No Mediator shall evaluate or advise.

Termination of the Mediation

5(6)   Whatever the process used in Mediation, the Mediation shall be terminated:

(a)   by agreement between the Parties; or

(b)   if a settlement is reached by the Parties; or

(c)   at any time during the Mediation, if the Mediator in his/her absolute discretion decides it should be terminated in which case the Parties agree they shall not challenge that decision nor shall the Mediator give or be asked for a reason for the termination; or

(d)   no agreement has been reached in the time available and it is either impracticable to take further time, unless the Parties and the Mediator agree to adjourn the mediation; or

(e)   a Party does not wish to continue in Mediation.

5(7)   On termination, the Mediator will as soon as reasonably practicable destroy all notes and documents save for the Agreement to Mediate and any Schedules to that Agreement and/or the Rules.

6.   SETTLEMENT AGREEMENT AND FORMALITIES

6(1)   Any settlement agreed at Mediation will not be deemed to be concluded or to be legally binding until the Parties or their Representatives sign a Settlement Agreement at the mediation setting forth the terms thereof.

6(2)   The Settlement Agreement shall not be drafted or signed by the Mediator.

7.   EXCLUSION OF LIABILITY

7(1)   Neither the Mediator nor FreeMed or its staff, employees or agents, including shall be liable to any Party or Representative for any act or omission howsoever arising in connection with any Mediation conducted by the Mediator.

7(2)   Without prejudice to the Agreement to Mediate and to the exclusions or limitations set out in these Rules, should contrary to the foregoing provisions any liability be found to attach to the Mediator then the Parties agree that it shall be limited to the maximum sum of £1,000,000.

8.   FEES AND COSTS OF THE MEDIATION

8(1)   Mediation with FreeMed is free. No payment will be made to the Mediator or FreeMed.

9.   LEGAL EFFECT AND STATUS OF THE MEDIATION

9(1)   The Agreement to mediate and these Rules are governed by the laws of England and Wales and the courts of England and Wales shall have exclusive jurisdiction to decide any matters arising out of or in connection with this Agreement and the Mediation.

SIGNATURE

I have read, understand and agree the provisions of this Agreement and the attached Rules.

Signed: _____ for and on behalf of Party 1 and its Representatives

Signed: _____ for and on behalf of Party 2 and its Representatives

Signed: _____ Mediator (who also signs for FreeMed)

Dated this _____ day of _____ 2018

SCHEDULE 1 TO FREEMED'S MEDIATION RULES

CONFIDENTIALITY AGREEMENT FOR OBSERVERS/NON-LAWYERS

MEDIATION between

Party 1   and   **Party 2**

Held on   **2018; at**

I/we the undersigned, in consideration of the participants in the above mediation agreeing to us attending and observing the above mediation, hereby irrevocably agree to keep confidential all matters that I/we hear, read, or see at the above mediation and shall never disclose what I/we learn, hear, read, or see at the above mediation unless required by a Court in due process of law.

I am/we are:

Name	Address	Email	Telephone	Signature

Signed in the presence of the Mediator(s):

Mediator(s) name(s):

Signed:
Dated:

ANNEX C – MEDIATORS'
SELF-REFLECTION CHECKLIST

Mediators might find this a useful exercise, to complete following mediation in terms of self-reflection. A summary narrative could be added and the table used to monitor progress.

Factor	Always 4	Often 3	Seldom 2	Never 1
I worked to put the participants at ease.				
I used open-ended questions to encourage exploration and elaboration.				
I let the participants tell their stories as they wished to tell them.				
I kept the conversation focused on the participants' issues.				
I demonstrated genuine curiosity and interest.				
I used body language and non-verbal cues to encourage, acknowledge and empathise with the participants.				
I made eye contact with the participants.				
I drew out the background and context of the situation.				
I encouraged the participants to clarify ambiguous or vague meanings.				
I asked questions to clarify the participants' issues or interests.				

I asked questions to encourage the participants to reflect on perceptions, assumptions, inferences and intentions; as well as the facts.				
I recognised and acknowledged emotions.				
I kept my composure and responded appropriately when strong emotions were expressed.				
I picked-up and responded to non-verbal cues.				
I summarised and checked my understanding of the key facts or elements of the situation.				
I allowed for and valued silence.				
I handled internal and external distractions well.				
I tried to keep an open mind, even when I had doubts or made judgements in my mind.				
I avoided pushing my own interpretation, agenda or solution.				

ANNEX D – SAMPLE WORKPLACE AGREEMENT TO MEDIATE

This is an Agreement to Mediate between the following parties/participants namely:

A.

and

B.

collectively known as "the parties or participants", and

C.   (Inset Name)   "the mediator",

who all hereby agree to mediate on the following terms and conditions:

1.   Mediation Procedures

1.1   The mediation shall be held according to this Agreement to Mediate (Mediation Agreement).

1.2   The mediation is "without prejudice" and any settlement reached in the mediation will not be binding until it has been reduced to writing and signed by each of the parties.

1.3   It is an express and fundamental condition precedent of the mediator agreeing to act that the parties (whether jointly or severally) shall neither call nor attempt to call the mediator as a witness in any subsequent matter, or seek a witness statement from him/her, unless an Order to that effect has been obtained by the Court.

2.   Mediator

2.1   The Parties agree that (Insert Name) of, (Insert Name) will be the mediator.

2.2 The parties and the mediator recognise that the mediator is both impartial and neutral.

2.3 The parties recognise that the mediator does not offer legal advice or act as a legal advisor for any of the Parties.

3. Place and Time of the Mediation

3.1 The mediation will take place at a time and place to be advised by (Insert name of instruction organisation and point of contact).

4. Mediation Fees, Expenses and Costs

4.1 The Mediator's fees and any other expenses associated with the mediation will be met by the organisation.

5. Private Sessions

5.1 Information disclosed to the mediator in a private session is confidential unless:

- it is in any event publicly available; or
- the mediator is specifically authorised in the private session to disclose it.

6. Confidentiality

6.1 Anything said during the mediation is confidential to the parties and the mediator and the parties undertake to one another that they will maintain confidentiality in respect to all matters arising in the mediation. They may choose to reveal some or all of what has occurred during the mediation to colleagues, or their managers if all parties agree.

6.2 The only exceptions are where, for example, a potentially unlawful act has been committed or there is a serous risk to health and safety.

6.3   Any other individuals attending the mediation will be required to sign a confidentiality agreement.

7.   Termination of the Mediation

7.1   Any of the parties or the mediator shall be entitled, in their absolute discretion, to terminate the mediation at any time without giving a reason.

8.   Human Rights

8.1   The parties agree and acknowledge that the referral of this dispute to mediation does not affect the rights that may exist under Article 6 of the European Convention on Human Rights.

9.   Signature of this Agreement to Mediate

9.1   This agreement is signed as follows:

ANNEX E – SAMPLE WORKPLACE MEDIATION ATTENDANCE CONFIDENTIALITY AGREEMENT

Background

This document is to be signed by all those in attendance who have not signed the Agreement to Mediate, the parties' representatives, others present, such as lawyers, experts, and any additional advisors to the Parties, agreed attendees, and any observers.

Confidentiality Agreement

Anything said during the mediation is confidential to the parties and the mediator and the parties undertake to one another that they will maintain confidentiality in respect to all matters arising in the mediation. They may choose to reveal some or all of what has occurred during the mediation to colleagues, or their managers if all parties agree.

The only exceptions are where, for example, a potentially unlawful act has been committed or there is a serous risk to health and safety.

Attendance List

Name & Date	Role at Mediation	Signature

ANNEX F – KICKSTARTER QUESTIONS FOR PRIVATE SESSIONS 2017/18

(Remember the follow-up/supplementary: "Why?" "What?" "How?")

- What is important to you that was not addressed in the opening session?

- How do you feel about this dispute?

- How to you feel about (the other participants – use their names)?

- What do you really want out of the resolution of this dispute?

- If you could only achieve one thing from this mediation what would it be?

- If this matter went to trial, what are your expectations?

- What have you based those on?

- What is the strongest part of (the other participant's) case?

- What don't you like about your case?

- If the judge is going to pick on something in your case, what might it be?

- What law or fact in your case would you like to change?

- What do you think that (the other participant) sees as your weak point?

- What is the range of possible outcomes at trial?

- What has hindered settlement to date?

- What are the costs going forward if you do not settle today?

- How are you funding these?

- What is going on with (the other participants)?

- What do you think they will take to settle this case?

- Is there anything else that it would be helpful for me to know?

- What else can I do to help move this case toward settlement?

ANNEX G – EUROPEAN CODE OF CONDUCT FOR MEDIATORS

1. COMPETENCE AND APPOINTMENT OF MEDIATORS

1.1 Competence

Mediators shall be competent and knowledgeable in the process of mediation. Relevant factors shall include proper training and continuous updating of their education and practice in mediation skills, having regard to any relevant standards or accreditation schemes.

1.2 Appointment

The mediator will confer with the parties regarding suitable dates on which the mediation may take place. The mediator shall satisfy him/herself as to his/her background and competence to conduct the mediation before accepting the appointment and, upon request, disclose information concerning his/her background and experience to the parties.

1.3 Advertising/promotion of the mediator's services

Mediators may promote their practice, in a professional, truthful, and dignified way.

2. INDEPENDENCE AND IMPARTIALITY

2.1 Independence and neutrality

The mediator must not act, or, having started to do so, continue to act, before having disclosed any circumstances that may, or may be seen to, affect his or her independence or conflict of interests. The duty to disclose is a continuing obligation throughout the process. Such circumstances shall include:

- any personal or business relationship with one of the parties,- any financial or other interest, direct or indirect, in the outcome of the mediation, or

- the mediator, or a member of his or her firm, having acted in any capacity other than mediator for one of the parties.

In such cases the mediator may only accept or continue the mediation provided that he/she is certain of being able to carry out the mediation with full independence and neutrality in order to guarantee full impartiality and that the parties explicitly consent.

2.2 Impartiality

The mediator shall at all times act, and endeavour to be seen to act, with impartiality towards the parties and be committed to serve all parties equally with respect to the process of mediation.

3. THE MEDIATION AGREEMENT, PROCESS, SETTLEMENT AND FEES

3.1 Procedure

The mediator shall satisfy himself/herself that the parties to the mediation understand the characteristics of the mediation process and the role of the mediator and the parties in it.

The mediator shall in particular ensure that prior to commencement of the mediation the parties have understood and expressly agreed the terms and conditions of the mediation agreement including in particular any applicable provisions relating to obligations of confidentiality on the mediator and on the parties.

The mediation agreement shall, upon request of the parties, be drawn up in writing. The mediator shall conduct the proceedings in an appropriate manner, taking into account the circumstances of the case, including possible power imbalances and the rule of law, any wishes the parties may express and the need for a prompt settlement of the dispute.

The parties shall be free to agree with the mediator, by reference to a set of rules or otherwise, on the manner in which the mediation is to be conducted.

The mediator, if he/she deems it useful, may hear the parties separately.

3.2 Fairness of the process

The mediator shall ensure that all parties have adequate opportunities to be involved in the process. The mediator if appropriate shall inform the parties, and may terminate the mediation, if:

- a settlement is being reached that for the mediator appears unenforceable or illegal, having regard to the circumstances of the case and the competence of the mediator for making such an assessment, or
- the mediator considers that continuing the mediation is unlikely to result in a settlement.

3.3 The end of the process

The mediator shall take all appropriate measures to ensure that any understanding is reached by all parties through knowing and informed consent, and that all parties understand the terms of the agreement.

The parties may withdraw from the mediation at any time without giving any justification. The mediator may, upon request of the parties and within the limits of his or her competence, inform the parties as to how they may formalise the agreement and as to the possibilities for making the agreement enforceable.

3.4 Fees

Where not already provided, the mediator must always supply the parties with complete information on the mode of remuneration which he intends to apply. He/she shall not accept a mediation before the principles of his/her remuneration have been accepted by all parties concerned.

4. CONFIDENTIALITY

The mediator shall keep confidential all information, arising out of or in connection with the mediation, including the fact that the mediation is to take place or has taken place, unless compelled by law or public policy grounds. Any information disclosed in confidence to mediators by one of the parties shall not be disclosed to the other parties without permission or unless compelled by law.

For more information see the Civil Mediation Council site: www.civilmediation.org

ANNEX H – THE FUTURE OF MEDIATION TRAINING – A VISION

The authors include this essay as an Annex to distinguish it from the factual and practical content of the work. They believe, however, that it is relevant to look to the future which they, and the Charity to whom any proceeds from this work will flow, hope will develop as the need for a deeper and more professional training for mediators is more widely recognised.

Ten years ago, at the beginning of 2007, a group of eminent Austrian Mediators were visiting London. They had heard that there was a real resurgence in interest in the United Kingdom and wanted to know more. They were entertained for lunch in the Temple and they admired the historical setting before exploring the gothic fantasy that is the Royal Courts of Justice building in the Strand. All should have been well in the world.

After that, one of their number (the late Werner Kliendorfer) asked: enough history – tell me about the future? How will you train the mediators England needs? What is the requirement?

The author set it out – and his guests were astonished. Accreditation in Austria could take up to four years, and there could be a degree involved and the minimum training was 200 hours of theory and a great deal of practical work – more than 10 times the amount of time spent in the United Kingdom. Where they asked, had this retreat from professionalism begun. Had the Germans started it? Or even Belgium?

At that time, most mediation training in these islands, following Harvard and Notre Dame principles, with a nod to CEDR and others, took place over three brisk eight hour days. The Civil Mediation Council ("CMC"), then just five years old, required 25 hours but there was little analysis. Some trainers did not even assess students. Everyone received a certificate in return for fees upwards of £2,000 or more. No one required observations, and there were no real controls over mediator quality. The market would decide if the panels did not.

There were debates about change. But people worried about the great and the good who had never undertaken any training and were dominating the market place through three organisations. It was discovered that one organisation, in Exeter, was offering training that lasted five hours. Others felt that 15 hours over two days was ample. A summer workshop of the CMC called for evidence that 15 or 25 hours was any better than five hours. Work began.

The Australian model

Later that year, the CMC looked at the Australian model – and the report by Professor Tania Sourdin. From this it was seen that there was really strong research and the times had to change. The Australian model set standards that said:

1. Unless 'experience qualified' (see Section 5 (3) below), from 1 January 2008, a mediator must have completed a mediation education and training course that:

a) is conducted by a training team comprised of a at least two instructors where the principal instructor[s] has more than three years' experience as a mediator and has complied with the continuing accreditation requirements set out in Section 6 below for that period and has at least three years' experience as an instructor; and

b) has assistant instructors or coaches with a ratio of one instructor or coach for every three course participants in the final coached simulation part of the training and where all coaches and instructors are accredited; and

c) is a program of a minimum of 38 hours in duration (which may be constituted by more than one mediation workshop provided not more than nine months has passed between workshops), excluding the assessment process referred to in Section 5(2) below; and

d) involves each course participant in at least nine simulated mediation sessions and in at least three simulations each course participant performs the role of mediator; and

e) provides written, debriefing coaching feedback in respect of two simulated mediations to each course participant by different members of the training team.

This soon became adopted as a good basis.

Research from a senior Professor at the LSE led to a Civil Mediation Council training committee proposing much the same model. Transition periods were put in place and the move to a five day course became established, even if some found it awkward and unwelcome.

On 28th September 2007, invited back to Vienna, the author listened to Sir Brian Neill, then a most respected and charming Chair of the Civil Mediation Council, speak on this subject. He acknowledged the differences across Europe but even his vision could not have imagined a Europe without Britain. He saw mediators as trans-European creatures, building on the European Code of Conduct, and offering an effect alternative to legal warfare. No panacea, he said, but a well-trained body of mediators, working to proper standards, that met with judicial approval, would be a real force for change and good in legal reform.

A decade on

Enough, though, of the context. Almost a decade later where are we? The norm remains 40 hours of contact time with an examination and independent assessment by trained trainers, who are also experienced mediators. Some providers meet this standard.

Others have, through a march to profit or by adopting a different commercial ethos, elected to offer training people who may have done a course themselves, but have largely never worked as mediators. They argue that they meet the criteria of the CMC: arguably, they do.

This does lead to some challenging results. One course, notoriously, contends through its academic leaders who have not mediated, that mediators should never read any documents sent in advance in case they are biased. Another conducts training using stolen materials which it hawks into India and elsewhere without shame or acknowledgement.

There is, then, a real range of mediation training providers, even amongst those registered with the voluntary body that remains the status of the Civil Mediation Council. Whilst the standards set by the CMC are required by judicial bodies and some government tenders, such as the recent NHS Resolution tender for personal injury and clinical negligence, and for costs mediation, these are far from universally adopted and are not mandatory.

What of the future?

At a recent demonstration of mediation skills, by students from King's College London at the headquarters of Pinsent Masons LLP in the City, Sir Peter Cresswell, the Patron of the Society of Mediators and an eminent international jurist, called for mediation training to be made more effective and practical, to be focussed and to involve a deeper understanding of psychology, the law, conflict and the theoretical context.

The authors welcome his vision. The Society of Mediators ("SOM"), offering cost-price training at a third or a half of the cost of competent alternatives, will embrace this call. From 2019 Academic Year, all SOM trainees will be expected to embark on a much longer journey – with a total of ten days of classroom work, practicals, observations, and ultimately a diploma paper that will mean that to be a Fellow of the Society, some 200 hours of work, training, writing, and experience, on top of the examination, will have been performed to a properly assessed standard. The objective will be to train a Practical Mediator.

Members who train with the Society will be awarded a Diploma in Mediation if they pass the second in a series of examinations after 100 hours of work and tuition. This will enable them to progress to Fellowship with the preparation of a learned paper on an aspect of mediation.

This process will be backed up by research, engagement with academia, peer mentoring and support, self-reflection and coaching. In short, a proper professional framework which by 2020 should offer a cohort of mediators of whom Werner and Sir Brian would be proud. That is the SOM vision. That is the Practical Mediation commitment.

How SOM will deliver this vision

The Society believes that it must invest in quality. This book will form the basis of the 100 hours of training in which the delegates will, by 2019, be engaged in a strong practical education supported by suitably academic materials and studies. The Society will broaden its links with Universities to ensure that the academic side is paramount, not only at King's College but with the regional centres of excellence.

Every course is and will be led and tutored, by trainers who not only have mediated extensively, and are qualified to deliver training, but also who have attended advanced courses and have studied the psychological and social framework of mediation. Every student is therefore coached and mentored through the training and supported by a ratio of one tutor to every six students. There is time allowed and proper criteria with strong learning objectives set for each module.

This is, then a vision for Practical Mediation that SOM will deliver that accords with its status and governing document as a Charity. It is important and refreshing to know that this is attainable and in the minds of those who care. It is to be hoped that students looking for training probe the motives and real skill levels of every faculty, North, and South, West and Midlands, to ensure they are being offered a truly effective and coherent course where the first concern is the needs of the student, and the least (and in reality non-existent) – lining the pockets of the owners.

In doing so, the Society believes that it has taken that ethical first step on the journey to a place the Austrian visionaries would have recognised a full decade ago.

For more details of how SOM is working to make this change, and how those interested can help or learn with the Charity, either in the United Kingdom or oversea, please contact the Training Manager (+44 (0) 207 353 3936) or email courses@218strand.com for details.

MORE BOOKS BY
LAW BRIEF PUBLISHING

A selection of our other titles available now:

'Ellis and Kevan on Credit Hire, 5th Edition' by Aidan Ellis & Tim Kevan
'RTA Allegations of Fraud in a Post-Jackson Era: The Handbook, 2nd Edition' by Andrew Mckie
'A Practical Guide to Holiday Sickness Claims' by Andrew Mckie & Ian Skeate
'RTA Personal Injury Claims: A Practical Guide Post-Jackson' by Andrew Mckie
'On Experts: CPR35 for Lawyers and Experts' by David Boyle
'An Introduction to Personal Injury Law' by David Boyle
'A Practical Guide to Running Housing Disrepair and Cavity Wall Claims' by Andrew Mckie, Ian Skeate, Simon Redfearn
'A Practical Guide to Claims Arising From Accidents Abroad and Travel Claims' by Andrew Mckie & Ian Skeate
'A Practical Guide to Cosmetic Surgery Claims' by Dr Victoria Handley
'A Practical Guide to Chronic Pain Claims' by Pankaj Madan
'A Practical Guide to Claims Arising from Fatal Accidents' by James Patience
'A Practical Approach to Clinical Negligence Post-Jackson' by Geoffrey Simpson-Scott
'A Practical Guide to Personal Injury Trusts' by Alan Robinson
'Occupiers, Highways and Defective Premises Claims: A Practical Guide Post-Jackson' by Andrew Mckie
'Employers' Liability Claims: A Practical Guide Post-Jackson' by Andrew Mckie
'A Practical Guide to Subtle Brain Injury Claims' by Pankaj Madan

'The Law of Driverless Cars: An Introduction' by Alex Glassbrook
'A Practical Guide to Costs in Personal Injury Cases' by Matthew Hoe
'A Practical Guide to Alternative Dispute Resolution in Personal Injury Claims – Getting the Most Out of ADR Post-Jackson' by Peter Causton, Nichola Evans, James Arrowsmith
'A Practical Guide to Personal Injuries in Sport' by Adam Walker & Patricia Leonard
'A Practical Guide to Marketing for Lawyers' by Catherine Bailey & Jennet Ingram
'The No Nonsense Solicitors' Practice: A Guide To Running Your Firm' by Bettina Brueggemann
'Baby Steps: A Guide to Maternity Leave and Maternity Pay' by Leah Waller
'The Queen's Counsel Lawyer's Omnibus: 20 Years of Cartoons from the Times 1993-2013' by Alex Steuart Williams

These books and more are available to order online direct from the publisher at www.lawbriefpublishing.com, where you can also read free sample chapters. For any queries, contact us on 0844 587 2383 or mail@lawbriefpublishing.com.

Our books are also usually in stock at www.amazon.co.uk with free next day delivery for Prime members, and at good legal bookshops such as Hammicks and Wildy & Sons.

We are regularly launching new books in our series of practical day-to-day practitioners' guides. Visit our website and join our free newsletter to be kept informed and to receive special offers, free chapters, etc.

You can also follow us on Twitter at www.twitter.com/lawbriefpub.

INDEX

Lightning Source UK Ltd.
Milton Keynes UK
UKHW02f1708240518
323163UK00003B/78/P